Advance Praise for

Workforce Crisis:
How to Beat the Coming Shortage
of Skills and Talent

by Ken Dychtwald, Tamara J. Erickson,
and Robert Morison

"From a CIO's perspective, the coming shortage of appropriately qualified IT talent is one of the most significant issues we face. This book provides practical ideas to attract and retain the talent we will need for continued success."

— Carl Wilson, Executive Vice President
and Chief Information Officer, Marriott International

"*Workforce Crisis* offers practical, innovative solutions to any business concerned about losing its most experienced workers to retirement. The book may help turn a potential "brain drain" into a "brain trust.""

— Robert J. McCann, Vice Chairman and President,
Global Private Client Group, Merrill Lynch

"*Workforce Crisis* is an indispensable source for understanding how the dramatic demographic shifts now taking place will affect organizations and their work force. It is essential reading for every manager."

— Warren Bennis, Distinguished Professor of Management,
University of Southern California, and coauthor of
Geeks and Geezers: How Era, Values, and Defining Moments
Shape Leaders

Workforce
Crisis

Also by the Authors

Ken Dychtwald

Bodymind and *Age Wave* with Joe Flower

Age Power

The Power Years with Daniel J. Kadlec

Tamara J. Erickson

Third Generation R&D with Philip Roussel and Kamal Saad

Workforce Crisis

HOW TO BEAT
THE COMING SHORTAGE OF
SKILLS AND TALENT

Ken Dychtwald
Tamara J. Erickson
Robert Morison

HARVARD BUSINESS SCHOOL PRESS
Boston, Massachusetts

Library of Congress Cataloging-in-Publication Data
Dychtwald, Ken, 1950–
    Workforce crisis : how to beat the coming shortage of skills and talent / Ken
  Dychtwald, Tamara J. Erickson, Robert Morison.
     p. cm.
    ISBN 1-59139-521-6
    1. Manpower planning—United States. 2. Personnel management—United States.
3. Labor supply—United States. I. Erickson, Tamara J., 1954– II. Morison, Robert.
III. Title.
    HF5549.5.M3D93 2006
    658.3'01—dc22

                            2005029060

For the future workforce, including:

Casey Dychtwald

Zak Dychtwald

David Erickson

Katherine Erickson

James Barrett-Morison

Demography is destiny.

—Auguste Comte

Contents

PART I

The Management Challenges of Changing Workforce Demographics

"In the developed countries, the dominant factor in the next society will be something to which most people are only just beginning to pay attention: the rapid growth in the older population and the rapid shrinking of the younger generation. Politicians everywhere still promise to save the existing pensions system, but they—and their constituents—know perfectly well that in another 25 years people will have to keep working until their mid-70s, health permitting.

What has not yet sunk in is that a growing number of older people— say those over 50—will not keep on working as traditional full-time nine-to-five employees, but will participate in the labor force in many new and different ways."[1]

—Peter F. Drucker

1

The Coming Shortage
of Skills and Labor

How a Brain Drain Threatens
Your Organization's Performance

T HIS BOOK began with a phenomenon and a realization. The phenomenon is the aging of the industrialized world, resulting in an unprecedented shift in the age distribution of the general population and, specifically, the labor force. This phenomenon is driven by the following three demographic realities—the disproportionate size of the baby boom generation, increasing longevity, and declining birthrates—that no organization can ignore. Managers must pay more attention to these trends and their implications.

The baby boom. Nearly one-third of all Americans—76 million people—were born between 1946 and 1964 (figure 1-1). That's a daily average of over 10,000 births in the United States, with 1,000 in Canada,

FIGURE 1-1

The baby boom: 1946–1964

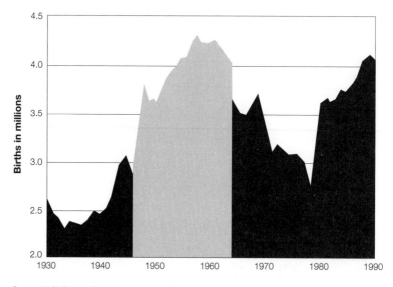

Source: U.S. Census Bureau

and comparable numbers across Europe and Australia. This fertile period was sandwiched between the baby busts of the Depression and World War II and the Viet Nam era. At such numbers, the boomer generation has repeatedly reshaped American life and fueled much of the productivity of the last several decades. As boomers reach traditional retirement age, how will corporations survive the massive exodus of skills, experience, customer relationships, and knowledge—a real brain drain?

The longevity boom. Throughout most of human history, the average life expectancy was less than eighteen. Around 1900, life expectancy at birth in the United States was forty-seven; now it is about seventy-seven (figure 1-2). A hundred years ago, only 4 percent of the U.S. population was over sixty-five; now it's 14 percent and rising. Thanks to breakthroughs in health care and other quality-of-life advances, more people are living longer. Consequently, all the milestones of life are shifting upward. What is middle age? When are workers no longer productive? At what age do employees stop learning or seeking new challenges?

FIGURE 1-2

Life expectancy at birth in the United States

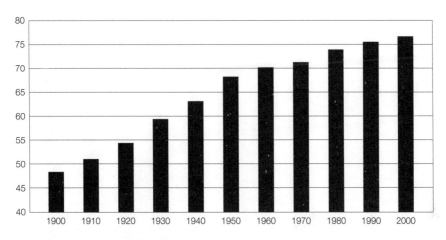

Source: National Center for Health Statistics

The birth dearth. After peaking at 3.7 in the mid-1950s, the average number of children per woman in the United States has declined to 2. Nearly 20 percent of baby boomers will have no children, and another 25 percent will have only one child. Declining birthrates across industrialized nations guarantee a recurrent shortage of native-born young workers (figure 1-3). Countries with birthrates such as Italy's (1.2), Germany's (1.3), and Japan's (1.4) are well below the replacement rate of 2.1 children per woman.

These three factors drive what we call the *age wave*, an unprecedented shift in the age distribution of the population. How global is this wave? Figure 1-4 depicts the projected growth or shrinkage of the working-age populations of eight countries. The United States appears to experience modest but steady growth, whereas the United Kingdom, after a grow-then-shrink cycle, will have the same number of workers in 2050 as in 2000. China follows a similar up-and-down pattern, ending with 5 percent more working-age people in 2050 than 2000—but that means 45 million more people. Unless birthrates or immigration rates change radically, the compound effect of the two declines depicted in figure 1-4 will reduce the German workforce by 25 percent in 2050, the Italian by 30 percent, and the Japanese by 38 percent.

FIGURE 1-3

Total fertility rate: 1960 and 2000

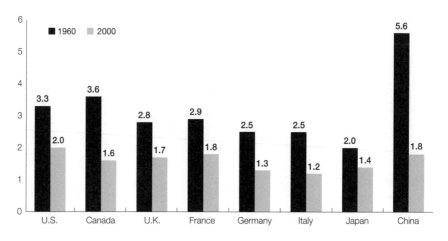

Source: United Nations Population Division

Throughout most of Europe, including Russia and most of the former Eastern Bloc, the pattern is much the same.

So that's the phenomenon. Here's our realization: few large organizations are really preparing for this transformation of the workforce.[1] While marketers are starting to target an older population of consumers, managers are still encouraging mature employees to retire early. Big mistake. Even though the total size of the U.S. workforce continues to grow, the *rate* of growth will decline from 12 percent this decade to only 4 percent between 2010 and 2020, then 3 percent between 2020 and 2030. That translates into a drop from today's annual growth rate of just over 1 percent to an anemic 0.3 percent by around 2020.[2]

If we look at workforce growth rates by age segment (figure 1-5), the patterns are dramatic. In the present decade, the ranks of youngest workers (ages sixteen to twenty-four by Bureau of Labor Statistics groupings) are growing by 15 percent, thanks to the "echo boom" as baby boomers' children enter the workforce. The twenty-five- to thirty-four-year-old segment is growing at just half that rate, and the workforce population between thirty-five and forty-four years old—prime executive development years—is actually declining.

FIGURE 1-4

Percent change in working-age (20–64) population

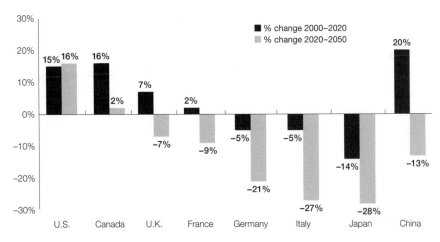

Source: U.S. Census Bureau International Data Base

FIGURE 1-5

U.S. workforce by age: percent growth 2000–2010

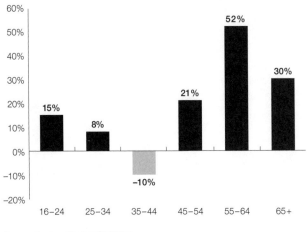

Source: Bureau of Labor Statistics

With the boomer generation moving through middle age and its vanguard nearing retirement age, the fastest growth rates are in the three oldest age segments.

In absolute numbers, the youngest of the three major workforce cohorts depicted in figure 1-6 (ages sixteen to thirty-four) will increase in this decade, then level off. The same goes for the midcareer cohort (thirty-five to fifty-four), but midcareers will outnumber younger workers. Steady growth comes only from the mature (fifty-five-plus) cohort, the fastest-growing segment. Today there are 84 million Americans of boomer age, with over 10 percent foreign born.[3] Their absolute numbers do not rival those of the younger cohorts, but mature workers will constitute proportionally more of the future workforce.

During the next fifteen years, 80 percent of the native-born workforce growth in North America—and even more so in much of Western Europe—will come from those over fifty. Between 1970 and 2000, the number of mature workers in the U.S. labor force remained steady at about 15 million, but as a proportion of a fast-growth workforce, matures declined from 18 percent to 11 percent. However, between 2000 and 2015, the number is likely

FIGURE 1-6

U.S. workforce by age: absolute numbers and growth rate

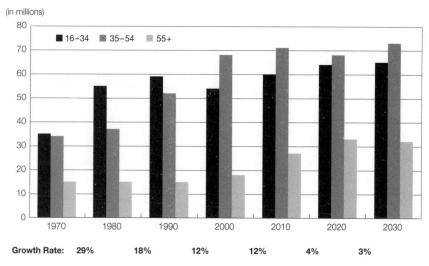

Source: Bureau of Labor Statistics

to double to over 30 million; and as a proportion of a slow-growth workforce, matures will increase to 20 percent. Already, fifty-five- to sixty-four-year-olds constitute over 12 percent of the workforce, up from 10.2 percent in 2000.

So employers should be planning to double the proportion of workers fifty-five and older. That's what we learned in our year-long study of an aging and diversifying workforce and in our later survey.[4] We identified unprecedented and, therefore, unfamiliar managerial challenges associated with all age cohorts in the evolving workforce mix—younger workers who eschew large corporations, disillusioned midcareer workers who burn out from work and family pressures, and mature workers who want to keep contributing to the organization and their community. But there's a more immediate threat at hand.

A Shortage of Skills Will Precede the Shortage of Workers

A widely repeated estimate of a 10 million worker shortfall in the United States by 2010 caught people's notice. But, like most broad estimates, it oversimplifies the situation.[5] Labor shortages affect different industries and employers in different ways. Where many public utilities will face a mass retirement of skilled technicians well before 2010, the medical profession has needed nurses for years. Demographic and economic projections suggest that the shortage of workers will start soon and grow significantly, but the Employment Policy Foundation (EPF) estimates that 80 percent of the impending labor shortage will involve *skills*, not numbers of workers potentially available.[6]

A complex set of variables shapes the nature, timing, and extent of these deficits. *Economic conditions* and the rate of job creation govern the demand for workers. The turn-of-millennium recession and the effects of September 11 on the U.S. economy reduced this demand and presumably delayed the shortages. Nonetheless, job creation has been accelerating, and the EPF estimate of 23 million net new jobs this decade will outstrip the supply of new workers by a wide margin.[7]

Productivity gains also reduce the demand for labor. The Bureau of Labor Statistics (BLS) workforce projections are based on the historical productivity growth rate of about 1.5 percent per year. Better automation and information flow enable companies to do more with fewer employees, and so economists no longer peg economic growth to labor force growth as they did when the economy centered on manufacturing and manual labor. Today's information-based work lends itself to more extensive automation and potentially higher rates of productivity growth. And so a sustained rate of 2 percent would reduce any shortage by two-thirds.

The *net export of jobs* delays or reduces labor shortages. However, the number of jobs currently offshored in an average year amounts to only two-tenths of 1 percent of total jobs. High-end estimates peg about 2 million jobs moving offshore this decade—a significant number, but not enough to offset anticipated skills and labor shortages. Twice as many American workers are displaced by the outsourcing of their jobs to other Americans than by the offshoring of that work to foreign firms. If you count jobs created in the United States by foreign companies, the country remains a net importer of jobs by a wide margin.[8] Labor markets, like consumer and capital markets, continue to globalize. More of today's information-based work can be performed anywhere in the world.

Immigration policies, including the number of work visas allowed for skilled workers, will affect the labor pool. By 2020, immigration will account for virtually all of the United States' net workforce growth. North America is faring better than some European and Asian nations where immigration is tightly controlled and birthrates fall far below replacement levels. By 2020, the overall European Union (EU) economy will need either a two-thirds increase in productivity or a significant enlargement of the labor force via immigration to avoid contraction; Germany alone is likely to need a million working-age immigrants per year to maintain its workforce.[9] EU members face a real dilemma in deciding whether to embrace proposed EU rules on the free flow of labor, or to protect local jobs.

Education—not just the number of workers but what they can actually do—factors heavily in almost every new job created. The technological demands of even "unskilled" entry-level jobs are increasing, and professional and technical fields are already experiencing labor shortages. The BLS estimates that 56 percent of workers gather, process, or use some form of automated information in their work. According to the EPF, 35 percent of the labor force works in management, professional, and technical occupations that demand extensive education, ongoing training, independent thinking, and decisive action. The BLS estimates that one in five new jobs this decade will be in business services, the fastest-growing sector. Other hot occupations include various categories of computer engineers and users (e.g., desktop publishing), nurses, medical and home care assistants, sales and customer service representatives, general office clerks, food preparers and servers, and security guards. By 2010, 25 percent of all workers will be in professional occupations, the most information-intensive of all. Overall, the United States will need 18 million new college degree holders by 2012 to cover job growth and replace retirees but, at current graduation rates, will be 6 million short.[10]

Finally, *workforce participation* rates will affect the labor pool. Obviously, if more people choose to work, then the talent deficit narrows. However, the overall participation rate of about 67 percent is holding steady. The rate among men, currently about 75 percent, is declining slightly; the rate among women of over 60 percent continues rising slowly, and every percentage point increase means another million workers. But compared with the increases of recent decades (the rate doubled between 1950 and 2000), women's participation has essentially leveled off. There does remain room for growth among older workers. Those in the fifty-five to sixty-four age range participate at a 60 percent rate, those over sixty-five at a 13 percent rate, and both numbers are trending upward. The EPF notes that there are 13.6 million college degree holders not in the workforce—predominantly retirees over age sixty.[11] As we argue in this book, to minimize the pending labor and skills shortage, managers must find mutually beneficial ways to retain older workers.

So when will these shortages hit and how severe will they be? It depends on whom you ask. Peter Cappelli of the Wharton School expects no labor shortage this decade in the United States, given positive trends in productivity, education, and retirement.[12] The National Association of Colleges and Employers estimates a shortage of 4 million by 2010.[13] Watson Wyatt pegs it at 8.9 million.[14] The Employment Policy Foundation projects a shortage of several million workers this decade, 10 million by 2015, and 35 million by 2030. The EPF approach makes the most sense to us because it compares the projected labor force available against that needed to produce enough goods and services to maintain the historic growth trend in per capita consumption. The current U.S. annual gross domestic product is about $12 trillion. Given that the average worker produces about $78,000 worth of goods and services (in today's dollars), a shortfall of 10 million workers means an economy three-quarters of a trillion dollars smaller; a shortfall of 35 million means an economy almost $3 trillion smaller. In other words, a large and prolonged worker shortage could severely reduce our standard of living.[15]

In figure 1-7, note that the lines representing labor needed and available are just starting to diverge. Right now, we are at the crossover point where overall labor shortages are predicted to accumulate. Note also that our bigger problem is not the number of available workers but the availability of skills to fill today's and tomorrow's jobs. Nearly 7 million people in key managerial,

FIGURE 1-7

Labor force needed to maintain economic growth

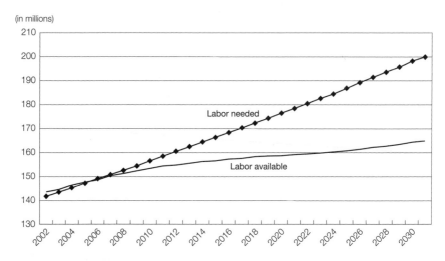

Source: Employment Policy Foundation analysis and projections of Census, Bureau of Labor Statistics, and Bureau of Economic Analysis data

professional, and technical jobs may exit the workforce in the next ten years, and the predicted educational shortfall could hobble our economy as much as a labor shortage could.[16]

To summarize, we will have too few young workforce entrants to replace the *labor, skills, and talent* of boomer retirees. The more immediate loss of skills and experience is already threatening the performance of many corporations. Since the generation after the boomers is much smaller, companies can no longer rely upon a relative profusion of younger workers. Even when they successfully hire and retain young workers, they are still trading experience for inexperience.

A World of Implications

The social, political, and economic implications of increasing longevity, declining birthrates, and the aging of the baby boom generation are enormous. Most industrialized nations established sophisticated checks and balances between political parties, church and state, and corporate and public sectors one or two hundred years ago, when the average life expectancy was thirty and the median age was fourteen. How could any founding father have imagined an imbalance of power between young and old? Currently, for every U.S. federal tax dollar spent per senior, only 14¢ goes to a child. The average senior receives $7,000 annually in medical benefits; in 1965 it was only *$1* a year. How will seniors' increasing dependence on social resources affect nations' and world economies?

Politically, the United States is fast becoming a *gerontocracy*. Today's senior citizens have the lowest poverty level, are the richest segment of society, and wield unrivaled and ever-increasing political clout. People typically vote in proportion to their age (less than one-third of twenty-year-olds vote, but over 70 percent of seventy-year-olds do[17]), and so politicians have learned to cater to the senior vote. How will seniors' political power affect future generations?

How should companies and governments plan for the shrinking number of young workers, young taxpayers, and young consumers? Most marketing is still youth oriented (or "youth obsessed") even though today's mature adults (those over fifty) control two-thirds of the accumulated wealth in the United States.[18] Boomers will be the most financially powerful generation of mature consumers ever. What happens to marketing and product development when 80 percent of the consumer growth comes from the fifty-plus age group? How will businesses maintain brand loyalty when customers reinvent themselves at forty, sixty, and eighty years old? Will boomers, who have been active spenders in their middle years, become more frugal as they mature?

What happens to our families as we find ourselves giving more care to our parents than we give to our children? Thirty percent of the workforce is already sandwiched between obligations to children and aging parents. In the coming decades, four-generation families will become the norm. How will couples reinvent their marriages repeatedly because of the length of life?

Finally, what will be the sources of economic and productivity growth as workforce growth slows? Will equity markets be driven by higher savings rates or by flagging consumer markets? How can countries continue to support generous pension programs when the ratio of workers to retirees continues to diminish? Already, General Motors and other long-established corporations have far more retirees than active workers. In the United States, there are more retired military than individuals in service. Can developing countries with relatively young population distributions develop the business and educational infrastructure to capitalize on the situation?

All of these issues merit far more attention from governments, businesses, and social organizations. But they are beyond the scope of this book. We raise them here to give you a sense of the pervasiveness of change that an aging population brings. This book focuses on a specific arena of change—the workforce—and the specific business problems of maintaining the much-needed labor and skills supply as we lose our demographic equilibrium.[19]

Ignoring the trends in workforce composition guarantees an organization's decline, but this isn't a bad news book. Far from it.

A World of Business Opportunities

This is not the first time the American workforce has undergone upheaval. We assimilated waves of immigrants during the early decades of the last century (and on a proportionately smaller scale continue to do so today). During World War II, we employed millions of women in production jobs to replace servicemen, then reincorporated the servicemen who returned. In recent decades, the workforce has absorbed tens of millions of women who've chosen to work outside the home. With every influx, employers have adjusted their work and employment practices. Simplified assembly processes and more systematic worker training enabled employers to put unskilled, and often non-English-speaking, immigrants to work. During the economic expansion of the 1950s, employers protected and rewarded their talent with implicit job contracts—generous pensions for loyal, long-term service—and the "company man" was born. During the 1970s and 1980s, employers expanded family-oriented benefits to attract and accommodate tens of millions of working mothers.

So we have positive precedent for both great change in the workforce and great adaptation in management policies and practices. But today's workforce upheavals differ from these earlier ones in two ways. First, as noted, we face an impending shortage of workers and skills, not a surplus, and so we must adjust to ongoing conditions of shortage. Second, employers must now retain the services of skilled older workers rather than discharge them with pensions to make room for younger workers. Companies have never dealt with this situation before. Given the increasing longevity, declining birthrates, and the disproportionate size of the baby boom generation now approaching traditional retirement age, we must look at the workforce quite differently and adapt our workforce management practices accordingly. That's what this book is all about. It's based on two bodies of extensive research, both qualitative and quantitative, yielding an extraordinarily rich portrait of the American workforce.[20]

The rest of this book sorts out the challenges and the opportunities before us. While most of our data describes the workforce in the United States, there are similar workforce demographics and challenges in Canada, Western Europe, Asia, and industrialized countries generally. Even though employment laws and practices (especially around health care) differ by country, most of our recommendations—and certainly our underlying philosophy— apply worldwide. We invite managers outside America to apply our patterns of workforce analysis and action to their own circumstances. Several of our research sponsors are based in Europe, and half are large multinationals headquartered in the United States. All have translated and applied our recommendations across borders.

The next chapter discusses related workforce demographics and trends. We emphasize how to overcome inertia and take action before the talent crisis hits full force. Part II focuses on the three career cohorts and how to engage their commitment and bring out their best performance:

- *Mature workers.* We focus on how to recruit and retain them, capitalizing on their knowledge and organizational connections. We describe how to overcome regulatory and organizational barriers to make "flexible retirement" work, and how to overcome age bias and develop a reputation as a mature-worker-friendly organization.

- *Midcareer workers.* We describe how to keep them engaged and productive by offering a wide variety of work, flexible work arrangements, and benefits that enable work/life balance. We emphasize career redirection and other means of personal reinvention and recommitment: fresh assignments, experience-sharing roles, new training, sabbaticals, and "late bloomer" entry into leadership development programs.

- *Young workers.* We describe how to recruit and retain them and minimize turnover, how to incorporate them into the organization rapidly and effectively, and how to keep them engaged and productive by giving them "say and stake" and fulfilling their desire for independence, learning, and rapid growth.

Part III focuses on three main components of the "employment deal" and how to customize the employee-employer "equation" to satisfy workers of all ages and lifestyles:

- *Flexible work arrangements.* We discuss how to embrace flex work as a natural and necessary facet of a networked, information-age economy; how to customize work schedules, locations, and formats to engender both productivity and loyalty; and how to enable teleworkers and other flex workers to stay connected with the organization, both socially and electronically.

- *Flexible learning.* Here we emphasize getting serious about lifelong learning for employees of all ages, work styles, roles, and career stages. We discuss the must-adopt multiple learning methods to meet the needs of diverse groups, while also using learning experiences to bring groups together, and how best to leverage the learning potential and efficiency of information technology.

- *Flexible compensation and benefits.* We describe how to enable employees to achieve better work/life balance by making compensation and benefits clear, accessible, manageable, and valuable, as well as how to make compensation and benefits part of a larger performance management system that motivates each employee toward high performance and business results.

Part IV examines management practices essential to business success as the workforce composition changes, starting with the fundamental role of the work itself in engaging employees—is it interesting, meaningful, important, motivating? We also discuss how to assess and anticipate an organization's own workforce demographics, then put that understanding to work. And we conclude with a summary set of questions, perspectives, and recommended actions for managers.

Throughout the book, we incorporate case studies and best-practice examples to help you see the problems and practices in action. Even though the management challenges weigh most heavily on large employers, be they major corporations, government agencies, or not-for-profit organizations, the specific employee engagement techniques recommended here should serve employers of all sizes. Note that we regularly use the terms *company* and *business* and rely on leaders of nonprofit and government organizations to make the simple translation.

Our goal in this book is to enable organizations and their leaders to make the most of their talent supply today and to ensure their talent supply tomorrow despite ongoing and impending changes in workforce composition. We provide *management perspectives* on demographic and workforce challenges, together with practical *management techniques* for addressing them. Along the way, we also hope to impart *management momentum* for taking early action and preventing problems with talent supply. We emphasize employment practices that will boost workforce commitment and performance immediately, at the same time that they position the organization to be an "employer of choice" in the tighter labor markets of the not-so-distant future. Those of you—especially those responsible for an organization's human assets and talent supply, namely the CEO and senior management team, human resource executives, and general managers—who act now will reap both early and ongoing rewards.

2

The Diverse and Demanding
New Workforce

Why You Need a New Workforce Strategy

A S WE EXPLORE the changing workforce, remember that the problems are bigger than we imagine. We've never had such an older age
mix in the workforce or a generation as large as the baby boomers
preparing to retire. The growth rate of the labor force has never dropped so
precipitously or stayed so low before. We've never before relied so heavily on
intellectual rather than physical labor. We simply cannot anticipate all of the
additive effects of these trends.

At the macro level, we cannot avoid skills and worker shortages entirely,
but these shortages are inevitable only for organizations that fail to anticipate
workforce changes and adjust in time. Since these changes are largely predictable and imminent, organizational leaders must start planning now. The
worst sin is doing nothing. The good news is, our research indicates that the

management techniques needed to accommodate tomorrow's workforce mix can be applied now to improve business performance, cost structures, and employee retention. Indeed, by overhauling your employment practices now, thereby distinguishing yourself in the labor market and ensuring your own talent supply, your company can lessen, or avoid altogether, the inevitable disruptions of workforce change.

So let the impending demographic changes described in this chapter prompt you to adopt more advanced, productive, and valuable workforce practices today—and position your company to thrive today as well as tomorrow.

Extreme Makeover of the Workforce

The demographic composition of the workforce is becoming more diverse than ever before, not just in age but in gender, ethnicity, country of origin, level of education, family status, personal ambition, wealth needed for retirement, and corporate loyalty. Put these forces together, and tomorrow's labor market will be characterized by more than slow growth and shortages: it will think and act quite differently from today's.

Gender

In the United States, two-thirds of working-age women work outside the home. These figures vary widely among industrialized nations, but gender and ethnic diversity are generally increasing. Sixty-one percent of women in the U.S. work and nearly 80 percent in the twenty-five to fifty-four age range.[1] A projected 1 percent increase this decade will mean another million workers, making women 48 percent of the total workforce. But their participation rate is leveling off, their entry into the workforce from school is declining slightly, and women over fifty-five tend to leave the workforce faster than men do. Thus, the overall gender distribution will remain fairly equal.

Ethnicity

Minority representation is definitely changing. Among the native population, birthrates are highest among people of color. In this decade, the total number of Asians in the U.S. workforce will likely grow by 44 percent, Hispanics by 36 percent, African Americans by 21 percent, and Caucasians by only 9 percent. White males have constituted a minority of new workers for years. Farther out, the pattern is even more dramatic. Between 1980 and 2000, native-born whites, male and female, accounted for well over half the prime age workforce growth. Between 2000 and 2020, their numbers will decline by 8 million. Minorities and immigrants account for most of the projected net growth in the workforce, especially at the younger end. In this decade, the population of workers under twenty-four is likely to grow by about 3 million, or 15 percent, and minorities and immigrants will account for 85 percent of that growth. The younger the generation, the more diverse (figure 2-1). The sixty-five-plus population of the United States is 84 percent white. Under thirty-five, it's around 62 percent.

FIGURE 2-1

Racial and ethnic diversity by generation

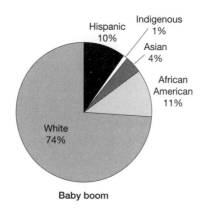

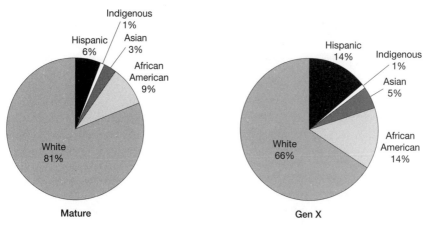

Source: U.S. Census Bureau, 2000

Immigration

Over 600,000 people per year legally—about 1 million total—continue to flow into the U.S. population, and the birthrates of immigrants are higher than for the native-born population. The 2000 census counted almost 7 million more people than the Census Bureau had estimated, a difference of 2.5 percent largely attributed to illegal immigration. Demographers estimate the current population of illegal immigrants at roughly double the official Immigration and Naturalization Service estimate of 6 million.[2] Immigration patterns have shifted, too. For much of the last century, the preponderance of immigrants came from Europe. Today, Europe accounts for only 15 percent, while Mexico and Central and South America together account for 50 percent. There are distinct patterns of destination—two-thirds of immigrants locate along the Pacific, Middle Atlantic, and South Atlantic regions.

Education

Rising educational levels have been driving economic growth over the last several decades. The baby boom generation is significantly better educated than its parents, and the percentage of the U.S. workforce over age twenty-five with college degrees has climbed steadily, from 22 percent in 1980 to 30 percent today. The number of workers with college degrees has more than doubled since 1980. But that rate is slowing, and if the trend remains steady, the rate will have increased to only 32 percent by 2020; and slower population growth curtails the number of graduates actually available. The absolute number of twenty-six- to thirty-five-year-olds with college degrees is actually lower than the number of thirty-six- to forty-five-year olds—the first time ever that a new wave of workers has brought fewer degrees than its predecessor.

Family

Not long ago, domestic life unfolded in a fairly predictable sequence. People married in their twenties, raised children in their thirties, paid college tuitions in their forties, cared for aging parents in their fifties, and enjoyed grandchildren in their sixties. Companies could reasonably anticipate the right mix of workplace benefits based on an employee's age. Not anymore. People marry and start families later, if at all. They divorce, remarry, and start second or third families. They find themselves caring for infants and elders simultaneously, sandwiched between generations and playing multiple roles.

They adopt, undergo fertility treatment, or raise grandchildren. Young adults move back with their parents; singles raise children on their own. No two households are alike.

Aspiration

Just as personal relationships and responsibilities progressed in a fairly straight line, so too did one's professional development. Everyone wanted to keep up with the Joneses. People more or less went to school, got a job, climbed the ladder, and retired. But that pattern is becoming more cyclical, with periods of education, work, and recreation overlapping or in parallel across a lifetime. Today, younger workers are demanding more time off, middle-aged workers are making radical career changes, and older workers are sitting on boards, starting new businesses, and giving back to their communities as never before. Two-thirds of today's employees plan to work at least part-time in retirement.[3] Professional aspirations are numerous and diverse.

Wealth

The generations born after World War II have spent lavishly and saved little. Not surprisingly, savings rates are generally low and consumer debt high. Many investment and retirement funds imploded a few years ago when the dot-com bubble burst, huge corporations went bankrupt, and global markets stumbled. What's more, the age wave is pressing heavily upon public pensions like Social Security, which rarely pay enough to maintain preretirement lifestyles. Truth is, many people in their late forties and fifties may have to work well beyond sixty or sixty-five, just to make ends meet. Retirement isn't an option. So employees' financial situations vary wildly in shape and size.

Loyalty

Like consumers, employees have access to all sorts of information about employment options, job opportunities, and labor markets, and they care about all the features of the employment package—work arrangements, development opportunities, compensation, benefits, and the corporate brand. The savviest comparison shop: they use the Internet to research employers, network with other informed employees, and manage their own careers. The more traditional are realizing that there are no jobs for life; work is more a series of employers and learning opportunities than a lifelong relationship with one company "until retirement do us part." So employees' degree of company loyalty and career opportunism varies as well.

Managerial Challenges of Demographic Diversity

As these forces of changing workforce (and customer) demographics build in strength and momentum, organizations must make course corrections to avoid costly workforce disruption. These costs will be direct, in terms of organizational performance and business profitability, as well as human, in terms of employees' struggle to survive organizational upheaval. Threats still loom on the horizon, but companies can seize the corresponding opportunities right away by considering how workforce composition will enable or impede business strategy. Managers should explore several key areas in particular.

- *Productivity and business growth.* What happens to an organization's productivity if it can't get the workers needed or if its young workers are continually turning over? What if many of its best workers leave via retirement or dissatisfaction with their total work package? What happens to business growth if an organization's human tapestry starts unraveling?

- *Work processes.* How does an organization get an unprecedented mix and range of diverse employees to collaborate productively? How does it capitalize on their diversity? What happens when employees' work-style differences—including productive team structures, preferred training methods, proficiency with technology, and attitudes toward authority—become more pronounced? With such diverse work arrangements as job sharing, telecommuting, and flextime, how can the workplace remain cohesive, communicative, and productive?

- *Learning processes.* What happens to institutional knowledge when those who truly understand the business, the customers, and the organization retire all at once? How can employers satisfy the thirst for deeper knowledge and continuous learning among the best and brightest employees? Does the organization really know how to reengage, retrain, and reignite a fifty- or sixty-year-old? Does it know how to accommodate the various learning styles of different age cohorts?

- *Leadership and management styles.* What happens when retirement depletes the executive ranks? What kind of talent will the organization need to lead a thoroughly ethnic-, gender-, lifestyle-, and age-diverse workforce? Can human resource managers model these skills and develop training programs? How about everyday management? How does one manage diverse and multigenerational groups effectively? What managerial or leadership style will bridge different generational expectations?

- *Culture and continuity.* How will the organization maintain its culture and identity with an increasingly diverse workforce, increasing worker mobility and turnover, and more geographically dispersed work groups? How will corporate mergers, divestitures, and other reorganizations factor in? What will hold an organization together if it outsources or offshores more work? How will the brain drain of retirement and other departures affect its institutional memory?

- *Competitiveness in global markets.* How does an organization remain globally competitive if its workforce demographics are strategically disadvantageous? How should it compete for top talent in increasingly global labor markets? How can it respond quickly and flexibly and serve global customers coherently, given the many forces fragmenting its workforce?

We recommend reviewing all elements of your business strategy and asking for each: How should changing workforce demographics shape this strategy or affect our ability to execute it? What would be the ideal workforce composition for its success?

Who Owns These Challenges?

Given the significant and unprecedented changes in workforce composition and the threat of labor and skills shortages, the challenge of managing workforce supply and demand carries greater magnitude, urgency, and complexity than ever before in the working lives of today's business leaders.

Who owns this issue? Who is responsible for an organization's talent supply? Two people primarily: the CEO and the head of human resources. As the integration point of an enterprise and the person responsible for its overall performance and sustainability, the CEO sets the organization's direction and goals and then makes sure that the organization has the business model, processes, and assets—including capital, facilities, technology, and people—to meet those goals. Depending on business conditions, the CEO may focus on different resources—for example, securing cash flow and capital in recessions or updating technology and production facilities during expansions. We

A Checklist of Trends to Count On

Based on our synthesis and analysis of these workforce demographics, we recommend that employers begin preparing for the following changes to safeguard their talent pool:

- *Aging.* The average age of employees will continue to rise, and the workforce will become more multigenerational. Proportionately, mature workers are the fastest-growing age segment, and large employers can expect to double their percentage of workers over fifty-five during the next five to ten years.

- *More women.* The proportion of female workers, already high, will continue to rise slowly.

- *More ethnic diversity.* By demographic standards, the racial and ethnic mix is changing very rapidly, with minorities now accounting for one-third of younger workers.

- *Increasing lifestyle/life-stage variety.* People are no longer "acting their age." Their life plans are no longer linear and predictable. They differ wildly in how they integrate work and other pursuits into their lives.

- *Tightening labor markets.* As the rate of labor force growth plummets to 2 to 3 percent per decade, labor markets will tighten and competition for talented people will intensify.

believe that, over the next five years, the CEO must address these people issues and talent supply.

Some CEOs make human resources a top priority, but most don't. General Electric is renowned for its investment in developing the performance and potential of its top layers of management—and insisting that these managers do the same in their parts of the business. The result is a cascade of attention to talent—especially the high performers—and the assignments and challenges that will stretch their capabilities. Beyond leadership development and succession, CEOs today should monitor the changing demographic composition of their workforces and recruiting pools. They should understand the overall flow and bottlenecks of talent throughout their organizations as well as how the corporate brand attracts or repels employees and prospects alike. Most fundamentally, CEOs should insist on a coherent,

- *Shortages of skills and experience.* As the baby boom generation reaches retirement age, organizations face a potentially debilitating brain drain of skills and experience.

- *Shortages of workers.* Overall demand for workers is already beginning to exceed supply. The gap is projected to grow to millions, perhaps tens of millions, of workers, with potentially profound effects on economic output and standard of living.

- *Shortages of educated candidates.* Despite continuing progress in average educational achievement, colleges will graduate too few candidates to fill the technical, information-intensive, judgment-intensive jobs five years from now.

- *Pressure on training and development.* Employers must not only encourage employees' continuing education but also provide that education directly to maintain needed skills levels.

- *Tension around HR policies and practices.* The whole range of management practices—compensation, benefits, and especially work arrangements—must appeal to the new workforce and accommodate the expanding variety of workers' needs and preferences.

- *Strain on organizational coherence.* As the workforce diversifies and disperses—adopting flexible schedules, telework, and other technology-enabled arrangements—leaders must find new ways to cultivate and nourish organizational culture and identity.

forward-looking workforce strategy that maintains the talent supply during turbulence and shortage.

To jump-start the development of that strategy, the CEO and executive team must own these challenges visibly and collectively because many of the tactics that will serve and appeal to present and future employees will require breaks from past practices and ingrained attitudes. Programs as fundamental as flexible work arrangements often require the genuine commitment of senior leaders before the rest of management will embrace and support them.

CEOs oversee the overall resource mix but rely on functional managers to supervise categories of resources—money, people, technology—and on line executives to deploy these resources effectively. And so the second owner of this challenge is the human resources executive, who must develop and execute the right workforce policies and practices. To synchronize the HR strategy with the enterprise's overall business strategy, HR executives must provide expert, enlightened counsel to the CEO and executive team on all workforce matters. They must oversee the redesign and execution of the processes of employee recruiting, development, administration and retention. In short, the HR staff maintains and develops the organization's human assets to provide the right talent in the right place at the right time.

However, given the mounting demographic pressures, HR executives today must do more than ensure the cost-effective execution of HR processes. First, to anticipate and implement necessary changes in HR management practices, they must assess how workforce composition and employee preferences are changing. Second, they must obsess over what's happening at the intersection of workforce and business strategies. As jobs have grown more information intensive, more technically demanding, and more complex, the relative value of skills and talent in the business asset portfolio has steadily risen. Therefore, workforce strategy must become a bigger part of business strategy. The stakes grow higher still as companies face a prolonged period of skills and labor shortages. The HR executive must articulate how the composition of the organization's workforce will enable or impede business success and what to do about it.

Responsibility for ensuring the enterprise's talent supply rests on the CEO and the HR executive but is shared broadly. The CEO shares responsibility locally with every general manager and any manager responsible for the complete mix of business resources—money, facilities, people, technology. Each general manager must understand the changing composition not only of the customer base but also of the local workforce, how those changes influence performance, and how the local organization can best participate in and contribute to the flow of people, experience, and skills across the enterprise. Meanwhile, the HR executive shares responsibility across the HR function at large, and especially with HR managers affiliated with particular business units, major business functions, and general managers throughout the corporation.

Developing a Workforce Strategy

A workforce strategy balances supply and demand. That is, it ensures the supply of skills and talent that the organization needs to accomplish its business strategy and performance goals. That means that it must account for the labor market's constant movement in unprecedented directions. For example, boomer retirement threatens to shrink the labor pool, but immigration expands it. Globalization and outsourcing expand a company's options for finding workers but also potentially expand the competition for them. Companies expand and contract their workforces more often and more readily, thereby churning the labor pool. Information and communications technologies make workers more mobile, performing much of today's work anytime, anywhere. But we seriously doubt whether ready-made, already-qualified, locally available candidates will form a large enough labor pool to meet your organization's needs five years from now. And so your workforce strategy must *anticipate* the needed labor and skills in the context of the longer-term trends, and it must also *prevent* talent shortages by retaining key employees and tapping new sources of labor and skills.

Thus, the workforce strategy of most organizations must center on expanding supply and reducing demand. Organizations can achieve this balance by

- *Raising productivity.* Automate or redesign work processes so that you can do more work with less labor.

- *Exporting work.* Outsource noncritical work to a local partner or to an organization halfway around the world where labor and skills are more plentiful and cost-efficient. If the provider really specializes in and excels at the work, then you can enjoy simultaneous cost and performance advantages.

- *Importing workers.* Recruit among recent immigrants or recruit people with specific skills to relocate for you.

- *Amplifying skill levels.* Expand the capabilities of people already working for you, perhaps dramatically so, such as by preparing unskilled workers for skilled positions.

- *Expanding the labor pool.* Develop new recruiting channels, such as to mature workers and retirees, workforce reentrants (including women returning to work after raising families), career switchers, and the underskilled or underemployed.

- *Improving branding and recruiting.* Polish and publicize your brand as an employer so that more prospects will consider yours a desirable organization for employment. Emphasize different elements of your brand to appeal to different workforce segments. Improve targeting, attracting, and hiring methods to gain market share of prospective employees.

Each of these approaches has limitations and costs, and so a sound workforce strategy will consider all and incorporate most of them. We focus on the last three of these six tactics in this book. Note that improving your recruiting of traditional candidates or in traditional channels may not yield the best results, simply because your competitors will likely focus there as well. Expanding the labor pool may generate more results, even after factoring in additional training costs. Do you want to compete harder for your share of the current labor pie—or start with a bigger pie?

So think about your workforce in terms of supply, demand, and opportunity. How can you leverage the changing workforce demographics to forward business strategies involving growth, innovation, or customer value? Your workforce strategy must ultimately match the supply with the organization's demand for talent. To identify your organization's opportunities, we recommend asking yourself these two questions.

How can we leverage changing demographics to strengthen relationships with our customers? Employees are more than performers of work; they are your face to the marketplace, especially in such sectors as retail, services, and the media. Your organization's employees—and not just those on the "front line"—could reflect the ethnicity, gender, and age composition of the evolving customer base, thereby increasing customer retention and business volume. For example, as the population at large ages, and mature consumers exercise a greater spending power, retailers could show a more mature face to their clientele. Retailers could also recruit employees to reflect the ethnic diversity of their local markets. How well does your workforce demographic correspond with customer demographics? Does it mirror the distribution and diversity of ages, ethnicities, and lifestyles of customers? How can you improve and capitalize on that match?

How can we leverage changing demographics to enhance our capabilities? What can your organization do to become more innovative, more flexible, and more informed about customers, best practices, and business conditions? Workforce diversity means a greater range of backgrounds, perspectives, and approaches to decision making, problem solving, and creativity. How can you leverage these assets in product development and process improvement? On project and development teams, for example, you could enhance performance by mixing the experience of long-tenured employees with the fresh viewpoints of newcomers or by combining workers with very different backgrounds, experiences, and viewpoints.

Most importantly, how quickly can or should we move? According to our research, organizations can improve short-term human resource performance—including higher productivity and lower turnover—by implementing progressive workforce management practices sooner rather than later. The time is now.

PART II

The Three Worker Cohorts and How to Engage Them

"At fifteen, I set my heart on learning. At thirty, I was firmly established. At forty, I had no more doubts. At fifty, I knew the will of Heaven. At sixty, I was ready to listen to it. At seventy, I could follow my heart's desire without transgressing what was right."

—Confucius[1]

3

The Needs and Capabilities of Mature Workers

Why Older Employees Are Your Biggest Untapped Resource

COMPANIES already know how to shed mature workers through early retirement programs. But they don't know how to recruit or retain them. Why bother until we need them, right? Wrong—for two reasons:[1]

- Companies will need mature workers soon enough—well before the end of this decade in most industries in developed countries. As work-force growth slows and economic conditions improve, older workers as well as the already retired will become a key source of your skilled labor. In sectors such as petroleum and aerospace engineering, the impending skills shortage is only a year or two away; in others, such as health care, it's already here.

- A company cannot develop a reputation that will attract the most talented mature workers overnight. You must adjust the policies and practices of hiring and retiring, and you must cultivate an environment that clearly welcomes and values mature workers.

The pressure to incorporate mature workers may not be high yet, but the dangers of waiting too long are great. We recommend starting now, climbing the learning curve, and branding your enterprise as truly multigenerational. In the short term, you can fill the skills gaps (in areas like retail and customer service) and establish yourself as the employer of choice for the multigenerational labor market in the not-so-distant future. This chapter puts a face on this rich supply of talent, skills, and experience.

Profile of the Unretired

Age is no barrier to accomplishment. Just look at Bob Lutz. In September 2001, General Motors Corporation named Lutz, then sixty-nine years old, vice chairman of product development, overseeing worldwide vehicle development and, most recently, manufacturing. Robert Wagoner, GM's president and CEO, chose Lutz because of his energy and his reputation as a creative force. "There are no significant unfilled 'consumer needs' in the U.S. car and truck market," Lutz says. "But there are 'consumer turn-ons' that research alone won't find."[2] Finding those turn-ons is Lutz's specialty. His mission at GM was to create vehicles that would capture the consumer's imagination, just as he had done at Chrysler with the Dodge Viper, Plymouth Prowler, Chrysler PT Cruiser, and Dodge Ram.

In many ways, Lutz's career serves as a model for today's "ageless" worker. A former Marine Corps pilot, Lutz has advanced by moving continually from one automobile manufacturer to another, first at GM Europe, then BMW, and then Ford Europe. He rose to executive vice president of Ford U.S., then joined Chrysler in 1986 to work for Lee Iacocca. In 1998, Lutz retired from Chrysler, well past the company's mandatory retirement age.

His retirement ended in about four months, when he took over as chairman and CEO of the failing battery maker Exide Technologies. In fifteen months, he replaced most of Exide's top management and all of its directors, sold off unproductive assets, canceled poor contracts, cut the product line, and settled several lawsuits. When he left, Exide showed a profit for the first time in three years.

GM clearly expects Lutz to repeat his success. At the January 2003 Detroit Auto Show, Lutz unveiled five prototype vehicles: the Buick Centieme, which combines sedan and sport-utility features; the Chevrolet Cheyenne pickup; the Chevrolet SS and Pontiac G6 sports sedans; and a $250,000 Cadillac Sixteen car. Lutz's job has hardly been a cakewalk, since he has worked to remove bureaucracy, inject passion, and get designers and engineers to collaborate globally. But he's up to the task and remains close to the center of GM's attempt at a marketplace turnaround.[3]

The energy, imagination, and drive that characterize successful individuals like Bob Lutz characterize many other well-known older workers as well. (See the box "Never Retire.")

Never Retire

Called from retirement early in the baseball season, seventy-two-year-old Jack McKeon coached the youthful but underperforming Florida Marlins to the 2003 World Series championship. A caricaturist for over seventy-five years, Al Hirschfeld was still drawing when he passed away at one hundred. Winning Grammy Awards in 2000 were Tony Bennett, Tito Puente, and B. B. King at a combined age of around two hundred twenty. Clint Eastwood won the 2005 Academy Award for best director at age seventy-four. Musicians Mick Jagger and Keith Richards of the Rolling Stones are over sixty—and still touring. Mr. Richards told the *New York Times* a few years ago, "This is not something you retire from. It's your life. Writing songs and playing is like breathing—you don't stop."[4]

The business world has Sumner Redstone of Viacom, Rupert Murdoch of News Corporation, and Warren Buffett of Berkshire Hathaway. Executives called from retirement include John Reed, named interim chairman and CEO of the New York Stock Exchange, and former executive E. Neville Isdell, who filled the chairman and CEO roles at Coca-Cola.

William Safire, at age seventy-five, wrote in his farewell column in the *New York Times*, "When you're through changing, learning, working to stay involved—only then are you through. Never retire."[5]

Are Older Workers Less Productive?

Unfortunately, there are misconceptions and conflicting research on the capabilities and productivity of mature workers, so much so that, in a 2002 AARP survey, two-thirds of workers over forty-five believe that workers face age discrimination today, and 60 percent consider age as a threat to job security.[6] Do seasoned employees really produce too little value for the costs they incur? Not at all. The ageist stereotype is far from reality. Let's review the facts.[7]

Physical and cognitive abilities slowly diminish as part of the natural aging process. Vision, hearing, and balance decline gradually with age. Raw mental power apparently begins declining in one's twenties. But as health and longevity improve, the timing and pace of these physical changes are delayed. That said, in some occupations, older employees may work less swiftly, struggle with physically strenuous tasks, learn unfamiliar material more slowly, and have more difficulty juggling many tasks at once. However, contrary to popular misconception, workers over age fifty-five do *not* sustain more injuries or absences than their younger counterparts. But when they are ill or injured, their recovery times are longer. Of course, they have higher incidences of degenerative conditions such as arthritis and age-related illnesses such as hypertension and heart disease, and so their health-care costs on average rise with age. But employers can adjust the physical environment (e.g., better lighting and acoustics), offer regular health screening, and encourage or even provide fitness programs.

Do any of these diminished abilities lead to low productivity? No, absolutely not. With their extensive knowledge and experience, mature workers can compensate, often by filtering out "noise" and focusing on essential decisions or actions. They simply work smarter. An AARP study asked employers to rank the qualities sought in new employees generally and the qualities found in their older employees.[8] The two lists—with such traits as commitment, reliability, performance, and basic skills—corresponded remarkably.

There are strong correlations between work and health. People in poor health tend to leave the workforce earlier, have lower workforce participation rates, or are working part-time. Early retirees report more health problems than do workers of the same age, and 16 percent of nonemployed older adults say that they are not working for health reasons. But people who stay on the job (or in equivalently intensive volunteer work) remain healthier and live longer. They enjoy the psychological benefits of contribution and self-esteem and the social benefits of a workplace community and its intergenerational exchange. As several recent studies have shown, the best way to preserve one's brainpower is to keep using it.

Will an older worker be as productive as a younger one? It depends on the job and the individual. Electrical utilities anticipate a severe shortage of linemen when the current generation retires. The physical demands of climbing utility poles and stringing electrical cables cannot be met indefinitely, and many linemen "descend" to less physically strenuous jobs several years before retiring. In health care, many nurses retire early or change jobs before retiring because of the physical and mental strains of the work—hence the current nursing shortage. In aviation, research shows that older airline pilots perform as well as younger ones, and sixty-year-old pilots are the *least* likely to fail flight simulator tests. So U.S. commercial airline pilots are lobbying to drop the mandatory retirement age of sixty for their profession (or else extend it to sixty-five, on par with Europe and most of the world).[9] On the whole, jobs in a knowledge and service economy are becoming less physically strenuous, and health risks usually stem from too little physical or mental activity, not too much. So people of any age can perform the overwhelming majority of jobs today.

What's more, people do not lose the insights of a lifetime overnight. Lee Iacocca once told *Wired*:

> I've always been against automated chronological dates to farm people out. The union would always say, Make room for the new blood; there aren't enough jobs to go around. Well, that's a hell of a policy . . . I don't know if the Internet will . . . change stereotypes, but I hope so. I had people at Chrysler who were 40 but acted 80, and . . . 80-year-olds who could do everything a 40-year-old can. You have to take a different view of age now. People are living longer. Age just gives experience. Besides, it takes you until about 50 to know what the hell is going on in the world.[10]

Pushing people out the door because of your current retirement policy is bad business. Smart companies will persuade mature workers to delay or even eschew retirement entirely as long as they remain productive and healthy.

Portrait of the Mature Worker

Today's mature workers—those people fifty-five and older who are in the workforce—are relatively well educated and well off.[11] They hold college graduate degrees in the same proportion (about 35 percent) as the younger cohorts, but they have the highest incidence of graduate degrees and the highest average household incomes and investable assets. However, they are the least diverse cohort, the least comfortable with diversity, and least likely to say that they enjoy working with people from different backgrounds and cultures. Non-Hispanic whites constitute 88 percent of our survey, compared with 76 percent of the midcareers and 61 percent of the youngest cohort.

Born to the Greatest Generation

Most matures were born in the 1940s, though the oldest are children of the Great Depression and the youngest, of the baby boom. They grew up during the WWII years, characterized by great national pride and followed by economic growth. Compared with younger cohorts, they hold more traditional beliefs in authority and the role of government and expect government support, protection, and intervention when necessary. They generally value structure and fairness in following agreed-upon rules. They also tend to define success from the outside in, with wealth and status as indicators of success, though they are most likely to describe success in life as "being true to myself and not selling out."

Among our three cohorts, mature workers are least likely to describe themselves as ambitious, but most likely (though by small margins) to consider themselves reliable, hard working, confident, optimistic, sociable, spiritual or religious, high achieving, and—breaking a stereotype—open to new ideas.

Having grown up with primitive information technology, they are less adept than younger workers at using today's versions, and some shy away from computers and related devices. They are least likely to say they enjoy working with new technologies, but their behavior suggests otherwise: the fastest-growing cohort on the Internet today is over sixty. After exploring the technology, most matures adopt it enthusiastically. Of course, those in technical fields keep themselves current.

Matures' strengths include experience, emotional maturity, and loyalty. When they commit to a company, manager, or work team, they will do whatever necessary to finish the job. They practice teamwork and believe in service to others. Most prefer long-term connections with their employers, and they associate their career with the company—not "I'm in sales," but "I'm an IBM salesman." Since mature workers are more comfortable with the hierarchies prevalent early in their careers, some may struggle to adjust to today's more fluid, flattened, and networked enterprises.

Personal Matters of Mature Workers

Compared with the other cohorts, matures report fewer issues with finance or indebtedness, marriage or relationships, and parenting, but slightly more issues with health (32 percent versus 30 percent reported by the mid-careers), particularly their own rather than family members'. Not surprisingly, they are most likely to report becoming grandparents and caregivers of an elderly relative or adult dependent. Overall, age brings greater independence from family concerns—matures are least likely (53 percent) to say that they put family before work.

Mature Workers' Attitudes Toward Work

Of the three cohorts, matures are most likely to be self-employed (25 percent versus 15 percent of the workforce overall), to work from home or away from the office or other fixed location, and to work for nonprofits (15 percent), even though most of them work for profit-driven companies. Given their experience, matures are most likely to serve as managers or senior managers and have the longest average tenures—fourteen years—with their employers.

Matures have the highest overall satisfaction rates with their jobs (68 percent) and managers (54 percent). They are most likely to say that their pride comes from work and career (59 percent) and least likely to say that they have too much work on their plates (15 percent). They are also least likely to say that they are feeling burnout, experiencing conflicts with colleagues, or in dead-end jobs (so much for the stereotype of reaching late-career stagnation). They are most likely to report that the employer offers a congenial and fun workplace where teamwork rules and opportunities abound.

In our survey, matures scored highest on levels of engagement with the work (work is energizing, time passes quickly at work) and with the employer (really caring about the fate of the organization, proud to tell others you work for the organization). Only about half agree that top management displays integrity and morality, or that the organization's values match their own. Only 43 percent say that the organization really inspires their best job performance.

One "wrinkle" in this portrait: these traits are amplified in workers over sixty-five. To ensure statistical validity, our survey included an oversample of people sixty-five and older still working for a primary employer at least thirty hours a week. Their satisfaction and engagement levels are higher still than the mature cohort at large. They have the highest percentages of any age group of people who really care about the fate of their organizations and will spend extra effort to enable it to succeed.

Retirement Preferences of Mature Workers

Among our age cohorts, workers age fifty-five and older want most to continue working past retirement age. Those sixty-five and older have the highest desire to keep working. Those who do intend to "retire" from their employers plan to do so latest—at age sixty-six on average—and 80 percent of them aim to work in retirement, most often part-time or in periods of working and not working. According to one AARP poll, the top four reasons for working in retirement were staying mentally active (87 percent), staying physically active (85 percent), being productive or useful (77 percent), and doing something fun (71 percent). Other reasons included needing the money (22 percent of respondents) and needing health benefits (17 percent).[12]

Note that the growing ranks of mature workers include many who already "retired." Over 20 percent of those collecting employer pensions still work in some capacity, and among people under sixty collecting pensions, more than half are working. Among those age fifty-five and older who have accepted early retirement offers, one-third have returned to work.[13] But these working retirees are more likely working part-time or for themselves than their not-yet-retired counterparts—in other words, they're working on their own terms.

What Mature Workers Want from Employers

Employees of all ages want meaningful work and responsibility, opportunities to learn, a congenial and respectful workplace, fair pay, and adequate benefits, but to varying degrees. Matures expect the mix, especially such elements as pension accumulation and payout options, to reflect the value of their experience and their retirement preferences.

Table 3-1 shows what mature workers want among ten basic elements of the "employment deal." Not surprisingly, a comprehensive retirement package tops the list, followed by a comprehensive benefits package (with emphasis on health-care coverage). The next several elements entail the work experience. Matures value the conditions for personal contribution, enjoyment, and growth more highly than work arrangements (flexible schedule and location) and more than significant increases in compensation and vacation. Note that more money and vacation matter least to mature workers partly because they are probably well paid already and have earned longer vacations.

TABLE 3-1

What matters to mature workers

General elements of the deal	Relative weight
Comprehensive retirement package	16
Comprehensive benefits package	14
Work that enables me to learn and grow	13
Work that is personally stimulating	12
Workplace that is enjoyable	11
Flexible work schedule	8
Work that is worthwhile to society	8
10 percent more in total compensation	7
Flexible workplace	6
Two weeks' additional paid vacation	5

Relative weights add to 100

Source: The New Employee/Employer Equation survey

This pattern—valuing security highest, work and workplace next, and the work arrangement lowest—recurs in the other cohorts, but it's most pronounced among matures.

The New Career Trajectory

We tend to picture a "career path" as a straight line or a climb up the "corporate ladder" of responsibility and rank that plummets into the abyss at retirement. That's the wrong mental model for an extended career. As noted, many people want to adjust their roles, schedules, and other work arrangements as they approach retirement. They want to "downshift" or "decelerate" into a less intensive but still rewarding work pattern that can evolve through and past any official age of retirement. Figure 3-1 depicts three possible trajectories for the latter stages of careers, one of which is the traditional *retiring* path, where responsibility and contribution stop cold. The *downshifting* trajectory completes a bell-shaped curve with a "deceleration" phase on the later end that can be as carefully planned as one's career "development" at the early end. In the *sustaining* trajectory, high responsibility and contribution continue

FIGURE 3-1

Three career trajectories

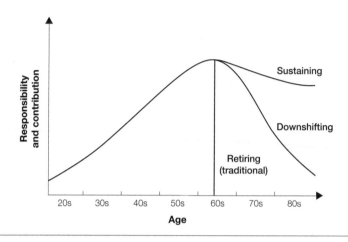

indefinitely as long as one remains healthy, eager, and able. In terms of economic productivity and individual well-being, the trajectory that makes the least sense is "retiring."

Sustainers may be special cases, though every field has those rare fertile minds who love their work, hunger for knowledge, and contribute meaningfully to society. Well-known examples are the late Peter Drucker in management and Jimmy Carter and Nelson Mandela in world affairs. We suspect that most employees will prefer—and employers must institutionalize—the downshifting model. Consider academia. Professors serve as faculty advisors, committee chairs, department heads, and research center directors, some reaching such leadership heights as dean or university president before returning to the laboratory, the field, or the classroom, with lighter teaching loads and fewer students until they join the faculty emeriti.

Employers must accommodate these evolving needs of mature employees to maximize their productivity. You cannot gratify and retain everyone, because people still use retirement to shift trajectory, and these trajectories vary greatly. Many people want to do less of the same work before or after the point of retirement. Some would rather do entirely different work for the same employer, often to "give back" to the organization. Some feel stale in their current situation and want to do the same work elsewhere, often in a smaller organization. Some want to do totally different work in a different organization—a late-career restart. And some want to provide service for nonprofits or volunteer outside the officially tabulated workforce.

What to Remember About Mature Workers

As you read later chapters, please keep in mind these three points about the mature cohort. First, matures want to contribute meaningfully, potentially assuming leadership positions relatively late in their careers and bridging leadership gaps during organizational transitions. Do not overlook the leadership potential of "late bloomers."

Second, like workers of all ages, matures want to continue improving their skills and stretching their talents, but companies continually overlook them for training and development, with retirement on the horizon. Big mistake. Since turnover tends to be lowest among older employees, the return on the educational investment in matures can be higher—much higher—than on an equivalent investment in young employees. To expand the contribution of these experienced workers, ask them to serve as trainers, coaches, and mentors instead of hiring as many outside consultants.

Third, flexible work arrangements, especially flexible schedules, will matter increasingly more as the proportion of mature workers increases. Flexibility must be a part of the employment deal both as workers phase into retirement and as retirees return to work. Master the practices of flex work and flex retirement sooner rather than later—and then use their success as a selling point with employees of all ages.

Stephen Wing of CVS/pharmacy summarizes nicely:

> Older workers stay at the company almost three times longer than others. They are very responsible. They care about the customers. They're good examples to our younger employees. They also relate well to CVS's older customers, who trust more experienced employees, particularly in vital positions such as pharmacy. We now the have reputation of empowering older workers, which puts us in front of the competition in attracting both older employees and older customers.[14]

The next chapter explains more concretely how you should change some of your current HR policies and practices to incorporate mature workers into your workforce strategy and establish your own reputation as a senior-friendly work environment.

4

The End of Retirement

How to Optimize the Services of Mature Workers

To safeguard and expand your company's talent supply, your workforce strategy absolutely *must* include specific plans for employing more mature workers, including those already past the conventional retirement age. Unfortunately, few employers have such plans in place. According to a 2000 survey by the Society for Human Resource Management (SHRM), two-thirds of employers did not actively recruit older workers, over half did not actively attempt to retain key ones, 80 percent offered no special provisions (such as flexible work arrangements) or benefits designed for mature workers, and 60 percent of CEOs said their companies do not account for workforce aging in their long-term business plans.[1] Many employers would *like* to offer flexible retirement, but most feel blocked by regulatory restrictions.[2]

This chapter focuses on three fundamental ways to begin changing your workforce strategy and your ability to execute it.[3]

- *First, hire mature workers.* The goal is to recruit mature workers, retain them, and leverage them as lifelong contributors. That means opening new recruiting channels, offering attractive employment deals, and, more fundamentally, rooting out the entrenched age bias in our management systems, human resources practices, and assumptions about people's capabilities.

- *Second, implement flexible retirement.* The goal is to give workers more freedom to remain productive, and employers more freedom to employ them. That means enabling people to adjust their roles and schedules as they approach and pass sixty-five, and expanding options for delaying and forgoing retirement altogether. "Retirement at sixty-five" is a quaint twentieth-century custom, born of economic necessity during the Great Depression—and we must end it out of demographic necessity in the early years of the twenty-first century.

- *Third, advocate reforms in pension and benefits laws.* The goal is to simplify the regulations on pensions, retiree benefits, and working in retirement so that people willingly stay employed. Flexible retirement depends on flexible pension and benefits arrangements, adjustable to mature employees' evolving work patterns and personal needs. But in many countries, including the United States, the Gordian knot of regulations not only impedes flexible work/flexible retirement arrangements but also motivates employees to retire fully from one company, only to jump to another.

All three involve the realms of social convention and government regulation as well as business operations and performance. Employers can act upon the first two directly; unions and businesses—especially large corporations with established lobbying processes and power—must band together to influence the third. The rest of this chapter suggests how.

Hiring Mature Workers

In 1967, the Age Discrimination in Employment Act (ADEA) banned discrimination against older workers (defined as those over *forty*) in hiring, promotion, retention, training, pay, or benefits. But age bias persists. Corporations operating in the United States might position themselves as unbiased, but their practices suggest otherwise. Advertisers have taken decades to discover the value of pitching everyday products (not just geriatric ones) to older consumers and to depict them as vital rather than senile. Employers must do the same, dropping their assumptions and subtle biases against older workers—and as soon as possible.

Unbiasing Hiring Practices

Hiring processes are generally aimed at younger applicants. Do managers, even young ones, know how to assess the résumé of a sixty-year-old applicant? How would a manager interpret an applicant's twenty-five-year tenure at one company? As a sign of stability and commitment—or inertia and lack of ambition?

Age bias can surface in the wording of a simple job advertisement. "High energy," "fast pace," and "fresh thinking" communicate "youth wanted here," whereas "experience," "knowledge," and "expertise" say "we value maturity." Recruiting channels such as newspaper want ads, "help wanted" signs, or the various job-listing Web sites may not attract older workers. Instead, travel programs for older adults (like Elderhostel), senior centers, country clubs, and retirement communities can all serve as productive recruiting venues. For example, CVS/pharmacy looked at national demographic trends fifteen years ago and concluded that it needed to employ far more older workers. But managers didn't know how to find them—older people shopped in CVS stores but didn't apply for openings. Now the company works through the National Council on the Aging, Experience Works, AARP, city agencies, and community organizations to locate productive new employees.[4]

Candidate screening and interviewing techniques can unintentionally put off mature candidates as well. People accustomed to more traditional approaches to demonstrating their skills may balk at having to build something with Legos or explain how M&Ms are made. One major British bank realized that its psychometric and verbal-reasoning tests intimidated older candidates, and so it used role-playing exercises instead to gauge candidates' ability to handle customers. Britain's largest building society, Nationwide, has begun short-listing job candidates through telephone interviews to reduce the number of applicants rejected simply because they look older.[5]

A Culture That Embraces Mature Workers

In the past thirteen years, CVS has more than doubled the percentage of employees over age fifty—from 7 percent to 17 percent.[6] It has no mandatory retirement age, so that people can easily join the company at an advanced age and stay indefinitely (six employees are in their nineties); and it boosts its age-friendly image through internal and external publications. Corporate and HR department newsletters highlight the productivity and effectiveness of older workers, and CVS teamed with a cosmetics company to produce a maturity-focused magazine, *In Step with Healthy Living*.

Older workers can see that CVS honors experience. After accepting a buyout package from his management job at a competing major drugstore chain, fifty-nine-year-old Jim Wing joined CVS as the pharmacy supervisor for the company's southern Ohio stores. Why? "I'm too young to retire," he explains. "CVS is willing to hire older people. They don't look at your age but your experience." Pharmacy technician Jean Penn, age eighty, has worked in the business since 1942. She sold her own small pharmacy to CVS five years ago and began working in another CVS store the next day. She recently received a fifty-year pin (because "they don't make sixty-year pins"). By crediting Penn for time served before she joined the company, CVS loudly communicated how it values experience. Since mature employees often work under much younger managers, CVS fine-tuned its approach to manager training. "You need to train managers whose average age is in the mid-thirties to work effectively with people of all ages. Our experience has helped us identify key issues in managing and motivating older employees," says Stephen Wing of CVS.[7]

Home Depot also has a widespread reputation for hiring midcareer and older employees by hiring dislocated workers—people recently laid off or retired, or those seeking new ways to apply their skills. The company works with senior organizations, community centers across the country, and partners such as the Department of Labor with its One-Stop Referrals program. Home Depot provides flexible schedules, part-time work, flexible vacations, and leaves of absence for various reasons, including once-in-a-lifetime family events or travel opportunities. Team Depot affords many employees the opportunity to "give back to others" through community volunteer projects. As a result, Home Depot enjoys a larger pool of candidates from which to recruit, and the candidates are more qualified. Turnover remains low relative to the retail industry.[8]

Other corporations that routinely hire mature workers include Wal-Mart, where 22 percent of the workforce is fifty-five and older—over a quarter-million employees—in positions ranging from greeter to senior management, most of them frontline with customers. Store managers recruit through senior groups, retiree associations, and church and community groups. Hotel chain Days Inn hires older workers as reservations agents, often part-time and often through a retiree job bank. They experience lower turnover among older workers, and higher customer satisfaction than with younger staff.[9]

The way to succeed in hiring mature workers is simply to get started. As John Rother, AARP's director of policy and strategy, puts it, "What speaks most strongly to the sincerity of the interest in hiring older workers is hiring older workers. If there are other people who have been brought into the company at an older age, that certainly is a powerful message."[10]

Implementing Flexible Retirement

For most of human history, people worked for as long as they could. The first U.S. mandatory retirement law was enacted in 1920—less than one hundred years ago—and covered only employees of the U.S. federal government. Then came the Great Depression, when unemployment reached 25 percent. Desperate to make room for young workers, governments, unions, and employers initiated retirement programs as we know them today, with social security and pension plans. But in doing so, they institutionalized and stigmatized old age. Today, we face a shortage, not a surplus, and so we must phase out "retirement" as we know it.

Flex Retirement

Most people have heard of "phased retirement"—that is, a staged reduction in work hours and responsibilities ahead of full retirement. For example, Varian, a leading provider of radiotherapy systems, allows employees over fifty-five to negotiate a reduced work schedule if they've served a minimum of five years and plan to retire within the next three. The program addresses employees' requests for flexible and reduced work schedules that ease them into retirement. They typically work four days per week the first year and three days a week thereafter. Half time is the minimum, and two half-timers can job share. Participants retain full medical and dental benefits. Other earnings-based benefits, such as 401(k) plan contributions and disability and life insurance, are prorated. Participants can request to return full-time if the new schedule creates economic hardship.[11]

Phasing is a variation on the traditional retirement trajectory for employees and, as we noted, a poor one because it eases people *out* of the workforce. We recommend *flexible retirement*, which encompasses flexible roles and work styles, attractive work assignments suited to one's experience and inclination, and reduced hours, flexible schedules, and more control over one's time—*before and after* the point of official "retirement," which loses its significance as flex practices become common.

Flex retirement means not only *partial retirement*, so that employees can enjoy other pursuits, but also *active retirement*, wherein employees remain productively and socially engaged in the workplace. It means *ongoing work*, often starting before retirement age and continuing decades later, and not shedding employees to reduce costs. Through it, employers can achieve five important business goals, namely to

1. Retain the services of key employees and top performers who might otherwise join your competitors for new responsibilities or reduced hours instead of full retirement.

2. Retain and transfer institutional, industry, project, and customer knowledge and expertise, as flex retirees remain available to train and mentor younger colleagues.

3. Provide highly experienced temporary talent pools and thus moderate fluctuations in staffing needs without tapping traditional temporary agencies or incurring recruiting costs.

4. Retain leadership talent to fill unexpected gaps, facilitate executive transitions, and groom the next generation of leaders for eventual succession. Retirees can act as leaders on demand and help to maintain the leadership pipeline.

5. Control unit cost of labor, getting the same skilled labor at equivalent salary levels but saving on the costs of benefits—not just health care, but pension contributions, vacation time, and others—because these part-time workers are covered by their retiree benefits, which the company is paying for regardless of whether it makes use of the retiree labor.

We estimate that only one employer in five offers phased-retirement or retiree-return programs. In a William M. Mercer study, 23 percent of the companies surveyed had formal programs to provide mature workers with flexible work styles. Of these companies, 47 percent offer reduced hours or schedules, 42 percent offer temporary work, 42 percent offer consulting work, 17 percent offer job sharing, 10 percent offer telecommuting, and 45 percent create special positions and assignments, most often involving mentoring, training, or research and development.[12] Moreover, such programs typically lack the scale to affect a corporation's overall staffing, except in organizations like The Aerospace Corporation, where its retiree buffer approaches 10 percent of staff capacity. Most programs function as internal placement agencies for people with sought-after skills and experience. As labor markets tighten, large corporations in other industries should bring these programs up to scale.

Since many pension calculations discourage people from reducing hours or responsibilities prior to retirement, and U.S. government regulations preclude most workers from drawing salary and pension simultaneously from the same employer, many of today's flex retirement arrangements manifest as "retiree return" programs. Typically, the employee takes regular retirement and then returns (after a specified break such as six months) as a contractor, often for a maximum of one thousand hours per year. The Internal Revenue Service (IRS) imposes the hourly restriction to discourage companies from substituting full-time employees with retirees, thereby avoiding such expenses as health benefits and Federal Insurance Contributions (FICA). Employees who work more than one thousand hours per year must usually work through an agency and offer their services to other employers as well. Employers with highly variable customer demand or work structured as projects of various length and effort—engineering firms such as The Aerospace Corporation and MITRE as well as professional services firms and companies with seasonal demand such as retailers and tax preparers—can benefit enormously from this contingent workforce.

Retiree Reserves at MITRE Corporation

MITRE Corporation values experience and expertise—the average age of its five thousand employees is forty-six, or about six years above the national average. Seven years ago, it realized that too many people with key knowledge and experience were retiring or leaving to join dot-coms. As a talent retention strategy, it formalized an otherwise ad hoc process for engaging retirees into what it calls Reserves at the Ready. Under the program, any employee with ten years of service can become "part-time on call," working up to one thousand hours per year. They staff projects, mentor younger colleagues, and convey technical expertise and organizational, customer, and project knowledge. Participants are ineligible for paid leave or regular health-care benefits, but almost all have health coverage as retirees. Those receiving pension distributions must wait six months before returning to work. Thereafter, current pension distributions continue, and pension program contributions (to the voluntary unmatched limit) may continue, but retirees cannot initiate new distributions.

On average, one hundred fifty to two hundred people are "at the ready." Because of its long history of engaging retirees as part-time contributors, the company need not advertise the program. But it regularly informs its very active retiree association and the company at large about the program. MITRE also has a part-time work program that some employees use to phase into retirement, assuming a "part-time regular" status and working twenty to thirty hours per week, with benefits. Currently, two hundred fifty to three hundred people (roughly 5 percent of MITRE's workforce) are in the program.

Bill Albright explains the philosophy behind the reserves program: "If you have a culture that doesn't recognize older workers, any retiree work program is going to fail . . . A lot of organizations believe if you're not in your twenties or thirties, you're a has-been or a cost issue. The corporate culture must value older workers and provide them with working flexibility and learning opportunities, and this must come from top leadership."[13] MITRE received AARP awards in 2001 and 2003 as one of the best places to work for the over-fifty crowd.

Ron Coleman, a former systems engineer in MITRE's Economic Decision Analysis Center, is among the reserves. Retiring in 1998 at age sixty-six after nearly ten years of service, he waited a year before signing up for Reserves at the Ready. "I had a lot of stuff to take care of and wanted to get comfortable being retired, and then I felt ready to come back." Since then, he's averaged two projects a year, each four to eight weeks in duration. "I like to golf in the summer, and so am available for work November to March. I can also choose days to go to the office—usually Mondays—and work at home other days— say, Wednesday and Thursday—for a three-day work week. I stay refreshed, keep my hand in, and can train younger people, which I enjoy most."[14]

Bob Bennie is a "serial employee," joining MITRE fresh from graduate school in 1965, then again after stints in academia, retailing, and independent consulting. He kept returning because "it's one of the best companies to work for—great bunch of people and a thoroughly people-oriented organization. MITRE kept offering me the opportunity to learn new things and try new stuff through the years." He's in high demand, essentially working half-time for his old boss, and nears or hits the one thousand–hour maximum each year, working two and a half days a week, half at a local air force base/MITRE office and half at home. "I can't understand why anybody retires. You become expert at what you do, and you make decent money—

why stop? To do all the chores that you never wanted to do anyway? I'd rather keep working and pay someone else to do the chores. You spend your career learning how a company works. You're at your peak in terms of knowledge and experience at age sixty or sixty-five. A company should have the foresight to keep you involved and take advantage of the expertise needed."[15]

While most reserves are engineers, any in-demand employee can participate. Theresa Powers joined MITRE as a secretary in 1993 and retired in 2002. She's on call and works when needed, usually a week at a time to replace vacationing secretaries, for a total of about two months a year. She enjoys the arrangement: "I keep my finger in the pot and keep up my skills. The extra money's nice. I see people I like. It's very convenient—just three miles away from my house. And I still have plenty of time to spend with my grandkids." Theresa goes everywhere in the local MITRE facility. "I get to work all over, meet new people, learn new software. And it's good for the company, since I know the systems and am already trained and experienced."[16]

Resource Re-Entry at Monsanto Company

Monsanto launched a similar program, Resource Re-Entry Center, in 1991. Liz Thien-Reich, the program head for several years, explains, "Coming out of the lean-and-mean era of the 1980s, we realized that we needed replacements—and that we had qualified, intelligent, and loyal retirees whom we wanted to maintain our relationship with." The program has about three hundred participants part-time, generating 132,000 hours of work and a payroll of about $4.5 million per year. Approximately 10 percent of retiring employees sign up.[17]

The program is open to all employees of any age who leave the company in good standing and want to return to a part-time position. Departing employees must wait six months after leaving a full-time job. Managers must use retirees for job sharing, cyclical spikes, and temporary replacements for unplanned leaves. They cannot reduce benefit costs by hiring retirees for long-term work: "If people are working long hours, then they should be made full-time employees and receive full benefits." Participants are eligible for company savings and investment plans as well as spot bonuses, though not the normal bonus structure. Originally, participants could work only one thousand hours a year so that the program wouldn't interfere with pension payouts, but Monsanto recently relaxed the requirement for those people whose pensions would be untouched, such as retirees who had received a lump-sum payout.

The company has carefully designed and managed the program by holding town hall meetings with retirees, workers, and managers to determine each group's needs, calling on participants as needed, and tracking their skills and hours in a central database. A small staff administers placements, payroll, and returning employee logistics, and a company newsletter advises participants of classes and other resources. Monsanto recruits retirees by including a flyer with their retirement exit paperwork, targeting those considering part-time jobs in retirement. It promotes the program to managers through an internal Web page and brochures, but most of the internal promotion is word of mouth.

The program has reduced Monsanto's agency fees by some $600,000 a year and has helped to set reasonable rates for contractors. Other benefits are more difficult to measure and also more profound, such as the value of veterans' passing the torch to their successors.

Variations of Flexible Retirement

Retiring from one job or career to begin a new one is becoming more prevalent. People in the military, law enforcement, public safety, and public education—where retirement benefits are available after as few as twenty years of service, and mandatory retirement ages are low—often take a break then begin whole new careers. But these public institutions have inadvertently institutionalized a brain drain. At the Federal Bureau of Investigation (FBI), agents must retire at age fifty-seven, and so 40 percent of agents (many recruited after 9/11) have less than five years' experience. The FBI is now recruiting retired agents as analysts to fill shortages caused by post-9/11 expanded responsibilities.[18]

Complex regulations muddle up a seamless transition into retirement, with the flexibility that employees and employers would like both before and after the point of retirement. But organizations such as Dow Chemical Company are striving to rectify that, enabling employees to move into different roles throughout their careers. Dow provides for "career deceleration," or what we call "downshifting" into less intense roles.[19] Mature employees at Dow can coach younger colleagues on everything from career advancement to technical work processes or can teach courses on Six Sigma or leadership.

British building society Nationwide is rewriting its rules of retirement to reduce turnover and retain experience. At the traditional retirement age of sixty, employees can opt to work another ten years, with a performance and attendance check at age sixty-five. For people who prefer shorter workweeks later in their careers, the company initiated a pension scheme that bases payout on earnings throughout a career rather than the three years before retirement. The company also initiated hiring campaigns aimed at people over fifty, revised hiring practices such as short-listing candidates by telephone, and included age in its equal opportunities policy. Ten percent of the workforce is now over fifty, compared with 1 percent fifteen years ago. According to a Nationwide spokesperson, "We're finding it's not about people's age; it's about their ability."[20]

Reforming Pensions and Benefits

In the United States, truly flexible retirement is still impossible for most employees of publicly held for-profit corporations. The IRS limits the timing and conditions of many pension distributions, and pension calculations often discourage people from reducing their hours with a current employer before retirement because their pay rate in the last few years of work often determines their payouts. Some combinations of pension programs and government regulations encourage retirement-age employees to "take the money and run"—sometimes to another employer, even a competitor—rather than staying with the original employer in an adjusted capacity.

Pension and benefits law and health-care benefits funding are complex fields. In this section, we outline what you should know about these issues, specifically how they complicate the hiring and deployment of mature workers and retirees. We describe the work-arounds available to employers under today's conditions and laws, and we endorse a set of legislative and policy reforms that would make employing mature workers easier. This discussion applies mainly to the United States. Countries with government-provided or -funded health-care services for all citizens will probably relate only to the pension section.

Pension Problems

According to an Employment Policy Foundation (EPF) study, 65 percent of U.S. employers want to offer flexible retirement arrangements, but most feel blocked by regulatory restrictions.[21] Three sets of regulations cover pension and benefits:

- *ERISA.* The Employee Retirement Income Security Act imposes rules of uniformity in the treatment of employees and their pension benefits. These rules inhibit making special arrangements for the skilled and valuable employees whom companies most want to retain.

- *IRS.* Internal Revenue Code regulations prohibit defined-benefit pension plans from making distributions until employment ends or the employee reaches "normal retirement age." Coupled with an ERISA provision, the code can prohibit distributions even *after* normal retirement age. Other tax laws impose penalties on the "early" (before age fifty-nine) withdrawal of funds from retirement savings accounts such as 401(k) plans and restrict the employee's ability to manage sources of income during career deceleration or phasing toward retirement.

- *ADEA.* The Age Discrimination in Employment Act requires equal benefits, such as health insurance, regardless of age. The 1967 law defines *older worker* as over forty. But plaintiffs have invoked the law not only to protect the interests of mature workers but also to challenge them. For example, if a sixty-year-old receives preferred treatment when an employer modifies a pension plan, then a forty-five-year-old can protest.

Given these obstacles and uncertainties, how can employers legally implement flex retirement programs?[22] There are four basic options or workarounds that companies can pursue. They can

- *Reduce hours as an employee phases toward retirement.* Continue pension contribution but pay no pension benefits. This option may entail changing or prorating pension payout calculations, because many defined-benefit plans base retirement pay on average pay during the final few years of work.

- *Implement a retiree-return program.* Hire retirees as contractors, subject to the current limit of one thousand hours per year, unless they are clearly "independent consultants." Pension and other retiree benefits are already in place.

- *Engage retirees as independent consultants.* Seek retirees who can set their own working conditions and offer equivalent services to other employers.

- *Invite people to continue work under revised arrangements.* Be careful to accommodate only those in-demand or highly specialized employees, and not everyone who wants to stay. Employees may have to delay pension payouts, and employers may have to adjust mandatory or customary retirement-age policies.

Most of the pension-and-benefit-related complications affect workers under sixty-five (or the organization's "normal retirement age"). Beyond that age, matters simplify a bit, and some recent legislation actually motivates people to keep working. The Senior Citizen Freedom to Work Act of 2000 removed the Social Security earnings test for those over sixty-five. Workers are no longer penalized by having their Social Security payouts reduced because they continue to earn income. The gradual raising of the "full payout" age for Social Security from sixty-five to sixty-seven not only improves the system's long-term solvency but also motivates people to work until full payment age. Not-for-profit organizations and their employees enjoy a great deal more freedom in pension management than for-profits do.

Health-Care Headaches

The costs of health benefits have been rising at double-digit rates annually. Consequently, employers want to reduce these costs by reducing coverage for employees and retirees. Since costs and premiums increase with age, employers have a disincentive to retain older workers. However, retiring people early may simply shift the costs from the employee health-care account to the retiree health-care account. As the number of covered retirees grows, their health benefits become a significant proportion of an employer's fixed costs. Many large, long-lived corporations—in the automotive and steel industries, for example—have more retirees than active employees. Even if pensions were fully funded, the exploding costs of retiree health-care benefits can debilitate the corporation's finances. General Motors, with 2.5 retirees per active employee, has a retiree health-care liability of over $60 billion. The EPF estimates the current total retiree health benefits liability of U.S. corporations at half a trillion dollars, half of which is borne by only twenty companies. By 2008, the number of companies with over $1 billion in liability will swell to over one hundred fifty.[23] So more employers are taking strong, sometimes draconian, action, such as increasing employee and retiree premiums and co-payments, lowering coverage levels and raising eligibility requirements, or eliminating retiree health coverage altogether.

Meanwhile, employees know that, with costs rising, health-care coverage is an essential benefit. They fear doing anything that might reduce or jeopardize coverage, and won't phase into retirement or negotiate more flexible work arrangements if their benefits will decrease or their health-care costs climb. The availability of health-care benefits can motivate employees to keep working. Even if covered by Medicare, older workers might continue working to maintain coverage for dependents. In other cases, taking early retirement might enable employees to lock in retiree health-care coverage benefits.

We face a mishmash of conflicting goals and incentives. Employers want to retain talent but must control current costs and reduce future liabilities. Employees fear to change their work arrangements lest their coverage erode further, but must absorb whatever changes employers succeed in imposing. What are the work-arounds here? Several are emerging, each with different cost and tax implications.

- *Multi-Employer Welfare Arrangements (MEWAs).* These enable smaller companies to gain economies of scale, pooling of costs, and access to expertise in contracting for and managing health coverage providers. MEWAs also increase the potential portability of coverage for employees.

- *Self-insurance.* Some large companies are becoming their own insurers of employee health coverage to reduce costs and gain more favorable tax treatment for premiums paid.

- *Retiree Health Accounts (RHAs).* These defined contribution–type plans essentially "prefund" the retirement health benefits provided by the employer. Employer contributions are not tax deductible. This plan encourages older employees to keep working to get more money in the RHA.

- *Voluntary Employees Beneficiary Association (VEBA).* These trusts are more like individual 401(k) accounts for health care. Employees self-fund their retirement health coverage, and earnings are tax-exempt.

- *Health Savings Accounts (HSAs).* In this most promising and flexible option, both employer and employee contributions are tax deductible, and earnings and distributions are tax exempt.

As with pensions, health-care coverage gets simpler once employees and retirees reach age sixty-five and qualify for Medicare. When employees have their health-care coverage already established, the employer's incentive reverses—it becomes *less expensive* to hire an older worker, not more, if you can avoid providing health benefits. However, some participants in such programs as retiree-return told us that, while they very much like working, they feel a bit exploited. We could argue for paying retiree-returns *more* than they earned as regular employees, given the value of their benefits-cost-free labor.

Control over Health-Care Costs

How can employers control health-care costs of employees and retirees? First, they control medical costs by working with hospitals, physicians, and other providers; identifying cost-effective practices and treatment protocols; encouraging use of generic drugs and mail-order fulfillment; and actively managing high-cost cases. Second, they encourage "informed consumerism" by offering wellness programs, helping employees plan for and prefund retirement health care, and educating and encouraging employees to understand their health-care costs and manage their consumption.

For example, Ford Motor Company has nearly two hundred fifty thousand retirees and dependents, representing 44 percent of the covered population but 66 percent of health benefits costs, with prescription drugs a major rising cost. The company uses its clout to improve quality and cost of service by building profiles and required performance metrics for vendors such as hospitals, and installing dosage optimization and generic drug programs with incentives for physicians. It has reduced cost structure by requiring retirees to contribute to premiums, making future coverage for new hires less generous, forming a VEBA trust for employee contributions to retirement medical premium accounts, establishing tiered co-pay levels on prescriptions and incentives to purchase drugs by mail order, and providing health education for employees and retirees.[24]

Vita Needle Company hires predominantly older employees precisely because the cost structure is lower when employees get health coverage through Medicare or previous employers. A fourth-generation family business, Vita manufactures needles and small metal precision products for major companies like Johnson & Johnson. It has hired older workers for almost twenty years, and the average employee age is seventy-four. As CEO Fred Hartman explains, "In the late '80s, we had to reinvent the company. We needed to find flexible employees who were willing to work part-time. At the time, that's the only segment of people we could find—people who had been laid off or retired. So we started with three or four people in this age category. Then the light bulb went on: This is better than just a short-term solution."[25] Vita Needle enjoys a dedicated, reliable, and experienced workforce and a lower cost structure—and both matter in highly competitive industries.

Policy to Pursue

Making flex retirement a productive reality today requires creativity, care, and persistence. But it's worth the effort both to retain key employees and to prepare for increasingly various and flexible work and retirement options that future employees will demand. That said, the U.S. government must remove the regulatory impediments so that mature workers can more freely work, and employers, more freely employ them. We support four important changes recommended by the EPF:[26]

- Amend pension rules to prohibit reductions in pension benefits if an employee's pay drops because of flex retirement. This amendment would protect the employee from pension calculation schemes based on average salary over the last few years of service and enable the employee to "decelerate" or phase into retirement without losing pension benefits.

- Eliminate the 10 percent penalty on early distribution to employees with thirty or more years of service, regardless of age, and allow distributions from 401(k) plans before age fifty-nine. These two changes would give employees much greater flexibility during periods of flex retirement.

- Allow people ages fifty-five to sixty-five to buy Medigap insurance at competitive rates. This option would give mature employees a bridge in health-care coverage until they reach the Medicare qualification age. (Of course, a provision for universal health-care coverage would do the same.)

- Liberalize nondiscrimination tests for flexible retirement plans so that employers could more easily customize work arrangements and offer them to employees with exceptionally valuable skills and experience without breaking antidiscrimination laws and uniformity mandates.

Recent attempts to change these laws have stalled, and the Social Security reforms mentioned earlier—gradual raising of the full-payout age and easing of restrictions on outside income—are incremental at best. Worse, the U.S. government lags behind several European Union members that are passing legislation to adjust retirement ages or require companies to give employees flexible retirement options.

We urge all employers to lobby for these reforms. Large corporations with significant government relations units should add mature worker employability to their lobbying agendas. Others can work through industry associations. Employees who will benefit from these reforms can make their voices heard, individually and through organizations for seniors.

ACTIONS TO TAKE

To Leverage Mature Workers

We recommend these basic steps to attract mature workers and retain their services as needed beyond the conventional retirement age:

☐ *Develop a mature worker strategy* with the overarching goal of maintaining your supply of talent and transferring valuable skills and knowledge from one generation to the next. Anticipate your company's short- and longer-term need to recruit and retain experience and expertise. Set specific goals for mature worker retention.

☐ *Assess recruiting channels and explore nontraditional sources.* Recruiting mature workers sometimes requires operating through new channels or partnerships with professional societies or seniors groups.

☐ *Review job descriptions and remove tacit references to employee age.* Mature workers are likely to interpret advertisements stressing "high energy," "fast pace," and "high ambition" as implicitly targeting younger workers, even when they possess these traits.

☐ *Review and adjust interviewing and hiring practices*, including the patterns and preferences of hiring managers. Watch out for hiring managers who implicitly favor younger job applicants or feel uncomfortable hiring older subordinates.

☐ *Review and adjust human resources practices generally.* Examine promotion policies, salary calculations, performance review procedures, and benefits to remove any implicit or explicit biases against older employees.

☐ *Build a reputation as an active recruiter and a good employer of mature workers.* An organization that publicly values the experience and capabilities of mature workers can safeguard its talent supply.

☐ *Assess mature workers' interest in flexible retirement.* Invite suggestions for how work might be structured, such as on a project basis or work from home, and experiment with such arrangements.

☐ *Adjust pension calculations and employee benefits* to enable career deceleration and flexible work arrangements before the point of retirement. Let long-tenured employees reduce hours and pay without lowering their ultimate pension rates.

☐ *Establish a systematic retiree-return program.* Set targets for availability and participation. Monitor not only policies and administrative mechanics, but also program marketing and retiree recruitment.

☐ *Institute procedures for career deceleration (or downshifting),* new roles and responsibilities, and flexible work arrangements for mature employees approaching or postponing retirement.

☐ *Articulate the desired public policy and legislative changes,* including how those changes will benefit your business and its mature employees.

☐ *Lobby policy makers and legislators directly*—especially at the federal level—and through business and industry associations and policy research organizations to recommend and enact these reforms.

☐ *Work with your union leaders* to change local pension and benefits so that union members can enjoy flex retirement, and to enlist union support of policy and legislative reforms.

5

The Needs and Frustrations of Midcareer Workers

Why the Boomer Bottleneck
Disrupts Productivity

W E SENSE real opportunity for employers to rekindle their midcareer workers. Employers can gain commitment and higher performance in the short term, and employees who are reengaged midcareer are more likely to opt for flex retirement and keep contributing indefinitely. The good news here is that rekindling careers doesn't require big new programs or great expense. Instead, as we shall see, it requires management attention and the application of existing career management techniques to a much broader employee constituency—the hitherto neglected middle class.

Profile of the Bottlenecked

An employee assistance counselor at a well-respected high-tech company shared a disturbing but increasingly common story about an accomplished middle manager in his late forties. A fifteen-year employee, this gentleman sought help not because of a specific event or health issue, but because of a deep general malaise. He was by all accounts a keeper: productive, highly professional, the kind of long-term presence who holds an organization together; not on the fast track to the executive suite, but nonetheless the kind of employee the company should retain.

He was "sandwiched" between obligations to his family, including high school and college-age children, and to his elderly parents, who had just moved to be close to his family. He longed to spend more time with his children before they flew the nest for good. A leader in a key functional unit responsible for service and field support for a profitable segment of business customers, he still found his work interesting but increasingly routine. The work group was still demoralized after two rounds of downsizing. He was putting in long hours, not so much in solving customer problems—which always excited and interested him—but in fighting fires and moderating workflow. He believed that his career had stalled. The company had flattened its structure and networked its operations, and there were fewer promotion opportunities than in the past. Most of the people higher in his organization were of a similar age, and some "fast trackers" were considerably younger. There didn't seem to be much room for movement at all.

The employee talked through all these pressures, the mental and physical tolls that they were taking, and then summarized: "This isn't how my life and career were supposed to play out. I was supposed to be accomplishing more and enjoying more. This isn't the deal I signed up for. And I don't know how much longer I can cope."

What's disturbing about the story isn't just the employee's situation—most people experience pressures like these in midlife and midcareer. It's that the counselor was at a loss as to what to do, and the company was ill prepared to make any adjustments to provide relief. The counselor offered empathy and localized advice, but the employee remained at risk to give up and quit.

Should Companies Worry About Midcareer Crises?

Midcareer crises take many shapes these days. Very capable people find their careers interrupted by corporate restructuring, or their promotion prospects bottlenecked by too few openings or too many fellow candidates.[1] They may be disillusioned and overwhelmed if corporate downsizing has left them with more to do and running harder just to stay in place. They may see their work horizon lengthening if they haven't accumulated the wealth needed for retirement. They may feel their skills and methods going obsolete as businesses reshape their processes, boundaries, and technologies. Meantime, at home they may be sandwiched between commitments to children and parents, frustrated by lack of time for family and community, and unable to adjust work/life balance.

Midcareer crises, like midlife crises generally, are hardly news. Especially in a society that prizes individual freedom, initiative, progress, and material rewards, people are raised to feel in control of their fates and ambitious to accomplish things in their lives and careers. When people reach age forty or thereabouts, the recognition of aging triggers the quest for change. They note that life's game is about half over and take stock in their progress and accomplishment, seldom with complete satisfaction and occasionally with debilitating disappointment. They've made compromises at work and at home, and career and life decisions may have painted them into corners. Even the most successful individuals typically note some missing pieces in their lives' plans. Midcareer crises vary greatly in intensity, and people emerge from them in different ways. Some become increasingly resigned and disillusioned. Some disrupt their lives—through divorce, career change, relocation—in search of a fresh start. Some adjust their goals and emerge renewed and recommitted to their personal progress. Our point here is that at this stage of their careers, employees are ripe (and sometimes desperate) for change and renewal, yet few businesses recognize and take advantage of that fact.

Table 5-1 summarizes midcareer workers' common sources of frustration. To reengage them and rekindle their careers, employers must understand and recognize these crisis points.

Why should management worry about midcareer crises? Why rekindle the careers of people besides the key performers and leaders at risk? Because your company needs them—for productivity today and retention tomorrow, when the labor and talent shortage hits.

Every day that an employee is less than fully engaged in the work and goals of the enterprise, energy and focus and contribution are left on the table—productivity lost and never to be recovered. Relatively straightforward changes—a fresh and challenging assignment, rotation to a different part of the organization, extra or specialized training, an in-house career switch, or a sabbatical—can quickly turn an unfocused employee into a reenergized one. Such changes benefit more than the employees and their individual productivity. The organization also benefits because the employee is better positioned

TABLE 5-1

Career crisis points

Crisis point	Explanation
Career bottleneck	The baby boom generation is large, and too many people are competing for too few leadership positions in organizations that have been shedding layers of hierarchy. Next to job security, this is one of the biggest concerns of managers in their forties and fifties.
Work/life tension	Midcareer workers are "sandwiched" between commitments to children and parents, often at the same time that their working responsibilities are peaking.
Lengthening horizon	Those who are not accumulating sufficient wealth for retirement face the disappointing prospect of having to work many more years. Many of today's midcareer workers have been lavish spenders and sparse savers.
Skills obsolescence	Some struggle to keep up with ways of working and managing in the information economy. Some hope that time and diligence will get them promoted or into better and higher-paying jobs, when what they most need is upgraded skills.
Disillusionment with employer	This includes insecurity and distrust following waves of downsizing, as well as resentment over the enormous compensation gaps between topmost executives and almost all other employees.
Burnout	People who have been career driven for twenty or more years find themselves stretched and stressed, find their work unexciting or repetitive, and run low on energy and the ability to cope.
Career disappointment	The roles employees play and the impact of their work fail to measure up to their youthful ideals and ambitions.

to share experience and innovate in the new role. We've all seen this kind of invigoration happen with individuals. The challenge—especially in most large organizations, where departments hoard talent rather than circulate it throughout the enterprise—is to rejuvenate careers more purposefully, more systematically, and for more employees. Longer term, your company will need these workers—and may want some to work past retirement age. Alleviating shortages and preventing a brain drain are not a matter of enticing just one generation of older workers to continue contributing; rather, working (at least part-time) past retirement age has got to become the norm. So you must retain not just the current generation of mature workers, but future generations as well. The most severe period of the worker shortage and brain drain will likely occur when most baby boomers—midcareer workers today—reach their sixties. Companies and economies cannot endure their retiring on schedule. But to retain midcareer workers tomorrow, you must reengage them today. Otherwise, the vast numbers who are less than satisfied with their employment situations will hang on only until they can retire or jump ship.

Rekindling the careers of midcareer workers is simultaneously a short-term and a long-term play. The same career changes and management actions to reenergize employees today also increase their effectiveness, commitment, and loyalty down the road. It's a win-win arrangement: win now with greater productivity and innovation; win later with better retention of employees with important skill and experience. Or a lose-lose, if too many employees remain frustrated in their careers, gradually disengage, and merely count the days until retirement.

Portrait of the Midcareer Worker

In terms of demographics, life stage, and career stage, midcareer workers are, naturally, in between the extremes of the younger and older cohorts. They are in the middle in terms of education, ethnic diversity, and income and investable assets. Many are well educated, twice as likely as their parents to earn high school and college degrees. This cohort is 76 percent non-Hispanic white (versus 61 percent for the young cohort and 88 percent for the mature). Perhaps most significantly, this cohort is gender diverse. The boomers were the first real industrial-age generation of working women, with 80 percent choosing to work outside the home for reasons other than the extraordinary circumstances of war.

Born to Be Wild

Born between 1951 and 1970, today's midcareer cohort includes most of the boomer generation and the older third of Generation X. Coming of age in the '60s and '70s—a time of global social upheaval—this cohort is cause oriented. Midcareers prefer to see the big picture and think in terms of a life's mission. The assassinations of Dr. Martin Luther King Jr., John F. Kennedy, Robert F. Kennedy, and Malcolm X, as well as the civil rights movement, women's liberation, and antiwar protests, sparked the desire to do something meaningful with their lives. Thus, they hope to embrace the vision, mission, and ambition of their companies. Ambitious, idealistic, self-reliant, and competitive—think young urban professional, or yuppie—they want to prove their worth, and so expect clear rules of performance measurement, focusing on both individual and group merit.

With such formative experiences as the Vietnam War, the impeachment of Richard M. Nixon, or the Cultural Revolution in mainland China, mid-career workers tend to eschew authority and distrust government, and so they tend to break rules, experiment, demand participative management, and value horizontal over hierarchical organizations.

Unlike today's youth, this cohort did not "grow up digital," though it witnessed the advent of space exploration. The older ones were among the last to take their mathematics and engineering exams with slide rules rather than personal computers or even handheld calculators. Yet, they have learned to apply information technology quite cleverly throughout their careers, pioneering such methods as business reengineering to reshape how corporations work. Among their strengths, today's midcareer workers are motivated, flexible, and people oriented. Their accumulated experience and knowledge are valuable, and they have more soft skills and customer-service orientation than the younger cohort. Among their potential weaknesses are a distrust of leadership and tendency to be self-absorbed.

Personal Matters of Midcareer Workers

Compared with earlier generations, today's midcareer workers lead very busy sandwiched lifestyles, full of pressures and priorities at home.[2] They report the highest incidence of financial and parenting issues. Just over half are coping with a financial crisis or debt reduction, and one in three is paying for their children's education. Over 40 percent are raising children, and 20 percent are adjusting to empty nesting as children leave home. The 30 percent who report serious health issues are only slightly fewer than the 32 percent among mature workers; however, for midcareers these health problems more likely involve a parent or an in-law. Regarding relationships, midcareers are most likely—almost one in five—to report coping with marital problems or divorce.

Midcareer Workers' Attitudes Toward Work

In *The New Employee/Employer Equation* survey, midcareer workers' average tenure is ten years, but that number can be deceiving: 42 percent have been with their employers for five years or less, and 39 percent for more than ten. One in four has supervisory or managerial responsibility, and among those, one in three is a midlevel or senior manager. While the preponderance are employed by for-profit enterprises, this cohort is the most likely (27 percent) to work in some form of government service (including government-provided education and health care). Most significantly, this cohort reports the highest number of hours worked per week—average of forty-five and median of forty-two, with 30 percent saying they work fifty or more hours per week. As in the other cohorts, there is a significant difference by gender, with men reporting almost five hours more per week than women. Not surprisingly, midcareer workers are most likely to report too much on their plate at work (22 percent), and 43 percent are coping with feelings of burnout.

Fifty-eight percent of midcareer employees express overall satisfaction with the job; that's slightly higher than the young cohort but 10 percentage points lower than matures. Almost one-third will express overall dissatisfaction with the job, the highest among the cohorts. Midcareer workers also express the lowest satisfaction rates with their immediate managers (48 percent). They are least likely to agree (only one in three) that top management displays integrity or commitment to employee development, and most likely (one in four) to disagree with the organization's policies on important employee matters.

Finally, midcareer employees are least likely to describe their workplace as congenial and fun, their colleagues as cooperative with teamwork as the rule, and their job as an opportunity to try new things. Over half seek some sort of change in responsibilities or arrangements at work, with 20 percent saying they are looking for a new job at another company, and 20 percent saying that they are looking for a major career change. Thirty-six percent, highest among the three cohorts, say they feel dead-ended in their current jobs.

Retirement Preferences of Midcareer Workers

The midcareer cohort is again in the middle in terms of planned retirement age, with an average age of sixty-three and a median of sixty-five (young workers plan to retire earliest, mature workers to retire latest). Two-thirds of this cohort plan to work in retirement, preferably to move back and forth between working and not working (as opposed to working full- or part-time). Many in this cohort identify strongly with their work, their disciplines, and their careers. They intend to learn, grow, try new things, and be productive indefinitely—often through a combination of commercial, volunteer, and personal pursuits. However, many have not saved enough to retire independently. With the decline in defined benefit plans, their employers' pension programs are less generous and less guaranteed, and many doubt whether Social Security will cover any shortfall in their financial needs in retirement.

What Midcareer Workers Want from Employers

Table 5-2 lists midcareer workers' relative preferences among ten broad elements of the employment deal. Like the mature cohort, midcareer workers value the security elements most, but with the order reversed—benefits, then retirement packages. Given their family responsibilities, midcareers heavily weigh the immediate benefits package, and the combined weight on security items (35 points of 100) is the highest among the three cohorts by 5 points. Compared with the mature cohort, midcareers place a little more emphasis on the workplace being enjoyable and on flexible schedules and vacation time.

We see a growing gap between employees' effort and satisfaction. Midcareer workers tend to be loyal and hard-working employees. The majority would contribute extra effort to help the organization succeed, yet only 43 percent say they are passionate about their jobs, and only 33 percent feel energized by their work. We also sense midcareer workers finding fault not only with employers, but with themselves—failure to live up to ambitious youthful expectations, to make a difference in their lives and careers. When

TABLE 5-2

What matters to midcareer workers

General elements of the deal	Relative weight
Comprehensive benefits package	19
Comprehensive retirement package	16
Work that enables me to learn and grow	11
Workplace that is enjoyable	11
Work that is personally stimulating	9
Flexible work schedule	9
10 percent more in total compensation	7
Two weeks' additional paid vacation	6
Work that is worthwhile to society	6
Flexible workplace	5

Relative weights add to 100

Source: The New Employee/Employer Equation survey

they reach whatever they define as *midlife*, many individuals find themselves reevaluating whether their lives have had the impact they anticipated when they were teens. Many in this group set out at eighteen to change the world, and their careers in corporations have not met their personal standard of impact. Keep in mind that their formative experiences were largely negative—assassinations, an unpopular war, a nuclear threat, a disgraced government, a declining economy, an oil crisis. Their ambition and idealism are interwoven with disillusionment, and for many in midcareer, disillusionment rears its head.

Those who feel frustrated in their careers naturally don't want to continue indefinitely with their current jobs and employers. They want to put their experience to work, but they want to work differently, in terms of both roles and work arrangements. Those who can afford to often make career switches into fields with greater social impact, such as teaching. And therein lies a problem for employers—capable and talented employees are opting out when their jobs lose variety and excitement. High performers aren't exempt from career frustrations. But they are more likely to have the personal and financial wherewithal to "call their own shots" and pursue alternative careers. Failure to identify these people and rekindle their careers causes a premature brain drain, as people depart before retirement age. Meanwhile, those who need role changes but can't afford to leave the corporate world can be increasingly disenchanted and disengaged. They stay, but often at minimal levels of commitment and productivity. They, too, and their employers, will benefit from rekindled careers.

What to Remember About Midcareer Workers

Midcareer workers need a mix of the pragmatic and the psychological. First, they need comprehensive benefit plans to meet their demanding life stage. These can commonly include elder care and child care, in addition to health and wellness programs. For many, especially those facing "lengthening horizons," financial management assistance matters more. Second, they need the flexibility to meet work and life commitments. Everyone values flexible schedules and time off. But compared with the other career cohorts, midcareers need flexible schedules and work arrangements (e.g., working from home on designated days) more immediately to accommodate all their commitments. Yet many have focused so much on their careers that they hesitate to request more flexibility, and many employers implicitly expect these experienced employees, especially managers, to work on-site or on call all the time. Third, they need stimulation, variety, and a change of pace, sometimes including the chance to reinvent themselves. Many midcareer workers are overdue for changes in role, an injection of training and development, or simply fresh assignments. They want to leverage their skills and experience in new directions, but they sense little opportunity to do so. The next chapter outlines more specific programs designed to rekindle their careers and provide more choices for workers of all ages.

Like everyone else, midcareer workers also need the fundamentals—meaningful and personally fulfilling work that incorporates responsibility, recognition, and personal progress, promotion bottlenecks notwithstanding. Since many of them remain idealistic and cause oriented, they most enjoy work that contains a service component and coincides with their "life mission." Unfortunately, too many feel sidetracked from their mission and ideals.

6

The Relaunch of Careers

How to Rekindle Employees' Passion for Work

How can employees rekindle their careers? First, by tackling a fresh assignment, perhaps elsewhere in the organization, designed to offer variety and challenge and to stimulate skills development. Unfortunately, many midcareer employees are "tracked" into specific functions or organizational units from which they fear to stray and their managers are loath to lose them. Second, by a heavy dose of training and new experience, sometimes through a refresher course, but often through a new discipline. However, as people well established in their careers and very busy on the job, midcareer workers may not readily admit the need for training and development—even when they crave a fresh start.

So we recommend three broad *tactics*, each aimed at unlocking more of the potential of midcareer workers. We detail them in the rest of this chapter.

- *Rekindle careers.* There are a variety of ways to rejuvenate people and their careers, engendering a fresh sense of accomplishment and renewed loyalty and commitment to the organization. These include fresh assignments or career switches, mentoring or knowledge-sharing roles, additional training and development, and sabbaticals. Change of pace, the opportunity to learn, and the opportunity to apply what's already known in new ways can all reengage midcareer employees, rekindle their ambition, and rejuvenate their careers.

- *Recruit reentrants.* Don't miss the opportunity to recruit midcareer employees, including people returning to the workforce (for example, women returning after raising families), people changing careers, and people displaced by other organizations' restructurings. These people are often highly capable and eager, but they may not have the recent relevant track record that forms the heart of most résumés and dominates most hiring decisions. Organizations hire young workers primarily on the basis of capability and potential more than immediate experience. They should be open to hiring people of all ages on that basis.

- *Expand leadership development.* Despite the size of the boomer cohort and the number of midcareer employees eager to fill the relatively scarce promotion slots available, many large organizations find their leadership "bench strength" surprisingly thin because their leadership development pipelines have gotten leaky. Take the opportunity to refill the pipeline with midcareer as well as young high potentials, and to recognize late-bloomer candidates for leadership. Also extend leadership development experiences to people who will be leaders within their organizations or functions, but are not necessarily on a path to the executive suite.

Few corporations put such attention and resources into reengaging their midcareer employees. After all, doesn't "the career belong to the individual"? That means the employee is ultimately responsible for his or her own skills acquisition, career progress, and marketability. The individual must learn about and seek the roles and assignments that forward a career. We agree, but also point out that the organization creates the conditions under which individual career initiative can flourish or be stifled. Too many companies pay mere lip service to the notion that employees manage their careers, hiding behind that declaration while leaving institutional barriers in place.

We're not advocating a return to the more paternalistic employment practices of yesteryear. Neither party is unilaterally responsible for determining what's best for the employee and then structuring a career accordingly. The initiative to make a career move is primarily the employee's. But it is in the enlightened self-interest of the employer to make career rekindling possible. In fact, we believe it's incumbent upon the employer—especially in the person of the employee's immediate manager—to keep the possibilities of career rekindling open, to recognize when the employee is in need of change, and to encourage the employee to seek change when the time is right. That's not paternalism—it's good management.

Rekindle Careers

The most fundamental way to engage any employee is through work that is interesting, important, and personally satisfying, including satisfying the need for a sense of career progress. Over time, the most inherently interesting and important work can become routine, and the most responsible and well-performed job can seem stagnant. For employment relationships to remain vital, people need variety, change of role, change of venue—they must stay in motion. But most of us reach points at least once—and sometimes multiple times in our working lives—when variety and momentum dwindle. We want to reinvent ourselves in some way, and our careers need rejuvenating. The best employers find ways to let that happen, because the alternatives are undesirable: some employees will seek opportunities elsewhere, and some will hang on but drift into low levels of productivity and commitment. In this section, we discuss five basic ways to enable career rejuvenation: fresh assignments, career changes, mentoring roles, fresh training, and sabbaticals.

Fresh Assignments

Often, the easiest way to reenergize an employee and a career is with an exciting new assignment, involving a new role and fresh challenge, sometimes in a different location or part of the organization. For midcareer workers, the best assignments mix roughly equal parts of old and new—the opportunity to leverage existing skills, experience, and organizational contacts while developing new ones. In some organizations, this type of internal movement across roles or units is commonplace, recognized as a facet of people's careers and valued as a means of "fresh blood circulation" throughout the enterprise. In many large organizations, however, talent is more often hoarded than circulated. There are subtle barriers to regular and widespread internal movement, and hence to using fresh assignments as an employee engagement technique. Openings are posted but not consistently, managers and departments strive to keep experienced employees in the fold, and there's no active agency for finding and matching assignments, for getting the fresh blood circulating faster. For most employees, next-assignment planning is part of an annual development planning exercise, and the options discussed tend to be conservative and close to home.

The bottom line is that some intervention may be needed to make more fresh assignments available to midcareer workers in need of variety and challenge. The means may include job-posting systems (in their basic form just passive listings), candidate locator systems (more active: who in the organization has the right experience or would be highly interested in an opening?), and assignment-brokering agencies (most active: seeking out opportunities on behalf of the employee). These means may need support from changes in managerial behavior—seeking "nontraditional" candidates for openings from across the enterprise, and willingly "releasing" employees to move elsewhere in the organization. The questions for senior management are two: Is our fresh blood flowing at a healthy rate? And are we motivating (through measurement and compensation) managers to do the right things to maintain the flow?

Some corporations are serious and systematic about keeping the fresh blood flowing. At Dow Chemical, the companywide expectation is that employees at all levels will continue to learn and grow, seek out new roles and development opportunities, and ready themselves for their "next career" moves.[1] At Duke Power, employees can post their jobs in search of swaps with others of equal grade level. At Lands' End, employees can request two-week trial transfers to other departments and then finalize the switch if all goes well. And many companies are deciding that it's finally time to relax or eliminate time-in-position requirements before an employee can seek a new role. Bell Canada both reduced its time-in-position standard for employees and set a transition time limit (thirty to forty-five days) for how long a manager could take before releasing an employee to a new position.[2]

Some organizations are very creative in making available fresh assignments. For example, General Electric targets interested midcareer managers for overseas assignments. Some empty nesters are suddenly more mobile and excited by very different assignments and locations. If the children have grown up or gone to college, and the employee is not constrained by commitments to parents or spouse's career, it may be a great time for a move, even offshore. GE also taps experienced managers to integrate new acquisitions—an ideal way for an experienced manager to get a change of scene and yet bring to bear a career's worth of organizational know-how. As GE's vice president of executive development puts it, "It's part of the DNA here to keep adding things to people's plates and making sure they have new opportunities."[3] In a similar vein, Principal Financial chooses empty nesters for high-visibility moves, particularly the relocations that they are finding difficult for the thirty-year-olds to make.

When considering employee relocations, some companies consider employees' life stage and personal needs. For example, one employee might want to move closer to children or parents. A second might for health or lifestyle reasons want to escape the smog and clog of the city. A third, perhaps facing heavy college tuition payments, might want to move where the cost of living is lower. The ideal fresh assignment for a midcareer employee may well fit the needs of both career and life stage.

Role changes can be particularly appealing to highly paid professional and managerial talent. For example, in 2000, Deloitte Consulting looked at the firm's demographics and realized that by 2003, 40 percent of its then eight hundred fifty partners would be fifty or older and eligible to retire at fifty-five. The firm didn't want to lose this talented group of men and women en masse, so it created what it called a Senior Leaders program, which enabled partners in their early fifties to redesign their career paths. (The program, along with a similar one at Deloitte's sister company, Deloitte & Touche, is currently on hold as the two companies reintegrate operations following the decision not to separate as planned.)[4]

Here's how the Senior Leaders program worked: Each year, a ten-member global selection committee assessed candidates who had made a unique contribution to the firm and would continue to add significant value. The committee then sat down with each nominated employee to customize a second career with the firm, including flexible hours and work location, special projects, and the opportunity to engage in mentoring, research, training and development, company promotions, or global expansion. Deloitte still has about a dozen active senior leaders, most of whom opted for full-time work in their rejuvenated roles.

The partner who launched the program describes two key benefits: "First, it enables us to keep people we are very anxious to retain. We must engage them in their early fifties because, in our experience, once they have decided to retire, it is very difficult to change their minds. Second, and the biggest surprise for us, is the prestige the program has developed. Being a senior partner is extremely prestigious both to the firm and to the clients. It gives our partners something to strive for."[5]

Career Changes

The most radical form of new assignment is a career change. Most people associate "career change" with something radical and therefore risky—jumping the corporate ship to pursue a passion or an avocation, such as teaching or starting a small business. They assume that changing careers is difficult and admire people with the fortitude to pull it off. We believe that the notion of a single career is becoming obsolete. The forces of technological progress and globalization alter—at a sometimes dizzying pace—how work gets done. Meantime, many people welcome the chance to reinvent themselves one or several times during a working career. A midcareer change is becoming a sign of success in adapting, not failure to thrive in one's original occupation.

We also believe that corporations should find ways to let the less radical career changes happen within the employment relationship. An employee may develop a new specialty, assume an altogether different job, and sometimes return from a management track to an individual contributor role. Such career shifts should be natural. In some Japanese manufacturers, assembly line workers regularly become product service technicians. After years on the line, the employee literally knows the product inside and out, and probably wants a change of work pattern. In many Japanese companies, workers are retired (so public pensions can kick in) and then simply hired back at half to three-fourths of their former responsibility and pay.[6]

Some companies retrain groups of people in new roles in response to changing business conditions and skills needs. For example, in response to skills shortages in areas like nursing, the U.K. National Health Service's "skills escalator" program trains capable employees to take the next step up the skills and job ladders, including from support roles into patient care.[7] Lincoln Electric's Leopard Program enabled employees to "change their spots." Rather than having to lay off workers in one part of the business while hiring others elsewhere when patterns of demand for steel fabrication products changed, the company trained a total of sixty-eight factory and clerical staff volunteers to be assistant salespeople.[8] As with the Japanese example, they moved product knowledge and experience into customer-facing roles, boosting sales and employee commitment simultaneously.

Mentoring Roles

Employees can also be rejuvenated by assuming mentoring, teaching, and other knowledge-sharing roles. Mentoring is a means for capitalizing on the knowledge and capability of experienced employees, and developing the expertise and organizational know-how of less experienced colleagues, through regular work and one-on-one consultation. It is also an excellent means for reengaging midcareer workers. For them, serving as mentors provides a personally fulfilling way to share experience, give back to the organization, and make a fresh set of social connections in the workplace. Being mentored by a yet more experienced colleague can not only expand knowledge and expertise, but also rekindle ambition and a sense of the possible. Mentor relationships are often stereotyped as pairings of old with young. In fact, they should be viewed as pairings of experience, skill, and tacit knowledge to share with experience, skill, and tacit knowledge to gain.

That's how mentoring works at Intel, where they abandoned the traditional notion of pairing up-and-comers with experienced managers for purposes of personal development and career advancement. Instead, the primary purpose is knowledge and skills transfer, and the partner may outrank the mentor. The program began in a chip-making factory in New Mexico in 1997, when Intel was growing and managers and technical experts were being transferred to new locations. The factory was suffering a brain drain and needed to accelerate the growth of new experts in a variety of fields. So they started matching partners with mentors on the basis of skills and knowledge in demand. Today the employee database, which tracks skills attained and desired, helps match partners with mentors, who may be local or in another country. Mentor and partner take a class to learn the key guidelines and detail the relationship in a contract with goals and deadlines. They decide together what to talk about, but the partner for the most part manages the relationship and calls the meetings. The best relationships last six to nine months.[9]

Other companies—Agilent, CSX Transportation, Southwest Airlines—have well-established mentoring programs that have become part of their organizational fabric and employee rejuvenation process.[10] But most organizations have more ad hoc programs. As with the other career rejuvenation methods discussed in this chapter, mentoring makes a real difference for the enterprise—in terms of employee engagement, development, and performance—only when it is practiced purposefully and at scale. The benefits of a regular and widespread mentoring program are many: directly developing skills and transferring knowledge and experience, sharing best practices across the organization, preparing employees for expanded roles and contribution, reducing the need and cost of formal training, and fostering a culture of teamwork, diversity, respect, mutual understanding, and common purpose and commitment. Mentoring also enables exchange of "tacit knowledge"—for example, about specific customer relationships—that can't be transferred via classes or information systems.

Because we're talking about experience, mentors tend to be older than their partners. But any age combinations are possible, including *reverse mentoring*, wherein the younger colleague shares the expertise, often in new technology or business technique. Procter & Gamble, Siemens, and General Electric have programs in which young employees coach midcareer and mature executives on new technologies and the Internet. When Jack Welch noticed that e-business knowledge tended to be inversely proportional to both age and rank in GE, he asked the top six hundred managers to find young Internet experts and become their students.[11]

Successful mentoring incorporates three key features. First, mentors and partners *work* together in some capacity, on some project or problem, or in pursuit of an explicit goal. This should be more than a career advisory relationship. Don't equate a true mentor with a senior person who sponsors the career progression of a junior colleague (even though the term *mentor* is sometimes applied to this role). Second, mentors must be trained in the rudiments of mentoring roles and techniques, while partners should be advised on their roles and what to expect from and how to comanage mentoring relationships. They should have a selection of capable mentors to choose from or "pilot test" the relationship. Third, every assignment must be designed for the growth and satisfaction of both parties. The mentor must be interested in sharing something, the partner in learning it. And every mentor relationship should have an element of reverse mentoring. The mentor should regularly turn the tables and ask for guidance, or find out what can be learned from the partner.

Because everyone in an organization can potentially have mentor relationships, mentoring is numerically the best way to put midcareer workers into knowledge-sharing roles. But there are others. Tapping experienced and expert employees to develop and deliver training programs is common practice. Experienced employees also teach and guide colleagues through internal consulting roles, participation in business performance reviews, and leadership of business improvement projects. Many midcareer workers are happy to take ownership of change initiatives, especially to assist colleagues, improve results, and serve the higher mission of the enterprise.

Fresh Training

Another basic way to rejuvenate a midcareer worker is fresh training and development. Today's midcareers tend to be educated and inclined toward education. They know that increasing their skills will also increase their chances for personal and professional advancement. Many jump at the chance to "go back to school" and learn new things of use in their jobs and careers.

Unfortunately, there are obstacles. Corporate training is disproportionately aimed at the young, especially new employees who must learn the basics. The tacit assumptions are that older workers have been trained, need less training, and get the training they need on the job. All three assumptions are, at best, only partially true. Meanwhile, many midcareer workers find themselves "too busy" to set aside time for extensive education and training. If their schedules and responsibilities, both on the job and off, squeeze their time, personal development time is typically forfeited. And some people, especially having reached positions of authority, stop seeking developmental opportunities because they hesitate to take risks or don't want to admit that they have things to learn. Too many organizations foster a silent conspiracy against education by making the training and development budget the first thing cut in lean times, by allowing managers to encourage employees to forego training in favor of "getting the work done," and by failing to institutionalize the practice of everyone's following a development plan. For this combination of reasons, many midcareer workers are overdue for a serious dose of training and development, would welcome the chance to take it, and would repay the employer with renewed commitment and productivity. By *serious dose* we mean in-depth education in a new or expanded area of interest, not a series of short courses to get the number of training hours up.

Serious education for midcareer workers can take several shapes. Formal educational programs offered by employers, universities, or industry associations can confer further certification in one's field, or may expand one's scope and versatility (e.g., marketing for operations people). "Action learning" experiences of the type usually associated with leadership development programs prove extremely effective. These usually combine classroom education, group work on a specific business issue or problem, and management review of the results. Groups combine people with various backgrounds and skills and from different parts of the organization, and the educational experience takes place in close parallel with one's regular job and responsibilities. Sometimes the best approach is to have employees design and direct their own education in subjects related to the job, thus enabling themselves to apply their knowledge and skills differently.

Motorola's "liberal education" program has elements of both formal and self-directed approaches. The company gives employees the chance to learn new subjects and discover how to apply their knowledge and skills differently and more interestingly. Motorola encourages employees to learn and update their skills, either through external academic institutions (with tuition reimbursement) or internal courses, which offer both leadership and business-related courses. Learning plans are part of employees' development plans, and must be related to the skill requirements of their jobs as well as to the business goals of the company. As with many other major organizations, Motorola is moving away from classroom-based instruction to more technology-enabled learning.[12]

Sabbaticals

Sometimes the best way to rejuvenate, personally and professionally, is simply to get away from the routine of the job for a significant amount of time. Sabbaticals are our final—but least used—technique for career rejuvenation. A common feature of academic employment relationships, sabbaticals remain rare and underutilized in corporations. Yet the sabbatical, paid or unpaid, is a powerful device for not only recharging one's batteries, but also rekindling one's commitment to an employer. Talk to people who have taken sabbaticals, whether for community service, further education, or personal endeavors. They are likely to tell you that the experience was a turning point in their careers or employment relationships. An extended "career break" can help renew commitment, prevent burnout, and maintain productivity. Sabbaticals also enable employees to refresh and recharge by pursuing opportunities that are not possible during a normal training or vacation period. People return with their creative juices flowing, with fresh perspectives on how to perform work, and often with new insight into customers and markets.

Anne Knapp, the managing director and executive vice president of HR, IT, and marketing at GMAC Residential Funding Corporation (GMAC-RFC), recently took a sabbatical. She and her husband spent six weeks in Japan, New Zealand, and Tahiti.[13] A once-in-a-lifetime trip? Yes, except that, like the rest of the one hundred fifty senior executives at GMAC-RFC, she's expected to take a six- to eight-week paid sabbatical every five years or so. The company's leadership recognizes the intensity of people's work in a high-performance financial services organization. They also recognize the need to escape that intensity and so have made work/life balance a core corporate value. The sabbatical program is one of the ways they make that value real.

The sabbatical program for senior executives officially began six years ago, "but it took two years before anyone dared." Now sabbaticals are both expected and prized. Half of the eight-member executive committee have taken them. The only eligibility restriction is two years with the company. People take sabbaticals for a variety of purposes, most often travel, education, a hobby, or simply time with the family. The only activity not permitted is looking for another job. Not that it's likely. Turnover is very low, and a sabbatical invariably both refreshes the individual and solidifies his or her commitment to the organization.

For the company's other forty-five hundred associates, the RFC Partner Program recognizes and rewards accomplishment in a variety of ways, including sabbaticals for about ninety people each year. And the company provides other ways for associates to get away and refresh—four hundred top performers and their partners recently took a Mediterranean cruise, for example. Because sabbaticals and other getaway opportunities typically include partners, commitment to the company becomes a family affair. "Our employees' spouses tell them they'd be nuts to quit this company."

For Anne, the sabbatical was a chance to travel in depth, spending significant time at each destination. It was also a remarkably refreshing opportunity to "live in the moment" in a way all but impossible in a demanding job. But the results also included a refining of her perspective as a manager: "I think more globally now. The world doesn't necessarily revolve around the United States. And, of course, I still think this is the best place I've ever worked."

We characterize sabbaticals today as "rare but there." In the 1990s, corporate sabbaticals started to gather some momentum when employees and prospective employees were in the driver's seat when it came to making employment deals. But under more austere business conditions these days, sabbaticals are less widespread, if no less desired by employees. Hewitt Associates has reported that of more than five hundred organizations surveyed, just 5 percent offered paid and/or unpaid sabbaticals. Among that small group, 77 percent say they offer sabbaticals to enable employees to refresh and recharge, 54 percent to increase employees' personal growth, and 35 percent to enable employees to contribute to the community or society.[14] The study also found that 5 percent of the surveyed companies offer a vacation bonus program, whereby employees receive one-time "bonuses" of extra vacation time (which can be taken as a mini-sabbatical) in recognition of reaching designated milestones (e.g., ten years of service) or of accomplishing extraordinary results.

A 2001 survey by Principal Financial Group found that over 50 percent of employees say they long for a sabbatical, but only 10 percent say they have taken or plan to take one. And nearly half say they would like to take one but feel they can't because of financial concerns or employer discouragement.[15] Employer reluctance centers on cost and, for key employees, potential disruption to business operations. However, the cost of replacing an employee in need of a break may be far more than that of a paid sabbatical. The forms of sabbaticals most palatable to employers focus on job-related education or community service. And employers tend to be conservative in their offerings, making sabbaticals available only to the best workers, limiting their duration, and, of course, offering them only after a designated period of service.

Employee reluctance comes from fear that, even with the same or equivalent job guaranteed upon return, they will somehow be marked by the organization or its management as less committed than others who don't interrupt their work. A study of 523 full-time managers of a big financial services company found that leave-takers were 18 percent less likely to be promoted than non-leave-takers and received 8 percent less in salary hikes.[16] Ironically, people are labeled as uncommitted precisely at the point when their commitment has been renewed.

Some notable companies still offer sabbaticals, typically of limited duration. Intel employees are eligible for an eight-week sabbatical, with full salary, after each seven years of full-time service. When combined with an annual three or four weeks of vacation, a sabbatical leave can provide up to twelve weeks of paid time off. Silicon Graphics' regular full-time U.S. and Canada employees are eligible to take paid six-week sabbaticals after four years. Adobe Systems offers three weeks of paid sabbatical after every five years of service.[17]

There are examples and variations outside of high tech as well. Arrow Electronics, one of the world's largest distributors of electronics and computer products, offers what it terms a world-class sabbatical program: up to ten weeks after seven years. Linchris Hotel Corporation's sabbatical program for its general managers and corporate executives entitles—and strongly encourages—them to take a paid three-month sabbatical every five years. And

Hallmark designs sabbaticals to get people out of the routine of work but still benefit the company by placing them into enlightening settings with the goal of "recharging the artistic talent of our people." Offerings range from a few days to several months at innovation facilities or artistic venues, where employees hone creative skills, or in settings that enable employees to study customers and social trends.[18]

Some companies have made creative use of sabbaticals to help weather business downturns. In the early 1990s, Virgin Atlantic Airways offered unpaid leaves of three to six months to six hundred employees, who retained their travel privileges on Virgin during their leaves. The sabbatical opportunity became institutionalized, and Virgin employees today can take "career breaks" of up to a year. Similarly, when Lonely Planet, publisher of travel guidebooks, was hit by the post-9/11 worldwide travel slump, its first move was not to cut staff, but to offer leaves of one to six months at 15 percent of pay. More than one hundred took advantage of the chance for extended time off.[19]

Wells Fargo's Volunteer Leave Program, more than twenty years in operation, offers team members (employees) with at least five years' service and a qualifying performance rating the opportunity to work in community service of their choosing for up to four months in a calendar year, receiving full pay and benefits while on leave. In 2003, twenty-four team members were selected for the program from over six hundred applications.[20] Among organizations with sabbatical programs, few have this explicit focus on community service.

Benefits to the individual participants are enormous—they have the chance to act upon their passions for specific causes and community service, and they return to their Wells Fargo positions energized, grateful for the opportunity, and additionally committed to the organization and their customers. The work they do is often inspiring: volunteering at a camp for cancer victims, traveling across the country speaking with high school students as a representative of Mothers Against Drunk Driving, returning to work in a homeless family shelter where the participant had gotten the training and assistance to land a full-time position with Wells Fargo, working in Armenia to help women develop small businesses—an initiative so successful that it was adopted by the United Nations, and the participant was allowed to extend her leave to assist the UN in setting it up. Meantime, the company reaps benefits on several fronts, including good publicity both within the corporation and in the local press in communities where participants are serving. The program also has positive effects on team member morale, commitment, recruiting and retention—not only among participants, but also among the broad population of people who like working for an employer that cares about the community and offers such service opportunities.

Sabbaticals are an extraordinarily powerful but underleveraged method of career rejuvenation, especially for midcareer employees. We recommend that employers make greater use of the technique, and we predict that as lifestyles become more "blended" and people want to mix work and other pursuits in creative ways, sabbaticals will grow more popular and important among employees. If you're thinking of starting or restarting a sabbatical program but want to proceed carefully, then we recommend making the ground rules clear, experimenting with a limited number of employees, studying the results, and reserving the right to adjust or cancel the program. Encourage sabbaticals that provide education and cross-training. Offer seminars on how to get the most from sabbaticals. And make sure that there are adequate backup personnel who themselves won't be stretched too thin.

Recruit Reentrants

Many companies today are, for economic reasons, carefully controlling their hiring. But as labor markets tighten and skills shortages loom, organizations will look to more midcareer and mature workers to meet their staffing needs. Those with an established history of hiring and incorporating midcareer and mature workers will enjoy an advantage over organizations just trying to get into the game. Whatever your organization's rate and timing of new hires, be sure to make midcareer workers part of the mix. The labor market has a lot to offer in the form of both workforce reentrants, including women returning after raising families, and people displaced by other organizations' restructurings. Most companies have learned that the latter group carries not stigma (of being laid off), but skills. Their salary cost may be on average higher than for younger employees, but they offer experience and skills—including in customer service—that younger employees lack. Midcareer hires should be part of the "fresh blood supply" of the enterprise.

Develop a recruiting strategy for the midcareer labor market. Do you know what your current midcareer employees want out of their jobs and lives? Turn that understanding into a value proposition and an employer brand for midcareer recruits. Be ready to offer flexible work arrangements, even for recent hires. Post recruiting notices on your company's Web site showing pictures of workers of all ages. Advertise your openings on Internet sites and in media that have a large number of older adult viewers. Make it clear that you value experience as well as youthful energy.

In the late 1990s, ARO, Inc., a business process outsourcer based in Kansas City, Missouri, had staff turnover of 60 percent per year. The turnover rate affected its efficiency as an operator of contract call center activities, back-office, outbound customer interaction, forms processing, and Web-based information solutions for clients in the insurance, health-care, and financial industries.[21]

Michael Amigoni, chief operating officer, made the decision to turn the business "virtual" in 1997, and did it gradually over five years. This was not difficult, because turnover eliminated many, and new hires were screened for the ability to work off-site. Amigoni, who manages operations and information technology at ARO's Contact Center, developed the model that allows some two hundred fifty employees to work from their homes. Several circumstances convinced Amigoni that going virtual was worthwhile. ARO faced a unique problem in recruiting: Kansas City hosts some ninety call centers, so the applicant pool was shallow. ARO did not want to move to a larger facility, which it couldn't afford, to accommodate more staff, which it needed. Once Amigoni saw the potential for both cost savings and improved client services, ARO upgraded the technology needed to accommodate virtual workers, then set about recruiting. The target: baby boomers, who represent a large potential pool of workers and bring desired characteristics. "Boomers are mature, experienced, and comfortable making decisions on the phone," says Amigoni. "ARO has clients in the insurance, financial services, and medical sectors, and a lot of the people we talk to are older. It helps that the people making the calls on financial services products are older, because they are in similar circumstances to the customers."[22] For insurance companies, a lot of ARO's work is underwriting, which involves asking questions about health, among other things. Again, it helps to have workers who are facing some of the same health issues—their own or perhaps their parents'—as the customers are. ARO has found that younger, entry-level workers cannot make these connections as easily.

ARO's at-home call center staff is over 90 percent female, and most are either empty nesters or have older children who do not need transportation to and from school. ARO at-home staff set their own hours; if a mother must pick up a child at 3:00 p.m., for example, she just logs off and then back on later in the day. Since the slack time for this work is usually in the afternoons, it is not a problem for staff to be offline then. Overall, ARO staff can match their work hours to business needs better because they work at home. All at-home call center workers are employees, not independent contractors; about 40 percent are full-time and 60 percent part-time. All full-time workers receive health benefits and have a 401(k) option. The bottom-line benefits are substantial—estimated savings of $1 million a year in reduced facilities costs, lower turnover, and higher productivity.

Expand Leadership Development

In the course of our research, a surprising number of corporations raised the issue of shortages in leadership ranks or their leadership development and succession pipelines. Surprising, because in terms of raw numbers, there are plenty of midcareer workers eager to move up the ladder and fill senior management slots. The problems follow these lines: "We have a wave of executive retirements in the next two to three years and, despite an adequate number of people one and two levels down, our bench strength seems thin. We don't have enough candidates *ready* right now. Meanwhile, the old career path to the top has evaporated. People aren't around long enough to accumulate the traditional set of leadership experiences. And the old path was too slow for today's business anyway."

We see three root causes behind these problems. The first is widespread organizational upheaval. Waves of industry consolidation, restructuring, and downsizing have disrupted organizational continuity. Job-for-life arrangements are history, average tenures are declining, employees are more mobile, and many potential leaders look for opportunities with small and entrepreneurial businesses. There are fewer candidates around long enough to make it through the old pipeline. Put simply, *the pipeline leaks too much.* The second cause is not-so-benign neglect. In periods of upheaval, many organizations tend to adopt a short-term, heads-down focus and pay less attention to leadership development and succession planning. Many of the company representatives we spoke with, having neglected leadership development in recent years, are now rethinking, reemphasizing, or even restarting their leadership development initiatives. *The pipeline hasn't been maintained.* Compounding these two problems is a third, the changing requirements of leadership. Markets are highly networked and interdependent. Organizations are global. Information technology suffuses everything an organization does. Workforces, organizational structures, and management methods are all evolving at an unprecedented pace. In short, what it takes to be a leader is very different from what it took ten years ago. *So the old pipeline may be the wrong one anyway.*

One executive described for us yesterday's highly structured and hierarchical leadership path: "In this hotel chain, you have to train in and supervise a variety of functions, then manage a small property, then manage a large property, then manage a region, then run one of our hotel brands. The problem today is that nobody's around long enough to complete the cycle—and it takes far too long to begin with." There's a lot to be said for learning a business inside and out through a progression like this, but today's career and leadership paths are much more various. Not one path but many. Forming not a ladder but a network. Organized not around a succession of specific jobs but around the expansion of responsibility, capability, and experience. If an organization has fallen behind in leadership development, yesterday's pipeline flows much too slowly. This situation is sadly ironic—midcareer managers are frustrated by the lack of promotion opportunities, while corporate executives sense a lack of candidates with the right experience. The solution to the problem is to refill the leadership pipeline and rejuvenate midcareer managers at the same time.

Leadership development training can be a powerful force for employee engagement. Participation is a form of recognition of an employee's value and potential, and employees "graduate" with renewed commitment and heightened sense of responsibility and ownership of the organization's results. However, in many organizations, it's difficult for midcareer people not already recognized as "high potentials" to get in line for leadership development experiences. We recommend reviewing participation criteria and making it easier for midcareer workers to take advantage of leadership development programs. Start by looking beyond those already in the high-potential pool and succession plan. Extend your leadership development programs to broader populations of employees who can exercise local leadership in their roles and functions.

Independence Blue Cross, based in Philadelphia, has put one-third of its top six hundred people, most of them midcareer employees, through a leadership program centered on individual development and action learning. They start with a "development council" rather than a traditional high-potential program. In each of four years, the council has selected forty managers for a special curriculum. It includes a week-long session at the Wharton School, individual coaching and development planning, and work on a special project— all atop the regular job. Many graduates were promotion-ready and promoted soon thereafter, and the personal networks people build in the process prove invaluable. They are now looking ahead to the need for a "graduate course" for people who have already been through the program. They try to maintain career momentum after the program through succession planning and finding nontraditional roles and assignments and having people move around the business more—but always with both business results and leadership development in view.

Turnover at the top is low, and there's no immediate looming retirement wave at Independence Blue Cross—so why the extra effort in leadership development? Because they must find ways to keep their best managers engaged and prepared for promotion. These people have a huge appetite for learning and development, and many were feeling bottlenecked. Leadership development and role expansion are seen as the key ways to maximize the progress and performance of their management ranks.[23]

RBC Financial Group felt it needed to develop the next group of leaders to run the fast-growing group of banks and financial services companies. They recognized a capability gap between the current executive team and the leaders to follow. So they created teams of current leaders and "next-generation leaders." Through direct experience sharing and involvement in decision making, the next-generation leaders learned both specific techniques and the core leadership values of RBC while simultaneously participating in the development of new strategy. Highly respected current leaders communicated these leadership values by telling real RBC "stories" that describe chaotic business situations, decision making, uncertainty, social interaction, and the like. The future leaders learned to implement strategy by sharing experience of real struggles of making decisions while maintaining values, trust, and fairness. Future leaders created development action plans and are mentored by their current-leader coaches.[24]

What must large organizations do to rebuild, refill, and speed up their leadership pipelines? Most must combine short-, medium-, and long-term actions. In the short term, delay retirements of selected leaders, or if the business is in some trouble and needs a steadying hand, bring back retirees as interim leaders. Meanwhile, give "almost there" candidates work as understudies with established leaders, where they enjoy ample coaching and mentoring. For the medium term, accelerate leadership development by having people in the pipeline (not just those in the immediate succession plan) participate in special programs, projects, or cross-organizational assignments designed to build capabilities and confidence fast. For the long term, build a different pipeline. Let many personal development paths replace "the one road to the top," and shape development plans around experiences to gain and capabilities to demonstrate or develop, not just jobs to hold. Then fill that new pipeline. Create more entry points. Remove implicit tenure requirements to admit earlier entry into the pipeline. Remove implicit age bias to admit entry by late bloomers, thereby rejuvenating the careers of more mid-career people. Also allow for exit points, to keep the pipeline filled with the best and most committed candidates.

Finally, stick with the leadership development process, even in times of business downturn and organizational upheaval. Measure the effectiveness of the process and refine it as you go—how good are we at delivering leaders with the right capabilities at the right times? General Electric is renowned for its track record in developing business leaders. In a sense, the "business model" for GE as a diversified corporation revolves around developing versatile leaders who can run a variety of businesses. Few organizations have management and leadership development so close to the core, but many would do well to adopt a bit of GE's constant and relentless attention to leadership development.

Reengage Now

In summary, if your organization wants to control its fate (and costs) when the boomer retirement wave hits with full force, start today systematically retaining and recruiting people with the skills and capabilities that you want to keep on hand for the long run. Recognize that many of your midcareer employees are, for personal and professional reasons, getting restless. Don't just assume they'll stay and hope for the best—reengage them by rekindling their careers now.

The techniques recommended in this chapter are not exclusively for mid-career workers, of course, but they will have greatest impact with this cohort. These techniques should prove neither expensive nor difficult to practice, and the payback of these employee reengagement actions—renewed commitment and productivity on the one hand, reduced replacement cost on the other—begin immediately. The actions we recommend are largely a matter of paying closer attention to the often silent majority—the midcareer employees who form the heart of your workforce.

To Energize Midcareer Workers

We recommend the following actions to reinvigorate the careers and maximize the productivity of midcareer workers:

☐ *Remove the impediments*, both procedural and attitudinal, to employee mobility. Educate line managers to recognize the signs that employees need a change, and motivate them to support and encourage employees to seek out fresh assignments. Set targets for employee migrations—among organizational units, disciplines, and roles (including into and out of management). Track performance against these goals.

☐ *Broker job assignments.* Establish an internal placement agency to help employees land the most rejuvenating roles and assignments.

☐ *Get systematic about knowledge and experience sharing.* Methods may include mentoring, training, best-practice sharing, "workout"-style business improvement projects, and information systems for knowledge management. Keep in mind that the most thorough sharing occurs when people work together in person.

☐ *Offer sabbaticals* for personal education and community service. Some employees—including key ones—rejuvenate best with a complete break from the work pattern.

☐ *Hire without bias.* As we stressed with respect to mature workers as well, make sure that recruiting channels, screening methods, and hiring decisions work for attracting midcareer workers. Make sure the organization can "take a chance" on reentrants with the right capability but without a recent track record. And be prepared to hire people directly into flexible work arrangements, including part-time work.

☐ *Incorporate new hires individually.* Midcareer hires, especially those reentering the workforce or changing careers, may benefit from training and incorporation activities different from what younger hires undertake. Find ways to put the new hire's relevant experience to work immediately.

☐ *Expand and accelerate leadership development.* As in the Independence Blue Cross example, make leadership development experiences available to a broader population of managers and employees—not just the designated high potentials or those in the official succession plan. If the next two generations are not on track, then create the ultimate action learning experience by having current and future leaders work closely together (as in the RBC Financial example).

☐ *Rejuvenate management careers.* Use leadership development experiences as a means of reengaging and rejuvenating the careers of midcareer managers, starting with those whose services the organization most needs to retain.

☐ *Admit late bloomers.* Enable people to enter the leadership pipeline relatively late in their careers, including after changing careers or reentering the workforce.

7

The Needs and Attitudes
of Young Workers

*Why the Best of the Young
Keep Leaving*

YOUNG WORKERS are in demand. As a proportion of the workforce, this younger cohort has shrunk dramatically over the last two decades. In 1980, over half the workforce was under thirty-five. Now that percentage has leveled off at about 38 percent. There simply won't be multiple young candidates applying for every opening. Competition for the best educated and most skilled of the lot will only intensify, as will efforts to retain them because they seem less loyal and more apt to job-hop than their parents were. The average tenure for workers in all age groups has been gradually declining for the past several decades. For workers under age thirty-five, the average is under three years; 80 percent of the young worker cohort has tenure of five years or less, and fully one-third are in their first year with the employer.[1] Even the promising employees who enjoy extensive early training and career advancement quit before the company can recoup its investment in their development.

Young workers are also unhappiest on the job. In our survey, this cohort had the lowest overall satisfaction and engagement levels. They are struggling to adjust to the demands of their professional and private lives, more than most employers might imagine. They distrust large organizations, and they often refuse to compromise work arrangements and workplace style. The employer who banks on youthful enthusiasm and desire to please, so characteristic of yesterday's young workers, is in for shock.

So how do some organizations beat the odds in retaining young workers? By understanding young workers, incorporating them quickly and completely, and making retention a top priority.

Profile of the Young and Restless

How do you treat new employees the first few weeks and months on the job? Do you give them a hearty welcome, a classroom or online orientation session, several hours of paperwork, and a "buddy" who springs for a couple of lunches and gives imprecise answers to the new recruit's questions? Does this probationary period center on procedures manuals, lectures from various department heads, and on-the-job training? How does a young person (who has never worked before) experience this process? How quickly does this new employee become really productive and engaged in his work?

Unfortunately, most training experiences are not very engaging. Training periods may be long and far removed from reality, consisting of weeks or even months of classroom work and practice sessions before "real work" begins. Such training unnecessarily delays the employee's sense of contribution. Some companies put people right to work without sufficient training or guidance. Low entry-level salaries may motivate new sales or customer service people to race through their training, to start earning commissions. Other companies overemphasize indoctrination into the company and its mission, its values and performance metrics, and its methods and "rules of the road." Such assimilation can never be too thorough, but it happens best when new employees are simultaneously learning and contributing.

But most employers treat young workers much as their parents had been treated, usually with superficial training, benign neglect, and blind faith. They expect new employees to train diligently, learn the ropes, and wait patiently for opportunity and recognition. That treatment will dampen the spirit, energy,

What Do Young Workers Expect from Work?

- Individual responsibility, freedom to make decisions
- Sociable and enjoyable colleagues and workplace
- Opportunities to learn and grow
- Opportunities to contribute right away
- Team-based work, collaborative decision making
- Lots of feedback, frequent and constructive reviews
- Accessible managers, open communications
- Respect from older coworkers
- Pay for performance
- Flexible schedules and ample time off

and ambition of today's young worker and, inevitably, will result in high turn-over, or "churn," among the young.

As summarized in the box, "What Do Young Workers Expect from Work?," their expectations are indeed high. They want individual responsibility despite any lack of experience, they want to collaborate in decision making and in their own performance management, they want access to and respect from managers and mentors, and they want to contribute immediately—not gradually as they "earn their stripes." In terms of compensation and benefits, this translates into pay for performance, benefits that are relevant and portable, and cash in hand now rather than longer-term rewards.

What Causes Young Worker Churn?

Many employers struggle to get young employees over what we call the "three-year hump," namely that point in an employee's tenure where newness is gone, routines become stale, wanderlust increases, and defection becomes likely. Just when the organization is about to recoup its investment in recruiting and training young workers, a significant number of these individuals resign, leaving the employer short of long-term employees who will grow up in the business and learn it thoroughly.

According to the *Economist*, the breakdown of the social contract between companies and employees coincided with the growing mobility of workers and portability of their knowledge-worker skills. Many young people expect no loyalty from their employers nor intend to give it, and they abhor the seemingly overwhelming economic and political power of large corporations. No wonder their tenures are brief.[2]

Twentysomethings are always experimenting with work and career, and, statistically, today's young workers job-hop as much as their counterparts did twenty years ago. Today, however, they make no apologies for hopping. Even the highly desired young employees—recruited from college, put in fast-track development programs, and expected to stay—are less willing to "play the company way" and more ready to depart. Their relative scarcity only amplifies the perception of their constant churning.

A few companies offer "stay an extra year" retention bonuses for recent hires, but that can get expensive and may often be just a matter of delaying the inevitable. The fundamental challenge goes deeper than retention tactics. Employers must become flexible enough—across work and worker management practices—to meet the changing needs, expectations, and methods of the first truly digital generation in the workforce. However, traditional management methods and styles prove ineffective in meeting these expectations. For example, giving feedback once a year in a formal review just doesn't meet young workers' expectations about the frequency and intensity of communication—many will be gone or emotionally disengaged from their jobs well before the first year is up. Similarly, the processes for recruiting and hiring need to adjust to the fact that young workers don't find the conventional employee deal, with its emphasis on long-term accumulation of benefits, attractive. Jobs, training methods, and everyday management practices have to be adjusted to young workers' needs and expectations, and older managers may have difficulty understanding young workers to begin with and respecting their differences.

Portrait of the Young Worker

Today's young workers are well educated, but not significantly more so than the older cohorts, perhaps because they haven't had as much time for continuing their educations. Well over half have college credits, and 35 percent hold a bachelor's or advanced degree. As to be expected in people still early in their careers, household income and investable assets are lowest among the three cohorts. Over half of young workers in *The New Employee/Employer Equation* survey responded to the question about investable assets with "unknown."

This younger cohort differs most significantly from the older groups in its diversity, including both racial and ethnic composition and attitudes toward diversity. In our survey, 61 percent of the young cohort is non-Hispanic white, compared with 76 percent of midcareers and 81 percent of mature workers. Nineteen percent of these young workers are Hispanic—twice the midcareers' percentage and six times that of the mature cohort. Thirteen percent are African American, versus 10 percent among midcareers and 5 percent among matures. Young workers are most likely to enjoy working with people from different backgrounds and cultures. Compared with older cohorts, they are more "color blind" and comfortable with diversity of all kinds.

Growing Up Digital

Today's young workers grew up as the first large generation of latchkey kids—in single-parent or two-working-parent households, many home alone in the afternoons after school, and on their own from a young age. Compared with earlier generations, more of their mothers were in the workforce, and their parents were more likely to divorce and often remarry. Just over 20 percent of marriages ended in divorce in the 1960s, but that rate jumped to over 50 percent by the mid-1980s. As a result, these young people are accustomed to having significant latitude and responsibility. They also tend to be libertarian in their social value systems and beliefs, and they cherish individual freedom and decision making. They are most likely among our three cohorts to describe themselves as ambitious, least likely to say they are spiritual or religious. They tend to be "tribal," with close relationships to a select but changeable group of peers. They are independent and highly networked, both personally and technologically. Compared with their parents, young people are "rule morphers"—applying rules and conventions when convenient but changing or ignoring them when necessary. This carries over to work style and ethic, where young people tend to be informal and situational and much less structured than older generations.

Very significantly, today's young workers have grown up digital, playing computer games as children, and now taking connectedness—via cell phones and the Internet—for granted. Heavily marketed to since childhood, they have lived their entire lives in an information-rich environment. For them, technology is not an occasional tool, but a constant extension of themselves. They are accustomed to instant communication and long-distance collaboration.

For many purposes, they may prefer phone contact, e-mail, or instant messaging to face-to-face communication. Technology, including the vast resources and undefined possibilities of the Internet, shapes how they approach and solve problems. Where an older generation tends to observe, analyze, plan, and act, the younger one tends to experiment from the start, to try things and learn what works. Such differences can be profound—not to mention mutually unfathomable across generations.

Also very significantly, many young workers hold an understandable bias against large corporations. Each generation rebels against the institutions of its parents, but something deeper is embedded in today's young workers' attitudes toward employers. They have seen their parents' careers disrupted by downsizing, restructuring, automation, and outsourcing. They have seen their parents' trust in corporations turn out to be misplaced, and are determined not to make the same mistake. Job-for-life expectations are ancient history, so their loyalties are short term, and they know they have to watch out for themselves. New to the business world and at the lower rungs of the salary ladder, they are astonished by the excesses of executive pay. Enron and WorldCom aren't viewed as isolated instances of malfeasance, but have become to them emblems of corporate America.

Personal Matters of Young Workers

The common assumption may have young people footloose and free of responsibility, but our survey paints a different picture. On the one hand, half are single (and never married), and young workers are almost twice as likely as older ones to say they go out and socialize a great deal. On the other hand, 20 percent say they're overwhelmed by responsibilities outside of work—highest among the three cohorts. Half say they are coping with a financial crisis or trying to reduce their debt, with one-third saving for or purchasing homes. They report fewer parenting issues overall than the midcareers do, but younger workers are naturally most likely to be in the process of having children. Also quite naturally, they report the fewest health issues, and are least likely (only 7 percent) to be caring for an older adult. Young workers do report the greatest number of relationship matters—most often getting married for the first time. And they are most likely—one in four—to be dealing with a recent relocation.

Young Workers' Attitudes Toward Work

Their distrust of corporations notwithstanding, young workers are willing to give them a try, presumably because that's where opportunity and money are perceived to be. Young workers are the most likely cohort (over 70 percent) to be employed by for-profit corporations, and least likely to work for governmental institutions. They do not seem to gravitate toward smaller organizations as older workers do.

Young workers bring some special strengths to the workplace. They are quick learners, adaptable and creative, and independent thinkers. Their experience as latchkey kids has helped develop emotional and intellectual attributes that play well amid the demands of a volatile marketplace and business environment. However, many have weak people and service skills—accustomed to doing things their own way, they have not been brought up or trained to exhibit the kinds of interpersonal skills needed in many roles in the workplace. And young people are by definition inexperienced—they don't have the benefit of learning from prior mistakes and successes.

Among our three career cohorts, young workers express the lowest overall satisfaction with their jobs (55 percent), and they are most likely to be neutral (neither satisfied nor dissatisfied—15 percent) and to express extreme dissatisfaction (8 percent). Young workers are certainly the most restless on the job, with two-thirds saying they are looking for a significant change. Twenty-six percent are actively seeking a promotion, 28 percent looking for a major career change, 28 percent looking for a new job at another company, and 16 percent planning to start their own businesses—in all cases the highest percentages among the three cohorts. Nearly half say that they are in the process of adjusting to new responsibilities or organizations.

Young workers appreciate some facets of the workplace. They are most likely to say they have ample opportunity to learn and grow on the job, that they get to work with bright and experienced people, and that their managers provide useful feedback and give employees flexibility to work on their own. But at the same time, they are most likely to say they fear being laid off and that they experience conflicts with managers, subordinates, or peers. Perhaps most disturbingly, 35 percent say they are in dead-end jobs (virtually the same rate as among midcareers), and 47 percent say they're coping with feelings of burnout (highest among the cohorts). So much for the carefree days of youth.

Young workers had the lowest percentages on nearly all of the engagement factors in our survey. They are least likely to agree (and most likely to actively disagree) that time passes quickly at work, that they are passionate about their jobs, or that they are energized by their work. In terms of investing themselves in their work, they are least likely (under 50 percent) to say that they are willing to put forth extra effort, that they really care about the fate of the organization, or that a great deal of their pride comes from their work. Only

28 percent think the organization's values are similar to their own, and the same low percentage says that the organization inspires the best in them. Young workers have a slightly less jaundiced view of the integrity of their employers' top management, but only one-third believe in it. One in five says he or she feels very little loyalty to the organization.

Retirement Preferences of Young Workers

The younger the worker, the more ambitious—and conventional—the retirement intentions. Young workers plan to retire the earliest, with 31 percent saying they'd like to retire by age sixty, and their mean planned retirement age is sixty-one. Forty-one percent say they prefer not to work at all in retirement (highest among the cohorts), and yet another 35 percent say that they plan never to retire completely.

How should we interpret these retirement preferences? Perhaps, with retirement a distant prospect and young workers still getting accustomed to the workplace, they haven't given the issue much thought and automatically buy into the prevailing view of retirement. Perhaps many see their parents hanging on to unsatisfying jobs to qualify for retirement pension and benefits, and they don't want to follow that example. Or perhaps young workers' desire for early escape from the workforce is another indication of their uneasy relationship with employers and work.

What Young Workers Want from Employers

What do young workers look for in their employment relationships? Quite a lot. A cynic might say that young workers have not yet learned to lower their expectations. A progressive might counter that employers have not yet learned to meet their expectations, which eventually they must do. A realist might point out that there are simply many ways for employers to fail in the eyes of young workers, and failure spells turnover.

Given their independence and libertarian leanings, they expect to be treated individually, they want flexible schedules, they know that their careers belong to them (not their employers), and so they value knowledge and skill more than tenure. Given their ambition, they want to contribute quickly, not work in the background. Given their technological proficiency, they appreciate up-to-date technology in the workplace, and they expect to manage their own information and communication. Young people are accustomed to being marketed to, and to morphing the rules to suit the situation, and so they want to be heard on the job, they want frequent and useful feedback, and they expect to make their work fit in with other life commitments and pursuits. Since they tend to be tribal and socially networked, they want sociable workplaces, they want to connect with others (including mentors).

Put these traits together, and young workers often seem disinclined to do things "the company way." Employers find, for example, that young employees are increasingly unwilling to accept relocations meant to forward their careers. Sometimes that's because a spouse can't relocate, but often simply because location is more important than employer. Many younger workers would much rather live in a lively community and work in a so-so job than they would work for a strong company but live in a dull place. For many of them, "where I live" is more important than "where I work."

Our survey of employment deal preferences reaches similar conclusions. Table 7-1 lists young workers' relative preferences among ten basic elements of the "employment deal." As with all workers, a comprehensive benefits package, with heavy emphasis on health-care coverage, tops the list. Young workers may be healthy, but they still value a benefits package, especially if

TABLE 7-1

What matters to young workers

General elements of the deal	Relative weight
Comprehensive benefits package	19
Workplace that is enjoyable	13
Work that enables me to learn and grow	12
Comprehensive retirement package	10
Work that is personally stimulating	10
Flexible work schedule	10
10 percent more in total compensation	8
Two weeks' additional paid vacation	7
Work that is worthwhile to society	6
Flexible workplace	5

Relative weights add to 100

Source: *The New Employee/Employer Equation* survey

they're starting families. Second, young workers value an enjoyable work-place more than midcareer and mature workers do, and they even value it above "work that enables me to learn and grow." They emphasize retirement packages least, perhaps because retirement seems far off, or perhaps because they doubt whether any retirement package will exist when they retire. The remainder of the list matches that of the midcareers. However, young work-ers place the highest relative weight of any cohort on three items: flexible work schedule, additional compensation, and additional paid vacation.

What to Remember About Young Workers

A lot of today's young workers are uneasy on the job, not because of inexperi-ence or lack of time adjusting to the workaday world, but because they seek a different kind of workplace, employment deal, and employer from what they encounter. Young workers highly value a congenial, enjoyable workplace, yet under half have it; and they value the optimal mix of work and life experi-ences, yet they are struggling more—at both work and home—than their eld-ers might assume. They want to believe in their employers but fundamentally distrust corporations and senior management.

To their older counterparts, young workers can appear brazenly demand-ing and impatient. Not willing to bide their time and earn their stripes, young workers are uncompromising regarding their workplaces and employers. Behind such "demands," however, are genuine differences. The younger co-hort is

- Independent, not only intellectually (as the baby boomers tend to be) but also functionally, having "grown up fast" and managed themselves from a relatively young age.

- Situational more than structured, and so they feel free to ignore poli-cies and procedures that they find restrictive.

- "Digital" in how they process information and communicate, and sometimes digital at the expense of interpersonal (by their parents' definition of the word, anyway).

- Diverse and comfortable with diversity, so that one-size-fits-all policies and management methods will likely alienate significant numbers of them.

Employers who label these differences as "poor work ethic" and expect these workers to outgrow them will suffer from endless churn. Those who respect these differences in thinking, communicating, and problem solving will try to meet young workers at least halfway—understanding their preferences, engaging their energies, and incorporating their methods.

In the next chapter, we discuss how to engage young workers, keep them engaged, and reduce turnover to manageable levels. Once again, our recommendations are not as much a matter of new techniques as of attentive management and focused effort—and the payoff in better productivity and retention should come today as well as tomorrow, as workforce demographics evolve.

8

The Retention of Talent

How to Connect with Young Workers

W ITH YOUNG WORKER CHURN a chronic problem and so many ways to fail at employee retention, what can companies do institutionally—in their employment practices and workplaces—to maximize the productivity and lengthen the tenure of young workers? First, adjust expectations downward. No company can stop churn entirely, but all companies can learn to cope better with the problem. Second, deepen relationships with young employees. In this chapter, we describe three key tactics for doing just that:

- *Rapid incorporation.* Establish the conditions for success from day one of employment by getting people up to speed as quickly as possible. Accelerating their learning and contribution builds satisfaction and commitment, not to mention business value, which lengthens their productive tenure and sets the cornerstone for retention.

- *Continuous retention.* Young workers remain loyal as long as the work, the workplace, and the management stimulate and engage.

Make employee retention an explicit, ongoing business process, and hold managers individually responsible for its execution and results. The process should include monitoring individual employee engagement and preempting an employee's possible departure.

- *Easy return.* When valued young employees do depart, their departure should be on the friendliest possible terms. Keep in touch with these former employees, remind them of the company's ongoing interest in them, enable them to return easily, and celebrate their homecoming.

Is it worth the effort? You bet. As we will see in this chapter, companies that have instituted and socialized these plans have indeed raised young worker tenure rates, increased their productivity, and retained a critical mass of key young talent for the management development pipeline.

Rapid Incorporation

The faster and more thoroughly a new hire comes up to speed, the better for employee satisfaction, business productivity, and retention prospects. The sooner young workers start producing results, the quicker the return on investment in their training. Successful incorporation begins in the recruiting and hiring process by setting recruits' expectations. For example, Cisco "peer recruits," matching prospects with current employees who personally attest to work and life at the company. On new employees' first day of work, their colleagues, work space, technology, and "peer" are ready to receive them.[1]

Incorporation then intensifies. At Whole Foods, store teams make the hiring decisions. New hires get a thirty-day trial period, during which team members have a stake in the hires' productivity, learning, integration, and success.[2]

Approaches to rapid incorporation vary with the nature of the business, the culture of the organization, the training needs of new employees, the talent of the individuals, and their destinations in the business. The mix varies, but the successful programs explicitly pursue and achieve these three goals: *accelerated learning* through deep immersion in business operations, *accelerated contribution* through early business problem solving, and *accelerated assimilation* through close association with experienced colleagues and mentors.

Trial by Fire at Newell Rubbermaid

Newell Rubbermaid, a global manufacturer and marketer of name brand consumer products with sales exceeding $7.5 billion annually and some

49,000 employees worldwide, emphasizes *accelerated contribution* through a "trial by fire" program named Phoenix after the mythological bird.[3] In this program, new employees work on the front lines of the business after an eight-day orientation on sales skills, product knowledge, and account management and a meeting with the senior management team and the CEO, who reviews company strategy and culture. Phoenix members follow new product and merchandising launches into the stores and capture valuable consumer-perspective feedback, including new product brainstorming from loyal customers.

Phoenix is essentially the "farm system" of Newell Rubbermaid. Hands-on experience with products, key accounts, and retail consumers provides the basic knowledge needed to reach one's career objectives. Whether the new employee aspires to sales, marketing, purchasing, finance, operations, engineering, or human resources positions, this initial exposure models the necessary behavior for high productivity and contribution. The program also builds strong bonds with the company and among the group. Many graduates communicate frequently in the field and swap merchandising ideas, the best of which are rolled out nationally.

Phoenix focuses on skills that will serve people immediately and throughout their careers: in-store merchandising and displays, product presentations, consumer interaction, building relationships with key accounts, and selling promotional concepts. Additional training occurs within assigned divisions, and during their first few years, new hires receive training in advanced selling, product and channel marketing, negotiation, and leadership.

The Phoenix program has increased innovation dramatically. One Phoenician designed a product display featured in six hundred Lowe's stores that boosted sales 250 percent. And the incorporation strategy is working—six hundred fifty Phoenicians have reached midlevel positions thus far. It has been so successful from a sales and marketing standpoint that Newell Rubbermaid plans to introduce the program into additional functional areas, including operations, purchasing, engineering, finance, and human resources.

This approach works best when the job does not require a long learning curve and where much of the learning occurs while performing the work itself. So people can get into the field quickly. Success hinges on challenging and stretching the new hires to continually raise the bar of performance. The best candidates are people driven primarily by the need for individual achievement and growth. Recognition, reward, and learning opportunities must be the payoff for high performance.

One key to success with trial-by-fire emphasis is to hire hungry achievers to begin with, but then find ways to encourage peer support and group camaraderie among them. While individual skills and ability are critical, it is vital to encourage teamwork and sharing of ideas among the group to avoid isolation and to ensure that new innovations will spread and take hold quickly. To really charge up this approach, top managers must make themselves accessible to these new hires, many of whom seek visibility and access at the top levels of the organization. For this type of pressurized incorporation to work, companies must also allow new hires to experiment and innovate. But they can't be too patient—results count. New hires should usually "get it" quickly. Those who struggle should be given support, but if there is not quick improvement, the chances for eventual success are slim, and the recruits should be culled from the program.

Boot Camp at Trilogy

At Trilogy, a rapidly growing provider of technology-powered business services, the approach to incorporating key employees combines extensive training and organizational induction with the actual work of the company, deploying existing knowledge and newly acquired skills to achieve important business goals. It is especially suited to jobs involving specialized skills (such as software development) and new product, service, or business development.

Most corporate "boot camps" focus on informing new hires about the company's products and markets and how to access key resources in the organization. Trilogy takes a more ambitious approach. It not only seeks to equip new recruits with the skills, values, and connections to work at Trilogy, but in the process also to develop the company's next generation of strategic ideas, products, and even leadership. Trilogy University (TU) is a three-month program held yearly, led and run by the company's top executives, including its CEO.[4]

In the first month, new staff are assigned to a section and an instruction track. Your section, a group of about twenty, is your social group for the duration of your TU experience. You share a section leader—an experienced colleague who serves as a mentor—and spend virtually all of your work time with these people. Tracks are designed to be microcosms of future work life at Trilogy. The technical challenges in TU exercises closely mimic real customer engagements, but the time frames are dramatically compressed. Each successive assignment is more challenging than the last. As in a Marine Corps boot camp, one purpose of these exercises is to practice intense teamwork and develop deep bonds with your peers. This period of training is lengthy in comparison with Newell Rubbermaid's, but the exercises are extremely realistic—people feel as if they're in the field already, even though they're not.

In the second and third months, the new employees tackle the challenge of coming up with a breakthrough new product or service idea. Teams of three to five people must develop an idea, a business model for it, the product itself, and its marketing plan—all at hyperspeed. This exercise proves exhausting and exhilarating because Trilogy's top talent teams with the new hires.

After graduation, the emphasis shifts to finding your place in the organization and having a broader impact in the company. Some staff continue work on their TU projects, while others find "sponsors" out in the company who take them on to work on projects. The graduation process involves rigorous evaluation of new employees and agreement among section leaders, managers, and graduates on next steps. Each graduate must develop a list of specific short- and long-term goals. Managers must lay out developmental job assignments and affiliations with coaches that will help the new hire to reach his or her goals. Upon graduation, new staff disperse to all parts of the company, and the trust and bonds they've developed with the company leaders and each other help to link and sustain them throughout their careers.

Trilogy University generates benefits well beyond that of the typical new employee boot camp. It has become a major research and development engine—projects have produced over $25 million in direct revenue and formed the basis for over $100 million in new business for the company. It doubles as a leadership development program and proving ground for the company's future generations of leaders, who work full-time for three months as section leaders. TU also provides the impetus and context for top management to continually challenge and evolve the company's strategic vision and direction, because these leaders must decide what they want to teach and how they want to focus the new hires.

This approach brings together high-caliber new hires with the best and brightest of experienced employees, including senior executives, and sets them to work on real, high-impact projects. It requires a significant commitment of experienced employee time and effort in teaching, leading sections, and guiding groups in their new product/service development projects. But the benefits can be enormous. The approach enables new hires to quickly and deeply engage with the organization and its most critical work, learning about the business alongside both one another and some of the most accomplished people in the company. It enables those experienced people to hone their leadership skills. And it delivers direct business results in the form of products developed and problems solved.

For this kind of incorporation program to work, the company must commit to staffing it with some of its most in-demand employees. Since this approach works best with the most talented recruits, the company can't compromise its hiring standards and candidate vetting processes. Participants—new hires and experienced staff alike—must stretch their abilities if breakthrough innovations and solutions are to emerge.

Mentored Entry at W. L. Gore & Associates

A third variation on rapid incorporation of new employees emphasizes assimilation through mentoring, sometimes by a combination of experienced peers and senior staff. This is a long-term and personalized approach to incorporating new hires into an organization and positioning them to make early and strong business contributions. The essence of this technique is working with new hires individually to make them professionally and socially comfortable with their jobs and the organization, with the goal of getting them "up to full speed" as quickly as possible. The approach particularly suits skilled workers in collaborative work teams.

W. L. Gore & Associates is a privately held and decidedly unconventional workplace. Founded in 1958, the company today has nearly seven thousand associates in forty-five locations around the world. Gore-Tex materials, the company's best-known products, are found in space suits and have been used in clothing worn by trekkers who have climbed the world's highest peaks and reached the South Pole. Gore attributes its steady growth not only to the innovative products they make from polytetrafluoroethylene (PTFE, better known as Teflon), but also to a "lattice" system of management first introduced by founder Bill Gore.

Gore & Associates has no management hierarchies, no predetermined channels of communications, and no job levels or titles locking associates into particular tasks. Associates don't have bosses; they have leaders and sponsors. They also do not have narrowly defined jobs; they make commitments within the general expectations of their functional areas. For example, the commitment might be to run a particular machine, do recruiting, or crunch numbers in finance. Gore's flat structure and egalitarian culture are meant to foster a creative and energizing workplace. The company believes that people take greater ownership of something they've volunteered for and committed to, as opposed to something they are told to do.[5]

Each new hire is assigned a sponsor who committed to help the new-comer succeed as quickly as possible. Nearly 30 percent of associates serve as sponsors. A key goal is to find a "quick win"—a project or an idea that puts the new associate on a fast track to accomplishment while getting him or her comfortable working within the organization. The sponsor gives the associate a basic understanding of what commitments mean and what it takes to be successful in those commitments. Sponsors provide encouragement, guidance on principles and practices, feedback on performance, help in securing resources, advocacy for the associate in compensation discussions, guidance in personal development planning, and role modeling.

Gore's mentored entry for new employees connects with its performance management process. The sponsors collect information and feedback from peers and leaders regarding the associates' performance and personal development. Meanwhile, the associates' peers rank each other based on each individual's contribution to the success of the business as well as personal skills. That information is then shared with the appropriate compensation committee—there are fifteen serving the various functional areas of the business. The committees take the feedback and individual rankings and come up with an overall ranking of the people doing that function. Then using guidelines based on external salary data, the top of the list will be paid more than the bottom. The objective is to be internally fair and externally competitive.

Mentoring of new hires is critical in a company like Gore that hires entrepreneurial, creative self-starters. "There is nobody responsible for your future except you," says Sally Gore, daughter-in-law of founder Bill Gore. "How successful you are and what you make of it is up to you."[6] Gore hires people who are motivated by opportunities to face new challenges, and Gore expects all staff to learn continuously. This type of work environment attracts bright young workers eager to learn and develop their skills and knowledge.

Mentored entry works well when work is demanding but relatively unstructured, where the productivity and success of new workers depend heavily on their ability to navigate the organization, connect and build relationships, collaborate and share knowledge, and learn on the fly. Mentoring facilitates the new hire's introduction into the organizational network and its processes, culture, and norms. In many cases, this process parallels conventional incorporation and skills training.

Since mentoring is labor intensive, companies should not assign too many people to any one sponsor. Experienced and effective mentors can set their limits—typically two or three mentorees at once. Nor should companies assume that everyone can be a mentor. Mentors need guidelines and training, and mentoring relationships need flexibility to evolve and dissolve as new hires mature within the organization, some to become mentors themselves.

Extending These Approaches

Gore's methods for rapid incorporation are thoroughly institutionalized, and they apply to all new employees. The more intensive and specialized approaches we've discussed at Newell Rubbermaid and Trilogy are naturally reserved for the new hires with the greatest skill and potential. However, companies can adapt the practices described here—particularly accelerated learning, contribution, and assimilation—for diverse incorporation programs for all employees.

For example, Household International, the financial services company now part of HSBC Holdings, implemented rapid incorporation techniques for call center staff. First, the call center representatives—not HR—interview and hire their new colleagues, so that everyone must commit to incorporation. Experienced reps and managers participate in the new hire training, and each new trainee has a "buddy." After initial training, each group of new hires spends a full week working in the "bull pen," where the supervisor/coach-to-staff ratio is 1:5, with plenty of individual support. Energetic and ambitious bull pens sometimes outperform the regular call center staff. Quickly assimilated, trained, and experienced—and with a sense of accomplishment—the new employees then join the regular call center.[7]

Such rapid incorporation experiences typify companies focused on young employees, especially recent college graduates with high potential. They are the contemporary, accelerated answer to the prolonged management development tracks of twenty years ago, where recruits had to rotate among jobs, functions, and locations for two to three years to master the business and demonstrate their dedication.

We recommend, however, that such programs open their doors a little wider—to welcome older employees with many good years left, career changers and capable workforce reentrants, and late bloomers and midcareer employees energized by challenges. Rapid incorporation techniques work for new hires and role changers of all ages.

Continuous Retention

Many employers struggle to cultivate a strong sense of organizational loyalty in young employees. But some companies we've studied—such as St. Luke's advertising, SEI Investments, The Container Store, and Intuit—employ a high proportion of workers under thirty-five who are extraordinarily loyal and committed to their organizations. Successful companies are not just in youth-oriented fields like technology and recreation, but in professional services, financial services, and retail as well. Their secret is understanding what keeps their young workers motivated and productive (and what will send them heading for the exits), and consistently providing them with what they seek most from the work experience. Their innovative work environments and management practices both engender loyalty and inspire outstanding performance in young workers.

The most talented and sought-after young employees know that they are in demand. They haven't been conditioned, as their parents were, to strive for long-term employment with a single company. As a result, many young workers (especially the well-prepared ones corporations covet) are uncompromising regarding their employers and work arrangements. As we've said, there are many ways to fail, from ineffective managers to lack of recognition, variety, or challenge. Such conditions can leave any worker dissatisfied; young workers are more apt to act upon that dissatisfaction sooner.

To retain young workers continually, employers must provide three basics, corresponding to what young employees insist on:

1. A thoroughly engaging workplace, featuring collegiality, teamwork, fun, and, most fundamentally, democratic participation

2. Ample opportunity to learn and grow, including assignments that expand skills and the leeway and mobility to try one's hand at a variety of activities

3. Attentive management, where the direct manager not only appreciates individual employees' points of view but also attends to the employee's needs and progress and explicitly encourages—and is accountable for—retention

We recommend that employers improve upon these basics not in isolation, but as part of an explicit and ongoing effort. Recognize and manage employee retention as a business process, with specific goals, performance measures, feedback loops, and process improvement activities. Do more than track retention rates. Describe the desired kind of workplace and how employees should respond to it, and track managerial performance and improvement against those standards. React not only when employees are unhappy but when they are doing well. Communicate with them; monitor their needs, concerns, and satisfaction; and act before an employee decides to leave. Again, these techniques will work for all employees, but they are absolutely essential for engaging younger ones.

Engaging Workplace

The thoroughly engaging workplace has six traits, namely three Ss—*say, stake,* and *stimulus*—and three Rs—*responsibility, recognition,* and *respect. Say* means having a real voice in the organization's goals and management relative to one's work responsibilities and work style. *Stake* means fair compensation, a sense of ownership (most directly through a share in equity or profit), and the sense of contributing to the organization's success. *Stimulus* is both environmental, from physical layout and collegial colleagues, and mental, from exercising one's abilities to accomplish interesting, important work.

The result: everyone behaves more like an owner of the enterprise. This behavior often requires a more democratic, participatory approach to management, carefully communicating the goals and performance of the company, and relying on teams to make decisions and take accountability for results. GE Capital, for example, regularly convenes under-thirty managers to advise senior managers on business issues and opportunities. Intel Corporation encourages entrepreneurial and ownership behavior by authorizing any employee to demand an "action required" of any manager on any issue. Continental Airlines' "no secrets" management philosophy motivates managers to discuss key company news with their employees before that news hits the street.[8]

The workspace can be engaging if the layout facilitates communication and collaboration, yet allows for quiet concentration. The organization can be fun, both spontaneously and purposefully, as organized by the Joy Gang and Grand Poobah of Joy at Ben & Jerry's.[9] But more important, employees need the stimulus of teamwork—colleagues interested in sharing, teaching, learning, and mutual success.

At SEI Investments, 46 percent of the workforce is under thirty-five years old, and 19 percent is under twenty-seven. The company believes that free and open communication of ideas among junior and senior staff alike drives creativity and innovation. Its structure is flat, with one hundred forty teams as the defining units. The physical workplace of the approximately eighteen hundred workers is open, mobile, and flexible, with none of the trappings of the typical white-collar workplace. No one—not even the CEO—has an office or a secretary. Everyone sits in an open floor plan with all desks, chairs, and furniture on wheels—the better to reconfigure them quickly for different projects and activities. Communications and electrical "pythons" hang from high, atrium ceilings, so that workers can plug in and unplug as needed. According to Al West, SEI's founder and CEO, "We don't use personal space to distinguish ourselves. Titles and seniority don't matter here. Workstations are open, flexible, and creative, and everything is on wheels to remind people not to get set in their ways."[10]

In many industries, young workers, not yet fully established in their organizations or confident in their careers, can feel disenfranchised when the value of their contributions is unclear and goes unrecognized—which brings us to the three Rs. Even inexperienced workers want *responsibility* for making decisions and delivering results, so that each role is meaningful. Explain how to do the work, clarify decision rights, give young workers more responsibility rather than less, and penalize no one for "rookie mistakes" when decisions and actions are sensible and well intentioned. Young workers want *recognition* for their accomplishments, individually and in teams. The right balances—between individual and team recognition, and between financial and other rewards—will sustain motivation and engagement day after day. Young workers want *respect* from coworkers and managers of all ages. They may have a lot to learn, but they also have a lot to contribute. If they feel "dissed"—by job assignments, coworker treatment, compensation systems, manager inattention, or public censure or discouragement—they communicate with their feet and quit. Younger workers will simply not bide their time until conditions improve, as older ones would. Organizations that carefully tailor recognition and reward practices to their young workers significantly improve both worker satisfaction and retention rates.

Intuit, a leading provider of financial software, mixes formal and informal recognition and rewards to motivate its staff. The company's Total Rewards program emphasizes noncash awards because those provide more effective and lasting reinforcement than financial ones in younger workers. Its Thanks Program features a variety of small noncash awards such as gift certificates to restaurants or movie tickets, together with written notes of thanks. Its Bright Ideas awards recognize employees for technical achievement and for everyday activities such as process improvements and eliminating bureaucracy. The On-The-Town award for contributing to outstanding business results can come with as much as $1,000 in merchandise or cash, depending on the magnitude of the achievement. Employee Choice, a Web-based service, allows employees to pick rewards from their favorite categories. To increase recognition and visibility of awards, the company is also developing a spot on its Web site to showcase employee achievements to the entire company and its customers. According to Jim Grenier, director of Total Rewards, "Noncash awards give employees solid, lasting reinforcement."[11]

Advertising agency St. Luke's effectively combines the Ss and Rs for its largely youthful workforce. The original firm of thirty-five people was formed in a management buyout from Chiat/Day in 1995. Today, it has ninety employees and has consistently grown its billings and profits. It has won numerous awards for its ad campaigns for clients and has won or been short-listed for ad agency of the year in Britain several years running. Its annual turnover rate is unusually low for an ad agency—only 10 percent, compared with the typical 25 percent. The majority of resignations pursue other careers, not competitors.

The agency's goal is to revolutionize the advertising business. It has created a culture comfortable with paradox. For example, the firm pushes its people to take creative risks and requires employees to evaluate each other's work every month, but it never fires anyone for making mistakes. Employees agree contractually to perform the job at St. Luke's that best suits them, often as determined in reviews by other employees. The company provides access to counseling to help staff deal with the emotional consequences of challenging projects and shifting roles.

Built on principles of openness, devolved authority, and individual potential, St. Luke's has a very flat organizational structure; the company is owned entirely by employees, and an elected body of six employees liaises with the management team and has responsibility for the welfare of all. People pursue their own initiatives and dare to question management decisions. There is a free flow of information on everything except salaries and personal information. The firm takes exceptional steps to avoid layoffs. To achieve this, it retains sufficient levels of cash to cover the potential loss of a sizable client account.

The company's main office in London is uniquely designed to promote collaboration. Employees use unassigned work spaces as needed, and the space is designed for people—to socialize, interact, and collaborate. "Brand rooms" are dedicated spaces that reflect a client's brand and the experience of its customers. For example, the Clarks team works in a room that displays Clarks shoes on shop shelves. Another brand room is fitted with a huge fridge and fruit trees—their client is a manufacturer of fruit drinks and smoothies.

Other inspiring spaces include the "café," designed for socializing and the "chill out room," where there are no phones or computers and employees can sleep, read, or get a massage.

The company holds weekly, monthly, and annual rituals and events designed to build the culture and bond employees. Every Monday, all staff gather in the dining area for a fifteen-minute "start the week" session previewing the company duty roster for the week. "Flag meetings" occur on the last Thursday evening of the month. These lively sessions are held under a flag emblazoned with the corporate logo (a winged ox) and involve reviews of their work, acknowledgment of individuals and groups for work well done, and focus on the demands of the month ahead. Each year, the entire firm comes together on October 18, or thereabouts, to commemorate St. Luke's day and to brainstorm and debate their collective future. According to St. Luke's joint managing director Neil Henderson, "We've created a company and a work space that benefits everyone—the people who work here, our clients and our suppliers and partners. It's uniquely collaborative and we have a real sense of team spirit you just don't get in other organizations."[12]

Opportunity to Learn and Grow

The second key ingredient in continuous retention of young workers is ample opportunity to learn, grow, and achieve. Many companies are surprised when young workers find their training programs, development experiences, and job options inadequate. The company may have traditionally thought of itself as a great place for young employees to get a start and learn a job or a business, but today's young hires still find the opportunities for learning and growth too few and too narrow. The problem is often not lack of formal training programs, but rather corporations' reluctance to allow new hires significant degrees of freedom to take on new roles and responsibilities at a rapid pace.

Yet that is exactly what many young people need most to feel happy in a company—continuous opportunity to learn and grow through frequent changes in roles, responsibilities, and projects. Challenge them, stretch them, stimulate them, let them try new things, allow them to learn by doing and failing—if you can do these things, you will keep more of the young talent you have, and word of the opportunities you offer will spread in the job market.

Young workers are at the beginnings of their careers, where it is only natural that they want to explore different roles and take every opportunity to experiment and learn. For these explorations to be successful and satisfying, young employees need not just training but *mobility*, the chance to work in different roles in different parts of the organization. Job rotation and comprehensive job-posting systems are two ways to facilitate this. Less formal means include reducing time-in-position requirements between transfers and removing any bureaucratic barriers to movement among departments or divisions. For some young workers, geographic mobility also has high appeal. At TGI Friday's, a qualified worker can be a "nomad" with five hundred restaurants in three hundred eighty places to choose from.[13]

Creating an active and mobile learning environment for young workers is not easy. The most effective approaches make learning and growing on the job a fundamental part of the culture and operations of the organization. Employees must be able, within reason, to move about the organization, learning new parts of the business and taking on different roles and responsibilities. They must also feel free to speak up—to contribute their points of view, ideas, and criticisms without hesitation.

Two good examples of organizations providing young workers with ample mobility, responsibility, and learning are SAS and Harley-Davidson. Software company SAS makes it easy for people to move laterally, in part by assigning people to work based on skills they have, not predefined tasks to perform. According to one of its HR executives, "There are no functional silos here— R&D, Sales, Technical Support, etc. In an intellectual capital organization like ours, the most important thing you can do is to engage the individual's energy so that they can apply it to the thing that excites them the most." SAS encourages people to discover what they are good at and want to do. The company assumes that people will have three or four careers during their working lives—it would like them all to be with SAS.[14]

Harley-Davidson offers a formal rotational program to its top young recruits that allows them to move across disciplines on a systematic basis to view and learn the operation from many angles. The company also provides ample cross-training opportunities to young individual contributors through its Technical Excellence Program, which provides exposure to a wide range of jobs in engineering and manufacturing. Young employees at Harley are allowed to change roles every eighteen to twenty-four months, and this mobility is supported through both individual coaching and a formal Performance Effectiveness Program.[15]

Founded in 1978, The Container Store is a Dallas-based retailer of storage solutions ranging from simple containers to shelving systems. Its steady growth and financial success are the result of attracting, training, and retaining a highly capable and fiercely loyal workforce. The Container Store's culture of teamwork and service proves very attractive for young workers and their lifestyles. Staff retention and loyalty are built upon both a unique compensation package and unmatched commitments to employee learning and customer service.

As a retailer of highly specialized and often high-cost products, the company depends on its floor staff to be engaging, informed, and enthusiastic. Employees are motivated by an open and trusting culture where helping customers is perceived as a public good. Underlying that motivation is an extensive and ongoing investment in employee training and indoctrination in company values. The Container Store puts extensive effort into attracting people who fit into this corporate culture and who reflect the demographics of the clientele. Employees, like many of their customers, are college educated and upwardly mobile. The company looks for people who embrace teamwork, are willing to help out with all aspects of the store, and see customers as people who need a problem solved. How important is recruiting the right people? It is the limiting factor for growing the business, more common in technology companies than retail.

To ensure that new recruits are indoctrinated into corporate culture and understand the many product lines, training is both immediate and intense. New hires in the stores, distribution centers, and headquarters all begin with Foundation Week. Designed to quickly convey a large amount of product and sales training, the week also gives employees an immediate understanding of the company's commitment to their success. For store employees, Foundation Week is especially critical, since some closet systems can mean single sales of several thousand dollars. Failing to meet a customer's expectations on a sale of that size can have lasting implications. Because of this, both full-time and seasonal employees receive the same training.

Foundation Week training begins before the week itself. Employees must complete all the HR paperwork and some reading before their first day. On the first day, the employee spends his entire time getting oriented to the new surroundings with his manager. Over the next four days, several coworkers join the manager in training the new recruit. Only after five full days of training does an employee get a regular schedule. For a retail store, the time a manager and coworkers spend away from their regular duties represents a tremendous investment in a new employee.

During their first year with The Container Store, all employees receive at least 241 hours of formal training, versus an industry average of about 7. In subsequent years, full-time employees receive an average of 160 hours of training. Sales trainers support stores for the ongoing development of the staff's solution-selling skills and knowledge.

Moreover, store and distribution center employees rotate—building teamwork, giving everyone frontline experience and focus, and ensuring that distribution isn't relegated to "backwater" status. Being part of a strong team, along with the occasional change of scenery, is a powerful motivator of younger workers. It also helps everyone understand the big picture of the company's operations and challenges. So does Continuing Education, three days of intensive training for career-minded employees from across the organization. With presentations designed by the staff of every department in the company, employees learn about the specific functionality of every facet of the firm.

To attract and retain talent, The Container Store uses the reliable method of generous compensation, based on the belief that all stakeholders should be enriched by the success of the business. While The Container Store hires fewer people than similar companies, it pays them double the industry average but does not pay sales commissions. Pay is linked to value to the company and position in the hierarchy. Even without commissions, merit pay still results in some salespeople earning more than their managers, and people can move in and out of manager roles. A comparatively generous benefit package is offered to all employees, both full-time and seasonal.

Several telling statistics attest to The Container Store's success in talent management: 97 percent of employees agree with the statement "People care about each other here," and over 40 percent of new hires are recommended by friends who currently work for the company. The annual turnover rate for all full-time staff is 7 to 10 percent (versus an industry average of close to 100 percent), and turnover among store employees is even lower than the company average.[16]

Attentive Management

Our third key ingredient in young employee retention is close attention by direct supervisors or managers. Studies of voluntary departures consistently show that the most common reason employees quit is the boss. For young employees, the perceived problem may well be of omission, not commission—failure to pay attention to the employee's needs and expectations. Benign neglect just doesn't cut it with this workforce cohort.

Younger workers want hands-on managers, but in the role of coach, not order giver. They want managers who

- Make work challenging.

- Demand personal responsibility in completing it.

- Are available and communicative.

- Include subordinates in decision making.

- Provide quick and immediate feedback and recognition.

- Have learned to relate to and respect younger workers.

- Can adjust their approaches to fit the individual needs and styles of their young colleagues.

- Are committed to delivering on the "employee deal" and making the employment situation work for the young employee.

- Serve as buffers between young employees and corporate bureaucracy.

Again, anyone would appreciate these characteristics in a manager, but younger workers—who haven't been through the mill, lowered their standards, and learned to cope with subpar managers—tend to insist upon them more than older cohorts do.

Being *hands-on* entails working alongside younger workers, providing regular guidance and feedback, and yet giving the employees room to experiment with their own methods. Managing by exception or intervening only when problems arise doesn't work. Young workers want to be mentored by and learn from managers with the skills, knowledge, and leadership styles that the organization values. Managers must always balance the goals and interests of the organization and the needs and desires of individual workers, but that balancing may be most challenging with young employees.

Managers must also be hands-on to ensure that employees have the learning and growth opportunities described earlier. They must not prejudge potential based on experience, credentials, or organizational status. Companies should prohibit managers from hoarding skilled people and top performers, lodging them in roles that suit the manager's interests but impede the worker's growth. Managers should enable and encourage employees to experiment within their current positions and should help young employees to design "next step" roles and responsibilities—but without locking people into career paths. Lateral movement and cross-functional experience can challenge and satisfy an employee as much as a promotion, provided that recognition and reward advance relative to responsibility.

To reduce young worker turnover, companies must—above all—make sure that managers, especially first-level supervisors and managers, are part of the solution rather than a cause of the problem. Tie mangers' compensation to staff satisfaction and turnover rates. Demand that they attend to their employees, and train them to manage more effectively. If first-level supervision causes tension in the organization, then these managers may require constant monitoring, appraisal, feedback, training, and coaching so that they recognize their pivotal role in employee retention—and then play it well. Also, provide managers with the role models who succeed at staff retention, and adjust management recruiting, development, and promotion practices to value not just individual expertise, but the people and leadership skills for working well with young workers. Don't automatically promote the most senior person or highest performer to fill a first-level management vacancy. Ruthlessly weed out managers who can't or don't deliver on their people development and retention goals. This focused investment in frontline management turns out to be a small price to pay when compared with the cost of high turnover.

Easy Return

This falls in the category of "obvious step to take but few corporations bother to do it." You will inevitably lose some share of young employees, and some "designated keepers" won't clear the three-year hump. To mitigate that loss, you can recapture some of your ex-employees. The best, most predictable, most reliable, most already-trained source of talent is people you already know—people who once worked for you and left in good standing.

Sometimes companies can recruit them back, and sometimes they return on their own, having explored the job market elsewhere. At Household International, ex–sales representatives are a major recruiting source. Many reapply for positions. When the company needs more staff, it conducts a letter campaign to ex-employees, sometimes recruiting dozens at a time.[17] In 1997 Microsoft began the Terminator Study, administered by ACNielsen, to ask ex-employees why they left. Meantime, the company treats departed employees "like family" and sends them regular updates about the company and industry. Thanks to such efforts, several hundred who left for start-ups returned to the company after the dot-com crash.[18]

Friendly Farewell

An easy-return program should prompt departed employees to think and speak highly of the company and to entertain the possibility of returning. A complete program makes sure that valued employees—the ones you'd most want back—depart on the best possible terms, even if the valued employee disliked the employment experience. The company can ease a departure by being flexible around timing and transition, even if the employee is going to a competitor. Never tell the employee to clean out his desk, show him the door, and tell him to reread his noncompete agreement. Use the process of departure to tie as well as loosen bonds with the soon-to-be-ex-employee. The social ritual of a departure lunch or party also sets a positive tone and provides a sense of closure among colleagues. Finally, conduct an exit interview (or interviews, if you're really serious about the process)—that is, a serious discussion about the employee's experience with the company, what worked and what didn't, and the reasons for departure. The company representatives must listen genuinely, and the company must treat the interview as an opportunity to learn, a form of market research into the effectiveness of the employment "brand." Departed as well as active employees are, after all, your brand representatives to the job market, for good or ill. The exit interview should also double as the first step in rerecruitment. Let the valued employee know that you'd be happy to welcome her back, and let her know how the company will keep in touch.

Alumni Associations

Another component of an easy-return program is keeping the door open and regularly reminding ex-employees of the company's ongoing interest in them and their careers. Techniques include communications and newsletters, "alumni" groups, and having individual executives and peers actively stay in touch. The goal is to redefine *retention* to include not only keeping staff on the payroll, but also keeping them "affiliated" with the organization over the long term.

Professional services firms like McKinsey & Company and Bain & Company excel at maintaining alumni networks because they serve two purposes, of which rerecruiting is the secondary. They stay in close touch with their alumni because many of them become senior executives and clients. Companies in many industries have this dual motivation for cultivating their alumni. In financial services and retail, for example, ex-employees can become lifelong customers and sometimes business clients. But even if your motive is simply rerecruitment, you can still learn from organizations like McKinsey and Bain.

They compete for the best and brightest talent to begin with, and then maintain extensive relationships with employees that leave. They seek lifetime affiliation, not necessarily lifetime employment, with star employees.

According to one Bain senior executive, "Ultimately, it's foolish to believe you can trap good people. The idea is to stay connected with them after they leave your payroll. How do you turn them into advocates, clients, business partners?"[19]

Bain was one of the first companies to adopt the university method of alumni programs, and it communicates with its alumni more often and effectively than some companies do with their employees. The firm has more people in its alumni network than it employs around the world. These people receive alumni directories and invitations to attend regional cocktail receptions. They visit an alumni page on Bain's Web site and read a newsletter covering both the firm and its alumni. Through these activities, the firm maintains the bonds formed among ex-employees as well as between individual employees and the company. According to the firm's head of alumni relations, "If people want to be successful somewhere else, you should feel great about that. The more successful our alumni are, the more successful we are."[20]

Welcoming the "Boomerangs"

A third component is celebrating people's return. This celebration serves not only to reincorporate the returning employee rapidly, but also to demonstrate publicly how highly you value returnees. Gensler, a San Francisco–based architectural and design firm, makes a special effort to welcome back returning employees. The firm has a staff of some nineteen hundred professionals in twenty-five offices around the world, and a client list that includes leading firms in every business sector. Visitors to the firm's offices see boomerangs hanging on the walls, each representing not a tour in the Australian office, but an employee who left the firm and then elected to come back. CEO Arthur Gensler explains, "There are all sorts of reasons why people might want to leave us at some point in their career. But we do try to keep the relationship going because many of them will decide to come back. And the people who do return become our most loyal employees and our best recruiters."[21] The boomerang is the firm's way of saying, "Welcome back."

The firm tracks its "boomerang rate"—a remarkable 12 percent of hires are ex-employees. The presence of these once-and-current employees has helped stabilize the firm, even as it has more than doubled in size in recent years. One advantage is that returnees already understand and appreciate the culture and workplace. They can hit the ground running when they return, and they introduce the company to new ideas, business partners, and processes they developed on the outside. Each boomerang is accompanied by a letter saying, "All Gensler Boomerangs enjoy a very special relationship with each other and with the firm. They're our prodigals returned, the old dogs who teach all the tricks to the new pups, the elite corps that we rely on and are delighted to welcome back. This boomerang is a token of our thanks—a frivolous reminder of the serious value we place on our association." By embracing its "boomerangs," the firm believes it's mastering the increasingly difficult arithmetic of talent. "There are only so many good people out there," Gensler says. "If you cross off the ones who've already worked for you, that's very limiting."[22]

Indeed, the best developmental experience for a valued employee may happen outside the company. When you succeed in rerecruiting an ex-employee, you capitalize on both that outside experience and the individual's familiarity with your operations. The results can be breakthroughs in innovation, contribution, and career progression. The best way to keep young employees may ultimately be to let them go—but with strong prospects of return.

Excelling at Retention

To succeed at retaining employees, and young ones in particular, you can't wait until they're unhappy and then scramble to recover the relationship. Instead, you've got to make retention a continuous priority and effort. At the very beginning, incorporate new hires, enable them to be and feel productive, as quickly as possible. Throughout their employment, offer responsibilities, a workplace, a community of colleagues, and a management style that constantly engages them. And for those who inevitably depart, make it easy to stay in touch and return.

To use the techniques descried in this chapter, you must begin with awareness. Be aware of the attitudes, characteristics, and experiences of young workers. Study and learn from them and start adjusting to their methods. They signal the workforce and work methods of the future, and they will be in the lead soon. Your successes and failures to engage and retain young workers will affect not only the turnover rate, but also your organization's reputation as an employer. You will no doubt struggle to get young workers over the three-year hump, but the only inexcusable failure is not trying. Never assume that today's young workers will eventually settle in and do things the good old-fashioned way. They won't, and that's good.

ACTIONS TO TAKE

To Retain Young Workers

We recommend the following actions for connecting with young workers and making their tenures last longer than average:

☐ *Poll new hires* about their incorporation experiences. You'll learn from them and simultaneously satisfy some of their desire to be heard.

☐ *Focus on day one*, so the new hire feels not just welcome to the organization, but equipped to perform.

☐ *Involve senior executives* in the incorporation process in meaningful ways—not just giving welcoming speeches, but meeting, listening, teaching, and learning.

☐ *Get in the field*—instead of limiting incorporation to the classroom—to give new hires realistic experiences and opportunities to make a contribution.

☐ *Talk with young workers* regularly, both individually and in focus groups. Don't rely exclusively on formal surveys. Ask them to evaluate the organization.

☐ *Make employee retention a real process*, with an owner, a design, performance measures, and improvement efforts.

☐ *Make line managers responsible for retention*, and measure and reward them accordingly. Provide them with the training and support to be genuinely hands-on.

☐ *Measure employee engagement, mobility, and learning.* Metrics will be useful even though not decimal-point precise. Set and pursue improvement targets.

☐ *Make exit interviews work* for you and the employee. Track what you learn, and make the interview the first step of rerecruiting a valued employee.

☐ *Evaluate the prospects* of each departed employee's returning. How much would you want the employee back, what are the circumstances of departure, and how likely is a return? Then personalize your later outreach to the best prospects.

☐ *Form an alumni association*, or at minimum a communications channel with ex-employees. Track their whereabouts and, for highly valued ones, career progress.

☐ *Ask and welcome people back.* Leave the door open, and periodically invite past employees to walk through. Then celebrate their return.

PART III

The New Employment Deal and How to Shape It

The majority of human beings cannot be safely regimented at work without relief in the form of education and recreation and pleasant surroundings.[1]

—Mary Barnett Gilson, factory personnel manager, economist, and educator

9

Flexible Work Arrangements

*Why You Need Them Now
and How to Make Them Work*

W HEN IT LAUNCHED in 1999, JetBlue Airways rejected many of
the industry's common practices. Among its technological and
operational innovations were its "paperless cockpit" flight technology, its implementation of e-tickets for 100 percent of passengers, and
its use of entirely home-based reservations agents—and all its reservations
employees still work at home, creating a virtual reservations center that decreases costs and increases customer service. David Neeleman, founder and
CEO of JetBlue, explains, "Reservationists are the people least compensated
in the company but generate its revenue and interface with the customers
more than anyone else except the flight attendants. We cannot afford to pay
them huge salaries, so let's just make them happier; let's let them work in
their homes. We train them, send them home, and they are happy."[1]

Julie Strickland, call center analyst for JetBlue, summarizes, "To be a customer-centric business, you must first be employee-centric." The airline aims to accommodate all the work preferences of its reservation staff—whether that means working only twenty hours a week or swapping shifts for a last-minute getaway—but balances those preferences against its business needs. Employees have unlimited shift-trading and self-scheduling privileges using an online community bulletin board. The company has experienced a 30 percent boost in agent productivity, a 38 percent increase in service levels, and a 50 percent decrease in management workload per agent. The airline can design staffing scenarios that satisfy the majority of its reservationists and still make business sense. JetBlue's revenues have grown from $100 million annually in 1999 to $1.27 billion in 2004. According to Strickland, "These motivational, productivity, and financial benefits ultimately mean our customers receive the best service and the lowest airfares."[2] The low attrition rate saves the company money, too.

New companies such as JetBlue have an advantage over established firms because they can implement flexible schedules and at-home work from the get-go, and flexibility in the scheduling and location of work matters significantly to specific employee segments:

- *Young workers* show the highest preference for flexible schedules. They often want time for education and recreation. They tend to be mobile and willing to experiment, many are not yet strongly attached to their jobs or employers, and they want ample time and opportunity to explore things outside of work.

- *Midcareer workers* want time for family and community. They often have family commitments—to spouses, children, and, more and more often, parents—and, unlike their parents, they refuse to miss key events in their children's lives. For work/life balance, midcareers may have the greatest need for flexible arrangements but a great reluctance to implement them for fear of setting their careers back.

- *Mature workers*, including many past the prevailing retirement age, want to keep working in a less time-consuming, pressured capacity so that they can pursue other interests. They want time for recreation and volunteerism, doing what their previous working lives did not allow. Naturally interested in reduced and flexible schedules, they show the highest preference for a flexible workplace and for experimentation, such as taking six months on, six months off.

Flexible arrangements are also more important on average to women, higher-income employees, and people who travel a great deal for work. Overall, 17 percent of employees are currently seeking a more flexible schedule, 14 percent to work more from home. That's all the more reason why today's corporations should begin changing their employment deal now to implement flexible work arrangements, and in the process enjoy improved productivity, reduced turnover, and lower facilities costs.

These next three chapters explain how to "flex up" your employment deal so that it accommodates and attracts a changing workforce. We start with work arrangements and continue with on-the-job learning and then compensation and benefits. As you read these chapters, please keep three points in mind.

- We define *employment deal* broadly. It includes compensation and benefits that motivate employees to perform well; work arrangements such as flexible schedules that allow them to meet their professional and personal commitments simultaneously; and opportunities to learn and grow on the job.

- The value of the employment deal depends entirely on the vitality of the work and workplace. No deal will bring out the best in employees if the work itself is unimportant and unengaging, or the workplace is uninviting and unsocial. The deal never works when the work itself, the culture, or the environment turns employees' stomachs.

- The employment deal evolves. Given precedents (especially in benefits) and regulatory restrictions, managers may consider specific changes impossible to make. However, if we study the deal over time (see the box "Evolution of the Employment Deal"[3]), we see how it has evolved to suit changes in workforce composition, employee and employer needs, and economic conditions. Given our changing workforce size and composition, we know that the deal must evolve further.

After decades of adding deal elements, especially in benefits, employers are scaling back coverage and shifting more costs to employees and retirees, as health-care costs climb and retiree pension and health-care liabilities grow. But today's employment deal is less paternalistic and more realistic, a more explicit give-and-take between employee and employer. With more choice and more responsibility in structuring their individual deals, employees are becoming more informed "consumers" of the deal elements. With better information systems and management methods, employers are trying to engage

Evolution of the Employment Deal

- A hundred years ago, workers had no benefits and little protection from illness or unemployment. Employers set the terms of employment; they paid people for time worked and trained them only to improve immediate productivity.

- In the 1920s, the U.S. government began offering many of its employees retirement and pensions. Many private employers offered paid holidays, some offered paid vacations to salaried workers, and some even began providing group life, sickness, and accident insurance, and access to a company doctor and to disability and death payments through benevolent associations.

- During World War II, with wage hikes restricted, employers offered pensions, paid vacations, and medical insurance to retain workers. After the war, employees expected these benefits.

- In the 1950s, amid economic prosperity and worker unionization, the modern deal began to form, along with the corporate human resources function. Defined-benefit pensions became standard, as did Social Security, eventually covering over 90 percent of the population. Subsidized medical coverage for employees, and then retirees, was available through local Blue Cross/Blue Shield companies and eventually a variety of commercial insurers. Fixed-amount life insurance and weekly disability benefits became common. Personnel departments organized around specialist units for hiring, training, industrial relations, and so on. Formal training and development moved away from a strictly short-term utilitarian focus on skills building. The American Society of Trainers formed, and General Electric founded the first corporate "university" in Crotonville, New York.

- In the 1960s, companies started taking more systematic approaches to instructional objectives, design, and evaluation of employee training and development. Personnel departments stressed employee productivity and associated management methods.

- In the 1970s, bonus compensation became more common for employees outside of sales. Paid sick and personal leave, precisely accumulated, became common. Employers started adding dental coverage and life insurance pegged to earnings. Retirees now had Medicare as a health coverage safety net, and were tempted by the option of collecting reduced Social Security benefits starting at age sixty-two. Companies emphasized organization-wide learning and performance management, and team effectiveness, using techniques like personality typing and competence profiles.

- In the 1980s, the phenomenal influx of women in the workforce fueled the proliferation of family-friendly benefits, including maternity, paternity, and family leaves and child-care support. Demand increased for technical training and supply increased through computer-based training, and the total-quality movement focused on continuous learning and improvement. The personnel department morphed more into a human resources function. Companies were learning how people management practices shape organizational performance and involving line managers in people processes and employee advocacy, with HR professionals as coaches and policy makers. HR executives were joining the CEO's inner circle.

- In the 1990s, the ubiquity of portable computers and telecommunications enabled the rapid expansion of flexible work arrangements, including flexible scheduling, telecommuting, compressed workweeks, and job sharing. Many large employers added eye-care and prescription drug coverage. The "cafeteria style" approach enabled employees to customize part of the deal while maintaining overall fairness. And HR learned to focus on both employee performance and workforce flexibility, just to contend with rapid changes in pay for performance, cafeteria benefits, flexible work arrangements, and corporate learning.

- Today, fully one-fourth of a typical employee's total compensation comes in benefits, not cash. Compensation more likely depends on performance (often involving stock options or profit sharing), and 401(k)-type savings accounts supplement (or replace) defined-benefit pensions. Medical coverage is available in umpteen formats, paid for partly through umpteen reimbursement accounts. The center of gravity of corporate learning has shifted from the company as provider to the employee as consumer, with distance learning, best-practice sharing, knowledge management, and the continuing integration of the tools of learning and work. Progressive HR staffs actively plan for and manage the corporation's human assets, talent supply, and employer brand, and must develop a systemic view of the interplay of employees, processes, customers, and technology so that HR execs can discuss the "people side" of every business strategy.

employees by getting the entire deal right. So employees are seeing some elements of the deal contract, but the deal as a whole opens up new options, especially in the area of work/life mix. The entire deal—work arrangements, learning opportunities, compensation and benefits—is in play, customizable as never before. This part of the book outlines some possibilities.

Forms of Flexible Work

Over the last decade, employers have learned how to validate opportunities for flex work and how to structure it so that it meets their business goals and employees' needs. Here are the three most basic options:

- *Flexible time* includes flexible hours and shifts (work schedules that permit flexible starting and quitting times within limits set by management) and compressed workweeks (for example, a forty-hour workweek compressed into four ten-hour days instead of the usual five eight-hour days).

- *Reduced time* includes part-time and seasonal work, job sharing (regular, part-time work where people share responsibilities of one full-time, salaried position with benefits), reduced hours or days worked, and various less-than-full-time contract assignments.

- *Flexible place* includes telecommuting (working primarily from home), mobile work (such as a salesperson who works predominantly on the road), and other forms of off-site work.

Flexible work is not new, and most major companies already offer some combination of flexible time, reduced time, and flexible place. According to the 2003 Society for Human Resource Management (SHRM) survey, 62 percent of large employers offer flexible hours, 33 percent job sharing, 43 percent telecommuting for part-timers, and 25 percent telecommuting for full-time employees. Among *Fortune* 100 companies, 87 percent allow telecommuting.[4] But employees have a different perception: only 42 percent said their employers offer some form of flexible scheduling (46 percent among large employers), and 21 percent said employers offer a flexible workplace.[5] According to the Bureau of Labor Statistics, about 29 percent of full-time wage and salary workers have flexible work schedules that allow them to vary when they begin or end work. That's double the number of workers in the mid-1980s.

There's a big difference between offering flexible arrangements to some workers and implementing flex work on a large scale that reaps real business benefits. Managers and professionals commonly enjoy flexible hours, but flexible shift and workweek scheduling can work as well for line workers in a factory or nurses in a hospital. Line employees on the plant floor might never work from their homes, but flex work can enable them to align child-care schedules, go to school part-time, or pursue a hobby. Unfortunately, today's programs are usually small in scale, appealing to new mothers and others with overriding family commitments, and participation rates are low, perhaps because employees believe that participants' careers will suffer for it. Companies with successful flex programs make them easily accessible without sidelining or overlooking participants for promotions—and so participation benefits both employer and employee.

For example, ARO, Inc., a business process outsourcer based in Kansas City, Missouri, implemented widespread telework to reduce call center staff turnover from 60 percent to 7 percent. Productivity rose 15 percent, because the deal attracted more experienced and mature people who preferred to work from home, and it cut facilities costs and avoided expanding into a larger building.[6]

At Hewlett-Packard, "flextime is not just a company perk or a negotiation for time off. It's a strategic business tool that improves productivity and quality of life for employees," according to the Work in America Institute. To illustrate, a group of HP field technicians had to work a 24/7 schedule to ensure two-hour response time to customer requests. The pressure was taking its toll, and so the group adjusted its team schedule to reduce the stress. Some members volunteered to work twelve-hour shifts Friday through Sunday and a four-hour shift on Monday, in exchange for reducing their workweek to three and a half days. The rest of the team worked their shifts in five-day weeks but got their weekends off. Overtime costs for the team dropped 36 percent—during a period of growing customer demand.[7]

The Home Depot uses several forms of flexible work arrangements, including flexible schedules and part-time work, to retain its many midcareer and mature workers, some of them workforce reentrants, whose knowledge and experience translates into excellent customer service in their stores. This flexibility appeals to those who are "semiretired" but keeping busy, and over half such employees have flexible schedules. The company also grants employees time to participate in community volunteer projects and offers flexible vacation schedules and leaves of absence for numerous personal reasons.[8]

The Mutual Benefits of Flex Work

Employers will gain from instituting effective flex work arrangements in substantial ways, starting with the shareholder value and the bottom line. Survey data from Watson Wyatt shows that a collegial, flexible workplace has a 9 percent positive impact on market value.[9] When workers can arrange their schedules to be on the job during their most productive times—and avoid prolonged and unproductive commutes—productivity rises. In a survey of fifty-nine thousand people in forty-eight countries, employees who worked at home rated themselves as more productive than workers in any other work arrangement category.[10] A company can save significant direct cost in real estate and facilities when employees work primarily off-site. Consumption of personal and sick days and attendant costs decline when employees have more flexibility to attend to personal concerns in the day-to-day flow of their jobs. A Commerce Clearing House survey showed that while personal illness accounted for the highest percentage of absences (33 percent), another 24 percent were because of family issues, 21 percent because of other personal needs, and 12 percent due to stress.[11] Non-illness-related reasons for missing work are increasing but could level off and decline if employees have more control of their workdays.

Flexible work arrangements also increase employee engagement, including satisfaction with the job, commitment to the organization, and willingness to put forth discretionary effort to help reach its goals. An employer's accommodation of an employee's need for work/life balance improves morale, loyalty, and commitment, thus raising retention rates and lowering hiring and training costs. Many employees will stay with an organization offering flex work rather than jumping to another employer offering more money. Beating the competition in flexible work arrangements also enhances employer brand and creates a strong recruitment advantage to draw in scarce talent during labor shortages.

Finally, flexible work arrangements can expand business flexibility. Flextime affords expanded hours for businesses with customers in multiple time zones. Telecommuting enables better management of unexpected peaks in work volume. For many jobs, no one must jump into a car and drive to work; people just log on and start immediately. Flexible scheduling lets employers position the best talent on special projects, which maximizes the usage of that talent and keeps workers interested in their jobs.

Trends in Flex Work

Our recent survey of workers nationwide revealed the importance of flexible work arrangements.[12] Seventy-one percent of surveyed employees work primarily from a fixed employer location—office, store, or factory. Eight percent work primarily from home. The remaining 21 percent are almost equally divided four ways: people working mainly on the road (such as salespeople), at frequently changing customer locations (such as management consultants), at a single customer location for an extended period (such as systems integrators), and "somewhere else." In larger organizations (over five thousand employees), the center of gravity of employer facilities is stronger. Seventy-nine percent work at employer locations, only 3 percent at home.

Overall, 24 percent of surveyed employees work in government (including public education and health care); but only 5 percent of those work from home. People working off-site are more likely to work for private or for-profit companies and not in any form of government service.

Employees in wholesale and retail trade, manufacturing, construction, financial services, and government are much less likely than the general population to work from home. But those working in information and technology are more than three times more likely to work from home than the general population, those in professional and business services more than twice as likely. Given that technology and business services are among the fastest-growing occupations by Bureau of Labor Statistics estimates, the ranks of telecommuters will inevitably increase.

In terms of gender distribution, people working from home reflect the overall average (55 percent male, 45 percent female); those working at employer facilities are more heavily female (50 percent each); those working on the road or at customer sites are quite heavily male (67 percent to 33 percent). Those working remotely report working an hour or two more per week. They also report slightly higher overall job satisfaction; people working from home more than twice as likely (26 percent overall) as others to describe themselves as "extremely satisfied." They score a bit higher on our employee engagement scale, with the greatest difference (3 points on a 100-point scale) between those working from home and those working at employer facilities.

Clearly, the employer and the employee must partner so that both the enterprise and the individual benefit from these arrangements. Here are two

Portrait of a Telecommuter

In many organizations, telecommuting is a temporary accommodation for people with significant family responsibilities, such as parenting responsibilities and health issues for themselves or close relatives. Telecommuters with children are twice as likely as other employees to be predominant caregivers (not relying on or sharing responsibilities with a spouse) and twice as likely (19 percent) to care for an elderly relative or adult dependent. For them, working at home is a necessity.

But many telecommuters are young. Employees ages eighteen to thirty-four compose 30 percent of our survey but 37 percent of those working from home. Given this youthful skew, large groups of at-home workers are single (never married) and childless. They prefer to work from home and mix work with nonfamily leisure pursuits. Least likely to work from home are people in the forty-five to fifty-four age group, whose on-the-job responsibilities are often peaking.

Remarkably, over half are managers (versus 36 percent of the total employee population) but not necessarily (less than one in five) front-line supervisors. Three in five describe themselves as senior managers. Thus, a small but doubtless growing cadre of senior managers, when they can call their own shots, choose to work from home and control their schedules. We also found that working primarily from home does not mean working exclusively from home. Telecommuters are more than twice as likely as their in-office colleagues to travel for work. Presumably these travelers are young professionals and the aforementioned senior managers. So you can see, working from home does not simply accommodate women with small children or others with family pressures.

Other studies have shown how productive and well adjusted telecommuters are, and our survey confirms some of those findings. More satisfied and better engaged, employees working from home are less likely to feel burned out, to experience work-related conflicts, and to feel dead-ended in jobs or overwhelmed by responsibilities outside work. They are also more likely to welcome a new project or assignment. But at-home workers are much more likely (31 percent to 18 percent for workers at the employer's facilities) to fear being laid off. Finally, some workers use telecommuting as a transition, seeking to reduce work hours or commitments or to start their own businesses.

examples of very large organizations that implemented flex work at a larger scale and reaped extraordinary business benefits as a result.

Flexible Work at IBM

"On any given day, worldwide, one-third of our people are not at an IBM location. They are working on-site with customers, telecommuting, or are mobile," according to CEO Sam Palmisano.[13] The company's mobile and telework program began in the marketing and sales organizations. In 1992, sales people were saying, "Why do I have to return to the office to get an answer to a customer's question? We're a technology company. I should have information at my fingertips." So IBM set a goal to improve responsiveness and profitability by equipping the sales force with mobile technology and support. By January 1993, the first set of employees started working primarily from mobile offices, going into the regular office only as needed. After four more pilot sites, the program was implemented nationally across the U.S. field marketing and sales operations offices in 1995. A rollout process that initially took nine months was refined to two weeks. The initial productivity of the mobile workers increased anywhere from 6 percent to 20 percent, and IBM realized initial real estate savings of $68 million per year. Employees now have a combination of mobility tools (ThinkPads, remote telephony access from home, printing/fax capability, wireless connectivity, and high-speed access) to allow them to work in the best environment to meet customer and IBM needs. Going by the office when needed has become the standard. Next, telecommuting was added as an option for other job categories within IBM.

Today, mobile/telecommuter is just one of six categories of IBM's supported flexible work options:

- *Compressed/flexible workweek:* a workweek compressed into fewer than five days

- *Individualized work schedule:* workdays varying from two hours before to two hours after normal location operating times

- *Leave of absence programs:* unpaid leave for an extended time

- *Mobile/telecommuter:* workers who are on the move and without dedicated IBM work space

- *Part-time reduced work schedule:* a regular employee with a reduced work schedule

- *Work at home:* working regularly at home and without a dedicated IBM work space.

All of IBM's flexible work options are available to employees around the world, and today over one hundred thousand employees have some form of flexible work arrangement, with satisfaction very high.

Recognizing the rising demand for flexible arrangements, the need for employees to find ways to improve work/life balance, and the issues of employees who were overworked because they were electronically "overconnected" to their work, IBM created a global work/life flexibility project office in 1998 as the catalyst for enabling flexibility and addressing workload across the corporation. The project office focuses on getting managers to embrace the need for work/life balance and act to make it happen, promoting the availability of the six types of flexibility programs, and ensuring that employees are working in the most appropriate work environment. The office also facilitates adoption of flexibility and mobility standards across all geographies, and it makes sure that technology and training are available, including management training, communications to employees about what's available, and tools for employees and managers to decide what will work best. The training is now Web based.

One of the initial pilot projects included the introduction of flexible work options in Latin America, where there were no "formal" flexible work programs in place. The project office worked with the country local management, human resource teams, and the senior leadership team to gain commitment to offer flexible work options, and determine which specific flexible work options were best suited for the employees in Latin America. As a result, flexibility was implemented in eleven countries within Latin America. Cultural training was conducted to ensure the overall success of the initiative, including addressing the myths of "face time management" and "are my employees really working?"

The most important ground rules for local implementation of flexible work are that management must be committed, and the arrangement must be a win-win for the employee and IBM. Many managers were relieved to have the new options, tools, and support information available. They had sensed the rising need for working flexibility but never had the focused support for addressing it before. And managers, including executives, are taking advantage of the enhanced flexibility within IBM. Note that as they continue to extend flexibility around the world, there's no such thing as "one size fits all." What flex work options are offered, what technology is used, and a variety of other matters include consideration of local legislation, local choice, and local need.

In 2001, the company put together a work/life strategy, with the primary goal of having eighteen countries (representing 89 percent of IBM employees) each offering at least three of the six flex work formats. They track progress with a Work/Life Scorecard, and all eighteen countries have now established at least three of the flexible work options.

With so many flex work variations, how do IBM units maintain work group and corporate cohesion? In addition to conference calls, videoconferencing, e-meetings, and team rooms, most recently teams are effectively using "Friday meetings in the office." IBM's global employee directory, called "blue pages," includes a persona page identifying employees by their function and allows employees to connect a face with a voice. IBM managers also stay in touch with remote employees via e-mail, cell phones, BlackBerries, and two different online instant messaging tools called "sametime" and "notesbuddy" (the latter will send a picture of the sender).

Telework at AT&T

AT&T's environment, health, and safety organization employs some 50 people and, under VP Brad Allenby, became one of the most thoroughly virtual groups in the company. AT&T has leveraged informal telework for a long time, starting in Bell Labs, where scientists kept flexible hours, were technologically equipped, and worked from home whenever they wanted. The company postponed formalizing telework arrangements because technology was originally inadequate for entire organizations, but today these barriers are lower. In addition, the business case for telework has become more apparent as firms continue to shift increasing functionality to their intranets.

In 1996, the environment, health, and safety organization—with some fifty people already somewhat geographically dispersed—went virtual, from an "our floor, our cubes" arrangement to one where everyone worked primarily from home.[14] Telework has since become formalized, with a policy and procedures statement, as well as a written agreement signed by an employee and a supervisor. The agreement spells out reasons for teleworking, company and employee responsibilities, equipment arrangements, and start and end dates, if the telework is on a trial basis. Senior management supports telework in general, although pockets of resistance still exist. Economic drivers for telework are increasingly powerful, however, and formal company policy now provides that anyone can arrange for telework if the manager and employee both consider the arrangement a win-win for company and employee. By recent count, 30 percent of AT&T management employees are virtual (i.e., primarily work full-time away from the traditional office, usually at home), another 41 percent regularly work from home an average of two days per week, another 19 percent work remotely when required because of "business continuity" reasons such as weather or building closures, and the remaining 10 percent work in the traditional office during business hours (although hours are flexible). Some employees, such as salespeople, who are on the road but do not work from home, find it harder to classify themselves.

The telework program has four major goals and benefits to the company. The first is cost reduction; estimated savings from existing telework (less office space, lower equipment expense, etc.) total $30 million per year. Second is productivity. AT&T estimates the value of higher productivity among teleworkers at $150 million per year. Teleworkers are seen as more efficient and put in more hours (they tend to "split" the saved commuting time with the company—in other words, work part of the time they would have spent commuting). On average, teleworkers have higher performance ratings than nonteleworkers. The third major goal is employee retention and job satisfaction. Telework can increase the quality of life for the employee and thus increase loyalty and retention. Many employees who have rejected competing job offers cite the company's telework arrangements as a significant factor in rejecting them. The fourth major goal is business continuity. When AT&T offices close because of hurricanes in Florida, for example, or when snowstorms inhibit commuting to corporate headquarters in New Jersey, employees are experienced and ready to work from home, and the technological platform is already in place. AT&T's widely dispersed workforce is a major factor in the firm's unmatched operational continuity.

Every telework arrangement is individualized, and managers must be ready and willing to structure win-win deals with employees. Teleworking employees are evaluated with the same performance measurement and management-by-objectives systems as traditional workers. Interestingly, feedback from managers with teleworking employees indicates that initial employee adjustment problems are more often related to overwork than lack of productivity. Many people have never had the freedom to balance their work and personal lives—they let the structure of the workplace and work schedule do it for them. When they have to establish that structure, that balance on their own, they initially tend to err on the side of working too much rather than not enough.

AT&T understands that a certain amount of face-to-face communication is essential, and emphasizes that communications—both by telephone and e-mail—must be explicit and regular for telework to be effective. Telework, the company has found, is easiest when work groups are fairly stable—that is, when turnover is low and people know each other.

The company cites three keys to success in its telework programs:

1. *A serious, determined effort.* The pressures for cost control and efficiency are strong, and telework is efficient. For example, companies should not maintain regular offices for people who work from home several days a week. Doing so forfeits the facilities savings. When teleworkers do come into the office, have them "hotel" in guest work spaces. Also, don't start with just a few people as telework "experiments"; it sends the message that these people are special cases and that telework isn't "ready for prime time." Additionally, AT&T's data indicates that telework is subject to the law of network economics—the per-person benefits of telework increase with the number of teleworkers.

2. *Top-notch telecom and IT support for home offices.* As firms move toward a more net-centric operations model, with functionality migrated to their intranets and a more virtual workforce, maintenance of network and individual computing capabilities becomes increasingly critical. To take full advantage of the cost reduction potential of telework requires that home technology packages be defined so as to control costs. It is also critical to ensure adequate technological capability and performance (for example, broadband access where available), and to incorporate corporate security and systems management into all equipment.

3. *Telework as part of a strategic business plan, not just a work arrangements tactic.* It should be part of a strategic transition to a network-centric and knowledge-economy business model. The transition is profoundly affecting business and society, incorporating the disabled, the retired, and the part-timers into the workforce. "We're all

the same in cyberspace." According to Brad Allenby, "We're going to reach critical mass and get culturally aligned behind the practice, and then it's going to take off. And the corporations and countries that embrace the net-centric workplace fastest will thrive."

Allenby summarizes AT&T's lessons: "We've been surprised at how many jobs can telework—our initial assumptions turned out to be far too limited. Do engineers need the water cooler as the catalyst of creativity? Not really. We also thought that secretaries and administrative assistants couldn't possibly work from home, but if all the people they support work from home or on the road, and with call forwarding and e-mail now being common technologies, what does it matter where the assistant is, as long as there is a basic or small office services support team in the office? Telework, and participation in the net-centric organization, is not limited to knowledge elites."[15]

Implementing Flexible Work

When determining whether and how a flex work program would operate in your organization, start by considering four key variables and looking for situations where all four are favorable:

- *Nature of the work.* How elastic is the work itself? Must it be performed at specific times or in specific places? In industrial settings such as assembly lines, or in complex tasks requiring constant team activity, options for flexibility are there—but limited.

  For flexible time programs, evaluate which positions are right for flexible hours and shifts. Define *core business hours* and earliest start and finish times. Can you refine schedules to ensure coverage of customer needs, and refine the system for recording hours, perhaps to include a monthly accounting of hours in credit or debit?

  For reduced time programs, evaluate what positions are right for reduced hours. Can you redistribute or reschedule work across existing resources, ensuring that workloads mesh with work times? Can you keep everyone informed of working schedules, and ensure that team members are not overloaded when others reduce their time?

  For flexible place programs, evaluate which positions are right for mobile work or telecommuting. Can you install collaboration tools and ensure communication and connectedness to those working off-site?

- *Employee needs and preferences.* Which kind of flex work do they desire, and which will benefit the most people? Preferences may vary, even among groups doing similar work. Survey employees and note patterns by age cohort and other relevant variables. Also realize that some employees need firsthand direction. Much depends on the maturity of the individual worker, experience in the job, performance, skills, and self-management style.

- *Employer opportunities.* How will flex work improve productivity, reduce cost, reduce turnover, increase employee engagement and commitment, and enhance the corporate brand as a desirable employer?

- *Manageability of the program.* Can the company initiate and administer flex work broadly, purposefully, and impartially? Improperly managed eligibility will cause friction between the eligible and the noneligible. Moreover, union contracts, local or federal regulations barring certain types of home work, local zoning laws restricting home offices, tax issues for employees, and even cultural traditions may constrain an employer's freedom to establish flex work programs.

The biggest obstacles to flex work in large organizations tend to be simple inertia ("We don't work that way around here") and, more profoundly, distrust ("We can't let our employees work without constant and direct supervision"). Perhaps inevitably, some employees will abuse the privilege of more flexible work arrangements. But it's foolish to deprive the organization of the benefits of increased productivity, loyalty, and efficiency because some employees can't be trusted or some managers refuse to change. Several of the organizations in our study have long-standing, large-scale, or high-impact flex work arrangements that have informed the following guidelines for improving your organization's execution of a flex work program.

Clearly define the business goals to meet, and pursue them relentlessly. True, these programs clearly benefit employees, but clear business performance motives such as productivity, cost, and employee retention must drive them. One executive in our study advises, "[Specify] which types of policies and programs meet company objectives and which don't, and educate your managers. We ran into problems when we left managers to create programs on their own—they tended to put employee personal needs over business needs. Invest the time and resources to identify the programs that work best for your company, then have mechanisms to assess and modify them as you go along." Set and measure performance goals such as requiring teleworkers to hotel (occupy shared desks or offices) at the central workplace: if they retain offices, the company forfeits facilities savings.

Carefully develop, regularly monitor, and continually refine companywide flex work policies. Managers who offer flexible work arrangements on a case-by-case basis can stray from business objectives. Experienced companies publish flex work policies and structure flex work arrangements as written performance "contracts" between employee and employer. Establish and communicate fair, consistent criteria, including application and approval processes, for participation at all levels of the organization. Publicize your flex work offerings and policies. According to one HR executive, "You must also educate employees about the program. We make sure people understand that not everyone is going to get picked. It's very important to set expectations." Develop teleworking policies and guidelines—covering equipment, communications, performance, training, and health and safety. Establish management policies covering goal definition, performance management, training, technology support, home office expenses, and visits to the office or regular workplace. With all types of flex work, backup resource planning and management gain importance. No one knows their jobs better than they do, and no one knows their exact set of assignments and their progress better than they do. They should help develop backup policies and plans.

Deploy flexible arrangements within the bounds of work schedules and performance goals. "We have had some difficulties with flexible work arrangements," said another company's representative. "For example, one manager started allowing his employees to work part-time. Within a couple years, he had effectively halved his headcount. We also had problems with part-time workers who aren't always around to get the job done. For part-timers, we have found job sharing to be most effective. With job sharing, no one overworks, the job gets covered, and someone is always there when you need him." Insofar as possible, use the same performance measurement and management systems for flex workers as for others.

Help employees anticipate changes and adjust. A compressed work-week with extended days, or variable shift schedules, can complicate the scheduling of child/elder care and family life in general. Employees with compressed workweeks can become physically and mentally drained from longer workdays. Telecommuters may face conflicts between work and home commitments—their families think that they are available simply because they are home. Alternatively, the workday for telecommuters can extend well beyond the norm, straining family relationships if the telecommuter cannot dedicate sufficient time to family. Workplace psychologists suggest setting strict "on" and "off" work times and substituting rituals for the commute home to disengage from work. Telecommuters may need some end-of-the-workday ritual, such as turning off the computer and the lights in the workroom and going for a walk or run or shopping.

Find new ways to build cohesiveness in the workplace. When participation rates in flex work increase, managers must somehow maintain continuity and community. Telecommuting and flexible schedules may reduce the opportunity for manager-employee interaction and for everyday recognition. Schedule regular social occasions for tele- and flex workers to gather with coworkers and managers, or give them communications technology and set clear guidelines for how and how often to use it. As one manager says, "If you send employees out to work remotely and don't give them the tools to do it, forget it. You are setting them and the arrangement up for failure."

Finally, publicize flex work in your recruiting and retention campaigns. Employer brands known for flexible work arrangements will attract workers of all ages. If anything, such flexibility matters most to the most talented professionals and managers. Help these employees to benefit from flex work opportunities without jeopardizing their careers. In short, make flex work part of your value proposition to employees and position yourself as an employer of choice.

All these guidelines are worth noting and following, but the most important ingredients for successful flex work are management commitment and trust in employees. As an HR executive from a major hotel chain put it, "If you don't have support from the top, you're somewhere in the middle trying to push up and spinning your wheels."[16] Support from the top includes developing and communicating an explicit statement of values supporting flexible work arrangements, publicizing the performance (and promotions) of flex workers, and never sending signals to the contrary. Both the statement and the act of communication across the organization signal the business importance and value of flex work.

Are You Ready for Flex Work?

The widespread use of flexible work arrangements can entail many levels of change—operational, managerial, organizational, even cultural. As with any such change, you can know and attempt the techniques for success and still fall short if the organization isn't receptive and conditions aren't right. How should you assess readiness to establish or expand flexible work arrangements?[17] We have identified ten organizational and management practices—which we term levers—to evaluate:

- *Policy.* Are there specific policy and strategy statements approved and communicated by top management that endorse flex work as a regular component of the employment relationship? Are there specific, pragmatic, and comprehensive guidelines about qualifications for and initiation of flexible work arrangements?

- *Employee commitment.* How much and how deeply are employees committed to the success of the enterprise's mission and to high achievement in their own jobs? Would their commitment remain high despite changes to schedules and work locations?

- *Management commitment.* Do their communications to employees and their everyday actions reinforce management's support for flex work? Do any senior managers themselves make use of flexible arrangements?

- *Workforce planning.* How adept is the organization at forecasting projects, deadlines, production quotas, and workloads; at scheduling workforce needs; and at allocating resources? Are workforce planning processes up to the task of anticipating and adjusting to the effects of flex work on a large scale?

- *Technology.* Are information technology and communications systems in place to support flex work in smooth, efficient, consistent ways? This includes connecting remote employees, enabling dispersed teams to collaborate, and providing sophisticated work- and worker-scheduling capabilities.

- *Training and orientation.* How effective are training content and delivery mechanisms for meeting the ongoing needs of flex workers (especially remote ones), and are there adequate guidelines and training to help people transition to flexible work arrangements?

- *Teamwork.* To what extent is work done in teams, and is there sufficient coordination to ensure coverage and to compensate for having team members on different schedules and/or in different locations?

- *Performance management.* Are there methods for performance measurement, employee appraisal, and staff development that are equivalent, if not identical, for flex workers and others? Are accountabilities and responsibilities clear on the part of both managers and employees, including communicating and reporting responsibilities? Are performance expectations clear?

- *Decision making.* Who holds decision rights and makes key decisions in the course of everyday work? Who advises on decisions? Does the organization's dominant decision-making style center on collaboration or delegation?

- *Communication and information dissemination.* How effective are the means, media, and frequency of communication of everyday business information? And how is knowledge, including about customers and best practices, developed and shared? Are these processes robust enough to keep flex workers in the loop?

You may want to assess these levers, especially the pervasive ones such as senior management roles and technology infrastructure, at the enterprise level. More importantly, however, assess them at the local level. How do the levers operate for specific types of flexible work in specific parts of the organization, such as telework in call centers or flexible shifts on a production line? Different flex work options will be appropriate for different employees, forms of work, parts of the organization, and management styles. By examining the levers locally, you can determine true fit and what actions to take to succeed locally.

We recommend evaluating both the *importance* and *performance* of each lever. How important is each to a specific instance of flex work that you're considering? Do you need this condition to be in place? For example, technology will be crucial for telework but may play a little role in enabling job sharing. To be systematic, use a 4-point scale (e.g., absolutely essential, important, needed, unimportant), or give each lever a simple yes/no. Then assess the degree to which the condition is already in place. How well do we perform in this area—well enough to succeed with flex work? Again, use a 4-point scale (e.g., condition is in place, mostly in place, partly in place, absent) or just a yes/no. Keep in mind that you are not evaluating the importance or performance of these levers to the enterprise at large (or for other business purposes), but whether and how they play in specific instances of proposed flex work. The answers indicate what issues need to be addressed in order to succeed.

For example, communication and information dissemination (the last lever) may be well established and technology enabled, and having workers change schedules or work remotely would neither interrupt nor cause problems for the information flow. This lever would score relatively low in importance and high in performance. Now suppose the organization's decision-making style (the ninth lever) is based on face-to-face discussion and consensus. In terms of enabling flexible work, this lever may have high importance and low performance. It's an area that definitely needs addressing if flex work is to succeed.

The purpose and value of this assessment come not from precision in scoring, but from getting people into detailed conversation about how to succeed. We recommend having a group of stakeholders—including managers, workforce planners, and prospective flex workers—score the local organization individually, then come together to discuss the areas of agreement and disagreement and to refine action plans.

You can plot the scores for each of the ten levers onto a four-quadrant matrix, such as the one shown in figure 9-1, to produce a graphical representation of your assessment of readiness for flexible work arrangements. The matrix can reveal not only your overall preparedness, but also levers that need immediate attention in order to increase your chances of success.

Levers in the *Unimportant* quadrant are just that. Those in the *Bonus* quadrant have performance higher than needed given their relative importance to flex work, but you might be able to leverage this performance to help the cause. For example, information systems may already be capable of supporting flexible work/shift scheduling; however, adding a Web-based scheduler for individual employees to use might make things easier. Levers in the

FIGURE 9-1

Flexible work readiness matrix

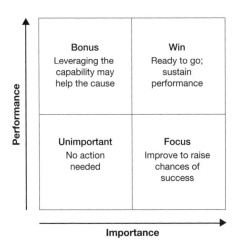

Bonus
Leveraging the
capability may
help the cause

Win
Ready to go;
sustain
performance

Unimportant
No action
needed

Focus
Improve to raise
chances of
success

Performance

Importance

Win quadrant are ready to support flex work. Those in the *Focus* quadrant demand the most immediate attention and action—importance is high but current performance not yet adequate. Here is where you need to improve methods and performance to increase the chances of success with flex work. Recognizing the need and putting attention and energy into such changes demonstrate to employees and the organization at large how serious and committed you are about making flex work work.

ACTIONS TO TAKE

To Implement Flexible Work

We recommend that you take the following four actions to expand your organization's implementation of flexible work arrangements and reap the business benefits:

☐ *Assess the situation.* Take a systematic look at flexible work arrangements already in place and at the organization's prospects for expanding them. Evaluate the ten levers we've just described. Determine what changes are needed to succeed at scale.

☐ *Pursue your business goals.* Set specific goals around cost, performance, and employees—including satisfaction, engagement, recruiting, and retention. Measure performance and insist on results. Keep track of what's happening where, and share lessons learned and best practices promptly.

☐ *Establish pragmatic policies and practices.* Appropriate patterns of flexible work will vary across the enterprise; however, you'll need a foundation of guidelines for all, covering basics like eligibility and expectations of employer and employee. Within the guidelines, be flexible and don't arbitrarily rule out flex work for any employee constituencies.

☐ *Enable the transition to flex work.* A teleworker may have a very difficult time quitting the office cold turkey. Make certain that flex work initiatives incorporate orientation, training, technology support, and any new communication procedures for employees and managers alike.

10

Flexible Learning Opportunities

*Why Continuous Education Matters
and How to Make It Pay Off*

ONE OF THE LARGEST COMPANIES in the oil and gas industry, BP LLP (formerly British Petroleum) is a federation of financially successful business units with over one hundred thousand employees. As BP's corporate leadership knows, size matters only if BP can leverage its knowledge of technology, customer relationships, and business methods across the company—without interfering with business unit autonomy. To promote such knowledge-sharing behaviors, BP implemented three explicit "peer processes":

- *Peer groups* of senior managers share know-how across business units and with the Executive Committee.

- *Peer reviews* of specific unit activities or business processes by senior professionals from other units identify strengths, weaknesses, and opportunities to improve or learn from other groups.

- *Peer assists* get the right corporate know-how to the right place at the right time. Anyone can request expert assistance from a peer anywhere in BP, and the in-demand expert must do his best to help.[1]

Such regularly shared knowledge and expertise has bolstered individuals' efforts, enriched customer outcomes, and improved BP's business methods directly. The collaborative learning here is more organic than systematic—that is, embedded in BP's culture and integrated into people's daily work. The increasingly valuable flow of knowledge among businesses and along leadership chains eliminates red tape and makes each business unit faster and more nimble. In short, BP's institutionalized learning through peer processes drives actual business results.

Not many corporations take this stance toward learning, but some of the most successful do. In his final annual report letter to shareholders (2000), General Electric's Jack Welch argued cogently for corporate learning: "The most significant change in GE has been its transformation into a Learning Company. Our true 'core competency' today is not manufacturing or services, but the global recruiting and nurturing of the world's best people and the cultivation in them of an insatiable desire to learn, to stretch and to do things better every day."[2] GE spends $1 billion annually in learning programs, including a pioneering corporate university and an enduring commitment to sharing best practices companywide, such as the Workout methods adopted by other companies. GE knows that learning enhances global growth and competitiveness.

Learning is integral to any organization's capability and productivity, recruiting and retention, and leadership and capacity for change. Learning—about customers, markets, technologies, competitors, and a variety of other business variables—boosts individual and organizational responsiveness, agility, and growth. It raises corporate performance and increases the value of talent. In short, lifelong learning is good for business.

More importantly, learning can mitigate the coming shortage of labor and skills in two ways. First, learning is an increasingly visible, important, and nonnegotiable component of the employment deal. Employees expect companies to invest in their professional development, thereby enhancing their "employability" within the company or in the job market; and the best and brightest—the ones worth retaining for the long haul—tend to be those who most enjoy learning. So *lifelong learning* has advanced from "nice phrase" to business performance imperative.

Second, with labor and skills shortages ahead, organizations must "grow their own" expertise by providing employees with opportunities, both on the job and off, to raise their skills level. Given the inevitable time lag in the capacity and performance of public educational systems, these shortages will especially enervate the skilled disciplines and fast-growing technical fields such as health care. The level of educational attainment continues to rise, but too slowly. Just over one-fourth of Americans hold college degrees, but most of the Bureau of Labor Statistics "hottest job" categories demand college education. What's more, the workforce population segments growing the fastest are neither the best educated nor the most upwardly mobile. Despite all efforts to improve access to education in the United States, academic achievement varies wildly among ethnic groups. Worse, the educational pattern of immigrant populations in the United States is skewed toward the extremes: even though the average number of years of schooling among immigrants is only about one and a half years less than that of the native population, one-third of immigrants do not have high school diplomas, whereas over one-fourth have college degrees, many with advanced degrees in medicine, science, engineering, and other professions. The Employment Policy Foundation projects a shortfall of 6 million college degrees in the workforce in 2012.[3] So, to safeguard their labor and skills supply, corporations must provide both advanced and remedial education.

Marvin Bressler, professor emeritus of sociology at Princeton University and an adviser to our research, argues, "A growing proportion of workers are inadequately schooled for their increasingly demanding jobs. Corporate education—technical, managerial, and humanistic—should thus not be conceived as an altruistic gesture but as an indispensable requisite for a robust bottom line. Moreover, since the American labor force is educated at immense public expense, it is in the enlightened self-interest of the corporation—and as a means of restoring its moral authority at a time of widespread distrust of big business—to exercise greater social responsibility in supporting education at all levels beyond its own walls."[4]

Thus, learning is both a marketing and a productivity tool—a means for attracting and retaining key talent, as well as for ensuring that employees are equipped with the right capabilities both to perform well and to maintain competitive competency levels. Simply put, your company must excel at enabling employees to learn.

Good News: Employees *Want* to Learn

In our nationwide survey of workers and their preferences, "Work that enables me to learn, grow, and try new things" ranked third among ten basic elements of the employment deal, behind a comprehensive benefits package and a comprehensive retirement package. It ranked higher than more pay, more vacation, flexible schedule, flexible workplace, work that is personally stimulating, and even (by a small margin) a workplace that is enjoyable.[5]

Which employees value learning the most? Well-educated ones, those with postgraduate work or degrees, rank learning significantly higher than do employees in general. Other eager learners include professionals and managers, especially senior ones; people who describe themselves as ambitious and leaders among their peers; and employees who describe themselves as "extremely satisfied" with their jobs, ranking learning number two among deal elements.

Based on our survey, we segmented employees by how they relate to their work. One group includes employees who are the most innovative, entrepreneurial, and energized by their work, the most proud of their careers, and the most likely to lead the organization. They have the highest employee engagement level and value learning extraordinarily highly, ranking it number one among the ten deal elements. That's *double* the average preference level for learning and growth opportunities. We noticed several other correlations to employee preference for learning:

- Employees at the two ends of the income spectrum—lowest and highest—value learning more than those in the middle.

- Both young workers and mature ones show above-average preference for learning.

- People with more time available—single, childless, with time to socialize—value learning above the average.

- Employees of nonprofit organizations show above-average preference for learning opportunities.

- Self-employed or part-time workers value learning higher than full-time employees.

- People in small companies value learning more than those in large ones.

- Employees who work over fifty hours per week show above-average preference for learning.

- Those who work primarily from home also have above-average preference to learn.

- People in professional and business services, information and technology, and construction show a significantly above-average preference to learn and grow than workers in other industries.

- People in education and health services show a slightly above-average preference to learn.

- Employees who are currently excited by a new project or assignment show a preference for learning well above the norm, ranking it number two among deal elements.

Workers of all ages need and want training in specific skills, as well as broader opportunities to learn and improve themselves, their performance, and their careers and lives. However, as we shall see, their needs, interests, and learning styles vary greatly. No single or standard approach is going to meet the needs of employers or employees.

Bad News: Employers Are Offering Too Few Learning Opportunities

Too many organizations fail to satisfy employees' desire and need for learning and growth, and the employer pays a price in lost capability, performance, and engagement. In addition to measuring employee preferences for the ten basic elements of the employment deal, we broke down the category of learning and development into four detailed elements.

People expressed the strongest preferences (almost a dead heat) for opportunities "to work with bright and experienced employees and managers" and "to grow through changes in roles, responsibilities, and projects." Third in the ranking, with about two-thirds' the preference level of the first two, came professional development opportunities—courses, seminars, conferences either inside or outside the company. In a distant fourth was formal mentoring programs, and such a low preference likely reflects their scarcity.

We also asked employees—yes or no—whether each element in the learning category is available to them through their employers. How many said yes?

- Professional development opportunities: 42 percent overall, 53 percent in large employers

- Opportunities to grow through changes in roles: 39 percent overall, 50 percent in large employers

- Opportunities to work with bright people: 36 percent overall, 47 percent in large employers

- Formal mentoring programs: 9 percent overall, 17 percent in large employers

Most employees also believe that their learning isn't high on top management's agenda. When we asked for a level of agreement with the statement "Top management is committed to advancing the skills of our employees," more employees strongly disagreed (14 percent) than strongly agreed (13 percent). A bare majority expressed any level of agreement (slight, moderate, strong), and here the large employers fare less well, with only 8 percent of employees strongly agreeing. Employees are certainly getting the message that learning isn't high on management's priority list.

Here's a third indicator of employers' failure to appreciate the importance of employee learning and growth. *One-third* of employees (38 percent in large organizations) feel at dead ends in their current jobs. One-third of the workforce has its growth initiative—however high or low that may be individually—stalled. That number is simply too high, especially compared with the smaller number (28 percent) who are working on exciting new projects or assignments. The percentage feeling dead-ended is extraordinarily significant because, regardless of segment, a low engagement score always correlated most strongly with the same variable—feeling at a dead end. So, to disengage employees, stall or appear to stall their growth.

Our survey revealed one other interesting phenomenon. Some 9 percent of employees (13 percent in large organizations) say they have inadequate training or knowledge for their current positions. Meanwhile, this group as a whole shows *lower* than average preference for learning and growth opportunities, and a significantly below-average engagement score. So an individual's general passion for knowledge prompts learning more than one's specific job demands do.

How to Become a "Learning Organization"

According to David A. Garvin of the Harvard Business School, a learning organization is one that is skilled at creating, acquiring, interpreting, transferring, and retaining knowledge and then modifying its behavior purposefully to reflect new knowledge and insights. To do this, the corporate culture must advocate and reward skill development, respect differences among individuals and viewpoints, provide timely and accurate feedback, and encourage appropriate risk taking and learning from mistakes. People should feel free, indeed obligated, to stimulate, test, and adopt new ideas. They share knowledge widely and their collaboration is rewarded. Garvin also offers a series of litmus tests for a learning organization: Are we open to discordant information? Do we avoid repeated mistakes? Do we retain critical knowledge when people leave? Most fundamentally, do we act on what we know?[6]

What does it take to become more of a learning organization, to operationalize learning as a business force? Start by following these three principles.

Give learning a short-term focus. Becoming a better learning organization may well be a long-term imperative, but short-term questions can yield immediate business payoff when the organization designs learning experiences around each. For example, what do we need to learn more about—starting with our customers and competitors? How can we use what we learn to improve performance? What must we decide faster, and which new information or conversations would accelerate action? How can we revise our business processes and reorient our technology infrastructure to learn more and improve faster? Answering any of these questions in specific terms leads to a series of learning actions beneficial to individuals and business performance.

Develop a business agenda for learning. Business strategy demands learning strategy, and learning strategy must be tangible—with targets, sources, and methods. Organizational learning is not a matter of goodness, though organizations are much the better for it. Rather, learning gets the right knowledge to the right people in the right jobs at the right times. It enables faster, more informed business decisions. It's the foundation for improving business performance, keeping pace competitively, acting decisively, and changing readily. Learning isn't a "soft" issue at all. Thus, learning plans must be specific and operational, and key learning processes, starting with best-practice sharing, must be explicitly owned, managed, and improved.

Expand the scope of learning. The learning process requires not simply training and development but also receptivity to new information and readiness to change; the performance of the processes of awareness, analysis, communication, and decision making; and the practical application of new insights. Thus, learning isn't a specialist activity in HR—it's a core management issue, a leadership responsibility, and an employee responsibility.

That last point is extremely important. Employees know that the most valuable learning happens on the job, in conversations with colleagues, through diverse assignments, and outside the classroom. To maximize the potential of learning, an organization must exploit all available channels, not just traditional one-size-fits-all courses. Think of organizational learning as a three-legged stool:

- *Training* delivers useful content and experiences to develop specific capabilities. Courses, conducted in person or virtually, plus on-the-job instruction and certification, compose most corporate training programs.

- *Development* realizes individual career and growth plans, orchestrating work assignments (especially stretch assignments) and training experiences to accomplish them. In aggregate, development ensures the right mix of skills and the right behaviors for learning companywide.

- *Knowledge networks* establish connections among people who can productively teach, learn from, and share information with one another. These range from passive directories of expertise and experience (who knows what and has worked where?) to active "communities of practice" that improve individual and network knowledge and capability. BP's peer processes simultaneously solve business problems and build knowledge networks.

Knowledge networks are the most prolific and underleveraged channels of organizational learning—prolific because they are the most natural, inherently interorganizational and intergenerational way to transfer knowledge, and underleveraged because relatively few organizations systematically promote them. In robust knowledge networks, people know where to go for expertise and advice, and everyone is socialized to seek and share knowledge in the network. The pace of communication and learning accelerates, the risk of brain drain (as when a very knowledgeable employee retires) diminishes, and the difficulty of tailoring training courses and assigning mentors decreases.

The most effective learning experiences are "blended" in several senses. The most common meaning is that they combine group and individual work, or classroom and online delivery, or academic activities and work assignments. But they also combine all three legs of the stool—training activities in service of development plans leveraged by knowledge networks.

Learning Opportunities for the Three Cohorts

Young, midcareer, and mature workers tend to approach and experience learning somewhat differently. These differences stem not just from generational characteristics, but also from the educational methods, technologies, and techniques prevailing during their respective "school days." Today's youth have a very different—and technology-based—educational experience from what their parents and grandparents had. Table 10-1 summarizes these differences.

TABLE 10-1

Learning styles of the three cohorts

	Young	Midcareer	Mature
Myth	Not motivated to learn	Know enough already	Slow learners and technology-phobic
Reality	Most vocal about their demand to learn and grow	Need to know more but too sandwiched, stressed, and short of time to ask for it	Eager to learn technology and more, but often overlooked
Preferred format	Self-directed, continuous opportunities to learn	Classroom, extended periods of education	Small group, regular refreshers
Role of technology	Enables multitasking, always connected and communicating	Solves problems, task specific	Gathers and disseminates information
Attention span/ thought process	Short segments, integrated, visual, multiprocessing	Scanning, classifying, planning	Reading, linear thinkers, focused on what they need to learn
Interaction	Role-play, experiment, question	Peer-to-peer discussion	Teach and learn, mentor
Short-term goal	Have fun, acquire skills quickly, increase visibility	Good grades, work/life balance, grow connections	Personal satisfaction, maintain connections
Long-term goal	Build résumé, be marketable	Succeed at work, change careers	Remain viable, give back
Insists upon	Relevance, personalization	Relevance, convenience	Relevance, authority, need-to-know now
Employer benefits	Rapid assimilation, long-term retention	Vibrant workforce, rekindled careers	Ready trainers, mentors, and leaders

This table is intended to help you recognize patterns, not to stereotype or predict the behavior of individuals. Though generational diversity is not new to the workforce, these age-specific differences around learning style are proving to be a particular challenge for companies trying to maintain a competitive edge in an increasingly technological business world while filling specific skills gaps and mitigating the effects of turnover and retirement and the associated brain drain.

How does an organization faced with these sometimes-pronounced differences in learning motivation and style go about developing training programs and other learning activities? Keep in mind that the goals of training are not only skills acquisition at the individual level, but also knowledge sharing and common commitment at the organizational level. The answer is in two parts.

First, given differences in preferred and effective learning methods, delivery must be flexible. The same content may need to be delivered in different ways at different times for different groups. A training course may be designed for a dominant group (e.g., entry-level skills for mostly younger employees), but it may also need alternative formats for other groups (e.g., choice of working individually online or in small groups face-to-face). Especially in this period of transition—when one workforce segment is thoroughly "digital" and others are not—there is no such thing as "one size fits all." For learning to be effective, it must be flexible. Second, an organization should make learning experiences a means of bridging generational gaps and fostering mutual understanding, knowledge sharing, and organizational cohesion. In other words, don't segregate groups by learning style and method. Instead, use a variety of occasions for learning—including special task forces and project teams, mentoring and reverse mentoring, and group training sessions—to bring diverse groups together.

These two recommendations appear to be in partial contradiction—tailor delivery to recognize differences and bring people together to overcome the differences. In fact, it's more a matter of recognizing the tension between two goals and knowing when careful design and implementation decisions are called for. Intergenerational learning is one facet of the *broad challenge of diversity*: on the one hand, recognize and respect and accommodate differences among groups; on the other hand, bring them together so their diverse experiences and perspectives can yield superior business results. So this isn't so much a contradiction—it's more like a core challenge of contemporary management.

Best practices in intergenerational learning start with being cross-generational where possible—in training programs and task forces and project teams. At Comcast Corporation, for example, intergenerational teaming and training quickly went from business necessity to everyday occurrence. Three years ago, the company was one-third its current size, with an age distribution skewed toward midcareer and mature employees. The acquisition of AT&T Broadband dramatically altered the company's size and age mix, and the two halves of the combined enterprise had to team and train together intensively. Today employees of all ages welcome the opportunity to learn with and from one another, and this intergenerational flavor extends to the Executive Leadership Forum and other bench-strength programs. The Forum is a year-long action-learning experience for forty-five high-potential people working in teams, with an age range from late twenties to early fifties.[7]

Formal classrooms may be the most problematic settings when differences in attitude and learning style arise. We specifically recommend the following:

- Train trainers to recognize and respond to generational styles, issues, and challenges.

- Nurture knowledge networks that include workers of all ages. Support them with technology, but make sure these groups enjoy face-to-face time.

- Include aging and generational issues as components of regular managerial training. For example, CVS, which actively recruits mature employees, often to work under much younger managers, incorporates into their regular training advice and techniques for managing older workers. "We need to train managers whose average age is in the mid-thirties to work effectively with people of all ages. The National Council on the Aging helped us to identify key issues in managing and motivating older employees," says Stephen Wing, director of government programs at CVS.[8]

- Provide managers with special training and coaching to handle the extremes: when peers or reports are much older, or much younger, or span an extraordinarily wide age range.

- Equip people to act appropriately when specific intergenerational conflicts arise—how they're handled sets the organizational tone and exposes hidden biases.

- Incorporate generational issues into diversity training and programs. According to a Conference Board survey, only 19 percent of companies give their employees training in age and generational issues.[9]

- Make management training more intergenerational, including by admitting nontraditional candidates—including midcareer and mature late bloomers—into the leadership pipeline.

In all these activities, bring out each group's strengths rather than fixating on improving one group's particular weaknesses. For example, reverse mentoring built into a specific work activity can enable mutual learning. A midcareer worker pairs with a younger worker to learn how to use the customer relationship technology (hard skills), while the midcareer worker helps the younger worker to effectively communicate with customers (soft skills), and as a consequence the two gain experience in working collaboratively.

Learning at Household International

Household International (now part of HSBC Holdings) has advanced its new employee training by realizing that people learn differently, at different rates, and so standard delivery doesn't necessarily mean effective learning. The Consumer Lending Group, including HFC and Beneficial Finance, employs approximately thirteen thousand people, with some eight thousand in fourteen hundred local sales branches and seven hundred to eight hundred in each of six collections and service processing centers.

In the sales branches, employees receive an entry-level base pay, and 40 percent of their total compensation comes from performance incentives. Given this compensation scheme, branch jobs tend to attract younger workers, and turnover is as high as 35 percent because many candidates lack the required extroverted personality. So the company administers personality/behavioral tests to job candidates to minimize the number of "surprises" for new sales staff. After initial screening by the branch manager and the behavioral test, an applicant gets a "realistic job preview" by observing an account rep for one to three hours while that rep makes outbound telemarketing calls and performs other job tasks.

Inexperienced people first learn the basics—for example, computer systems training. The curriculum is self-paced and modular. Sales staff have forty-three modules; after every ten or so, they are reviewed/tested, can brush up on what they've learned, and obtain their manager's sign-off before proceeding to the next modules. New employees train until they pass certain modules, but the organization does not penalize anyone who takes longer than average to complete the training. In fact, after concluding that too many salespeople raced through training too fast to start earning the incentive pay, they now provide a guaranteed fixed amount of incentive pay for the first two months before the new employee converts to the regular incentive pay system. This both encourages thorough training and eases the transition from training to operations.

The processing centers have employees with various skills and pay levels, with the most experienced and skilled people making the most. Most of the centers' staff are women, including many single mothers, and 35 percent of the employees are people of color. Each group of new hires receives initial training and then spends a full week doing the regular work in the "bull pen," where the supervisor/coach-to-staff ratio is as low as 1-to-5, ensuring lots of individual support. Wanting to apply learning immediately, the bull pen sometimes outperforms teams of experienced employees. Once on the center's "floor," each new employee is paired with a "buddy" from whom the new hire can comfortably learn. The combination of better integration of new employees and more employee involvement in shift scheduling has reduced turnover to a manageable 16 percent, low for the industry. Like the sales branches, the processing centers staff up in waves, and the January 2003 hiring wave was the most successful ever.

The company conducts ongoing training in two tracks, sales and management. It no longer forces successful people to move into management if they're happy and productive on the line. With the leverage of incentive pay, employees don't need rank or seniority to do well financially. Half of all new employees come via referral, and many former employees return, after deciding that the job outclassed others available

The company would like more people to view it as a long-term career, and so it encourages movement around the company—among branches, district management, centers, staff functions, and other Household units. It is pushing succession planning lower into the organization and actively identifying high performers, thereby "breaking up the old-boy network" and strengthening the loyalty of top performers.[10]

Leveraging Technology to Support Learning

Information technology is a very significant variable in implementing flexible organizational learning. IT is a powerful lever for corporate learning, and the Internet has amplified that power in extraordinary ways. IT plays in two ways: first, it is an indispensable tool for delivering training and enabling learning.

As part of the organizational infrastructure, information technology provides much of the flexibility in flexible learning. Second, it represents indispensable content and skill set for almost all workers. Everyone needs facility with both specific information systems and the general tools of information finding, communication, and collaboration.

Information technology supports learning through a wide array of capabilities—for example, repositories or libraries of information, especially about key entities like customers; systems for online delivery of training courses and modules; systems for online administration of training offerings, development plans, and other learning activities; performance measurement and management reporting built into everyday business applications of all kinds; specialized systems for capturing, managing, and investigating knowledge; and tools supporting knowledge networks, "communities of practice," and collaboration generally.

We know too well, however, that deploying technology never guarantees business results, in learning or any other domain. Fortunately, the basic success factors for using technology to support learning are known, though by no means universally followed:

- *Look at your overall learning infrastructure*, not just electronic delivery of courses. Online training can be extremely valuable, especially in providing needed knowledge and skills "just in time." Similarly, automating the administration of training is an obvious thing to do. But these are just two pieces of the learning infrastructure puzzle.

- *Distinguish between explicit and tacit knowledge.* Some information lends itself to electronic capture, storage, communication, and management. Other information—especially in the realm of experience and intuition—is much more elusive. The transfer of explicit knowledge can often be automated. The transfer of tacit knowledge almost always requires person-to-person contact.

- *Use technology to support human networks.* For purposes of business innovation and change, the network of human connections is far more important than the technological network. The most effective learning takes place when knowledgeable people find one another, converse, work together, and share best practices. But the technological network can support the human one—with basic communications facilities such as e-mail; collaboration systems that enable dispersed teams to work effectively and communities of interest to share knowledge and experience; directories to locate people and expertise; and repositories of best practices.

- *Build a "learning portal."* This is a Web site that serves as the organizer and entryway to all the corporation's learning resources and opportunities. It facilitates access, self-service, and just-in-time delivery of selected content. If well wrought, it motivates learning by making it both convenient and effective.

To capitalize on the technology, for learning or any other business purposes, employees must, of course, be adept at using it. But today's workforce covers the entire gamut in terms of attitude toward and facility with IT—from the occasional technophobe to a generation that has grown up digital. John Seely Brown of Xerox PARC, an adviser to our research, describes how different a digital multimedia upbringing can be. Young workers merge work and play, networking fluidly and without structure. Over time, this digital culture will permeate, and eventually dominate, organizational operations.

Relationship-driven and accustomed to personal contact and to following channels, older workers have different modes of operating. They call the help desk instead of going online and tinkering around. They must acquire and update their technical skills *again*, as in every preceding wave of transformational workplace technology. But this time, it involves not just the machinery and applications but also the mode of interacting with coworkers.

Given the "digital divide" in today's workforce, an organization must recognize this bimodal workplace and strive for coexistence between the two modes, without allowing any worker to forgo technology training or to avoid using up-to-date technological tools. Information systems and communications technologies are too embedded, too integral to business operations and management. IT has become a primary source of organizational coherence. You cannot hold a diverse and dispersed organization together without heavy reliance on and effective use of communication and collaboration tools. Teams and their information and decision rights may be distributed around the globe. Even when people are colocated, they still aren't in the workplace together, because they work flexible hours, telecommute, or work in the field. Organizations must therefore master the technologies of *electronic conversation*—not just how to use functions like e-mail, videoconferencing, and collaboration systems, but also how to *behave* in these channels, avoid the social gaffes, and work effectively even though remotely.

Information technology is simultaneously a force for organizational dispersal and organizational integration. Thus, the one topic about which learning cannot be avoided—by any age cohort—is how to use the technology to begin with. Participating in a modern organization simply demands it. You cannot accommodate everyone's preferences in regard to technology use (or avoidance). You need to step up to the challenge of enabling workers in all age cohorts to maintain reasonable facility with the technological tools of everyone's trade.

E-learning at Sears

Sears, Roebuck and Company has succeeded in rapidly deploying e-learning on a broad corporate scale.[11] The 875 Sears full-line stores (incorporating hard line goods, soft line goods, Sears Auto Centers, and online shopping) have significant, ongoing training needs, for both new hires and experienced associates. Because turnover in the retail industry is high, especially for entry-level positions, Sears has a variety of initiatives to attract new employees, get them productive and satisfied quickly, and retain the best. Electronically assisted recruiting includes in-store kiosks where job applicants can submit applications and take some preliminary tests; the system screens for each applicant's job interests and prints a suggested interviewing guide for the hiring manager. The company is also developing a new value proposition for associates and prospects, covering the work itself, management style, learning, recognition, and pay and benefits.

The company's major learning initiative has been to roll out Internet-based e-learning to every store. Each store used to have a full-time trainer, and the typical store training room was a chaos of videos and binders, many of them out-of-date. The training process was inefficient and costly. In the course of one year, Sears eliminated the trainer position at all the full-line stores, revamped the curriculum, and moved most of it online.

In the first part of 2002, the corporate training group worked with an e-learning vendor (who hosts their training site) and subject-matter experts to develop the online content. The goal was not just to automate what was already being delivered, but to deliver consistent, updatable content geared to the individual job, and make it all available on demand and as needed. Sears did not just put the old training manuals online for people to read, but rather capitalized on the inherent capabilities and advantages of online delivery to make the course modules both engaging and efficient. They worked from the conviction that to gain its advantages, you have to go "all the way with e-learning," which demands significant investment and leadership commitment.

Sears implemented the e-learning system in waves and, through excellent project and change management, rolled it out to every store between May and September 2002. The overall thrust of the new training program is "Here's what you need to do your job." Some eight hundred to one thousand training modules are keyed to job code. Each module ends with a survey, and workers young and old have offered very positive feedback on the e-learning content and site. The e-learning system also facilitates "onboarding" of new associates by delivering much of the new-employee content without class work. Every new sales associate also gets a "buddy" on the floor who helps him or her learn the job and become familiar with the company. Financially, e-learning has been a major success.

After such rapid and widespread implementation, the company continues to explore and define the right mix of online and face-to-face delivery at the most efficient cost. Some content requires facilitation. For example, there are three variations on diversity training—totally online, totally instructor led, and a hybrid—and store managers and assistant managers sometimes teach selected topics in their ongoing roles as coaches and mentors. This day-to-day interaction following e-learning contributes mightily to the success of employees and store operations.

Eight Approaches to Building a Learning Organization

Many of the management techniques we recommend in the chapters on the three workforce cohorts relate to learning. After all, learning is a key element in the employment deal for all employees. Here, we consolidate and review the most important of our recommendations for addressing the organizational learning challenges posed by changing workforce composition.

Fill skills gaps and enable skills transitions. Assess and anticipate skills needs and how much skills acquisition must happen through employee development (as opposed to recruiting). Find ways to fill specific gaps. As needed, work with educational and governmental organizations to prepare underskilled people for entry into the workforce. The U.K. National Health Service has a "skills escalator" program whereby interested and capable employees undergo extensive classroom and on-the-job training to prepare for performing higher-level, scarce-supply jobs. For example, orderlies escalate their skills to become nurses' aids, and aides escalate to nurses.[12] Follow the training basics: training must be continuous, not episodic. It should incorporate on-the-job as well as classroom activities. Where possible, it should involve work teams, not just individuals, so that people develop versatility, camaraderie, and loyalty to the team. It should reward people for attaining new skills and achieving related performance objectives. Show commitment by sustaining training investments.

Rapidly incorporate and train new employees. The goals are to minimize the time it takes a new employee to get up to speed, maximize the employee's productive contribution while with the organization, and increase the retention rate. The key is to make the learning and incorporation experience engaging from the start, which in turn requires a judicious mix of delivery methods—in groups, on the job, and online. It also requires careful weighting of content. To be fully incorporated, new employees need to learn both the specifics of performing their jobs and how the organization works—mission, values, and how performance is measured and managed.

Commit to lifelong learning for all employees. That means removing any implicit age bias, having individual development plans for employees of all ages and ranks, and providing a variety of learning opportunities for all. The number of officially counted training days is likely to still favor newer and younger workers who have need of formal skills training. However, on-the-job action learning and work assignments geared for employee growth must be available to all. At Dow Chemical, the companywide expectation is that employees at all levels will continue to learn and grow; as a result, employees regularly seek training and development opportunities, readying themselves for their next career moves. This expectation of continuous career and skills development continues even if later in people's careers they downshift into roles of lower intensity or responsibility than they held at their career peaks.[13]

Employ all channels of learning, all three legs of the stool—training, development, and knowledge networks. Expanding learning channels should not require large investment. It does require management processes, starting with work and project assignment, with a systematic eye toward learning needs and opportunities. It may require breaking down organizational barriers to enable freer flow of people and information. It may require either new technology or the use of existing technology in new ways, such as to support knowledge communities. But any major technology investment, such as implementing e-learning at scale, should have business payback.

Leverage information technology to enable cost-effective learning in a variety of contexts: on the job, in the classroom, self-paced at home, and through communities of practice and other knowledge networks. E-learning can simultaneously lower learning costs through automated delivery and raise learning effectiveness through engaging, interactive, and individualized presentation. The technological tools are available, and organizations such as Sears, Roebuck and Company have transformed their training methods to incorporate e-learning on a large scale.

Turn diversity into learning. Provide action-learning experiences whereby a variety of people learn to work together, appreciate one another's talents, and collaborate to solve business problems quickly, creatively, and with customer focus. Intergenerational teams are one of the most reliable means of knowledge transfer.

Brand your learning commitment and methods and make them a force for recruiting and employee retention. Training and development and opportunities to learn and grow are an ever more important part of the employee deal. As you articulate the deal for employees and prospects, be specific about the types of opportunities offered and the organization's commitment to employee learning. If lifelong learning really is a deeply held organizational value, proclaim it—with examples. But you've got to live up to the brand—half-hearted commitment to learning is quickly detected by employees and eventually the labor market.

Finally, *develop and follow a learning agenda.* Don't dilute focus and waste resources by letting learning initiatives operate in isolation. Pull the preceding pieces together into an explicit agenda of activities and objectives. Make sure they're aligned with business outcomes and talent management strategy. And articulate the role of learning in organizational and individual performance. Then follow through on the agenda with accountabilities and performance measurement.

ACTIONS TO TAKE

To Increase Learning Opportunities

To meet the learning needs and expectations of employees, as well as maximize the business return on learning initiatives, senior management should start by insisting on four things:

☐ *Look upon human capital as a basic business resource*, and upon learning as the way to maintain and increase the value of these assets. Don't waver in this commitment regardless of business conditions. The organization that gets out of the employee-education business stagnates.

☐ *Escape one-size-fits-all approaches to learning.* Incorporate the different means, human and technological, of enabling people to learn, and accommodate the variety of learning styles of a diverse workforce. Handling variety is difficult but absolutely necessary.

☐ *Build knowledge networks.* Give employees the means of locating knowledgeable colleagues, connecting and collaborating, and sharing experience and expertise. This primary method of learning goes underutilized in many organizations. Yet a little effort here can go a long, long way.

☐ *Measure learning's effects.* The business return on organizational learning cannot be measured with mathematical precision, but that's no excuse not to measure. Keep track of how and how much specific learning initiatives help specific business initiatives. Monitor how knowledge networks operate and contribute. Measure progress against your learning agenda. Over time, build your understanding and appreciation of the business role that learning plays.

11

Flexible Compensation
and Benefits

*Why Variety Will Rule
and How to Leverage It*

T HE WORLD'S LARGEST privately held software company, SAS,
Inc., provides data warehousing, business intelligence software, and
industry-specific systems to large companies, with forty thousand
customers in more than one hundred ten countries. Based in Cary, North
Carolina, SAS is renowned for its rapid growth, minimal turnover, and peer-
less product quality and customer satisfaction.

SAS is also widely known for the benefits that it offers its employees,
nearly ten thousand worldwide. The package includes free on-site full-service
primary medical care; low-cost preschool child care and kindergarten; extensive on-site recreational, exercise, and massage facilities; on-site discounted
automobile maintenance, dry cleaning, and hair salon services; subsidized
cafeterias; three weeks of paid vacation plus a Christmas–to–New Year's

shutdown; and domestic partner benefits. Unlike other high-tech companies, SAS does not trade on-site amenities for sixty-hour workweeks. Managers encourage SAS employees to spend their evenings and weekends with families or neighbors. Salaries are competitive but not extravagant.

Meanwhile, SAS does demand productivity and results. Founder and CEO James Goodnight explains, "I like to be around happy people, but if they don't get that next release out, they're not going to be very happy."[1] He simply believes that stressed-out workers produce bad software. "It turns out that doing the right thing, treating people right, is also the right thing for the company."[2] One employee sums up the success of SAS's approach: "You're given the freedom, the flexibility, and the resources to do your job. Because you're treated well, you treat the company well."[3]

The approach works: SAS maintains 98 percent annual customer retention and consistent growth in revenue and profits, and its annual staff turnover rate has been consistently below 5 percent, even during the 1990s technology bubble, when the industry's was 20 percent.

That's the lesson of this chapter: compensation and benefits should work for employees and for the business—as levers with which the company can meet employee needs, enable their productivity, and improve their performance.

A Changing Scene for HR Professionals

HR veterans know that, not long ago, benefits were similar for all employees and often based on a union contract. Levels of certain benefits linked to tenure, and perks escalated as employees climbed the corporate ladder, but choice was limited. Compensation was primarily market based, consisting predominantly of wages, salaries, or commissions. People might jump to a new employer for a large raise, but many would stay to protect their pensions and retiree health-care benefits, generally generous and seemingly guaranteed.

Today's situation differs dramatically for several now-familiar reasons.

- Increasing workforce *diversity* in ethnicity, gender, age, and background means more variety in workers' needs and preferences for compensation and benefits.

- Increasing workforce *mobility* and weakening worker loyalty because of downsizing and poor governance means a greater desire for portable benefits, and so portability in the employment deal becomes a valuable recruiting and retention tool.

- Increasing employee *consumerism*, especially among talented workers, means that employers must provide specific (and increasingly lifestyle-dependent) combinations of benefits.

- Flatter organizations mean fewer hierarchical promotions. Organizations must find ways to recognize employees and meet their needs for status through expansions of role and responsibility rather than rank.

- A higher proportion of mature workers means more people transitioning to less intense roles. As organizations turn to mature workers, many of them partially retired, to meet labor and skills needs, they must adjust pay, role, and rank in accordance with career downshifting. We must break the expectation of steady advancement and make it okay in the minds of workers and organizations for careers to have ebb as well as flow.

- Virtual organizations and telework mean no offices, corner or otherwise. With flexible work arrangements and dispersed workers, the physical signs of status, such as a fancy office, lose much of their power. We need more reliance on other forms of employee recognition.

As a result, today's worker-consumer looks at the compensation and benefits "package" in two new ways. First, it is one part of the overall employment deal, which also encompasses the often dominant variables of the work itself, work arrangements, learning opportunities, and the organization's mission, culture, and management style. Second, workers look for very specific elements of the employee deal and combinations of benefits—for example, flexible hours together with child-care or elder-care support, or the option of making "trades" between pay and time off. To underscore how compensation and benefits are in transition today, table 11-1 lists the fundamental changes.

To attract and retain talent today—and to compete tomorrow as slow workforce growth tightens labor markets—organizations must handle the variety of employee needs, accommodate employee mobility, customize more employees' deals, and get all facets of the deal "right." Most organizations have taken large steps in these directions: cafeteria-style benefits, portable defined-contribution pensions, and compensation plans with long-term components like stock grants. But there's much more work to be done as workforce composition changes and competition for skilled people intensifies.

TABLE 11-1

Trends in compensation and benefits

Element	From	To
Pay	Tenure based, mainly cash	Performance based, more equity
Pension	Defined benefit	Defined contribution, cash balance
Health benefits	Employer managed and provided	Cofunded and comanaged
Other benefits	Standard	Many choices, cafeteria-style, customized
Recognition and reward	Formal, periodic	Formal and informal, on the spot

A "Perfect Storm" of Market Conditions?

Organizations feel the pressure of increasing complexity—handling growing variety in employee preferences and increasing customization of the employment deal demands unprecedented flexibility in management processes, information systems, and HR staff. The lines of delineation among compensation, benefits, and other facets of the employment deal are blurring. Start with the growing list of benefits-related payroll deductions, not just for government and employer pensions and health-care premiums, but also for insurance, stock purchase, and (in the United States) before-tax self-funding of additional medical and educational accounts. Employees must make constant trade-offs between money and benefits. Then overlay the complications of a variety of flexible work arrangements, including the fact that many employees consider control of their time or extra time off as the most important "benefit." What, for example, is the definition and measurement of *vacation time* for someone who takes time off, but clears e-mail, voice mail, and important matters, and even conducts meetings via teleconference, almost every day during "vacation"? Thus, benefits categories—and the management responsibilities for them—increasingly overlap, and more people, processes, and information systems must work together flexibly to shape and administer employment deals.

Are these the ingredients for a "perfect storm," when all the unfavorable conditions converge at once? Competition for talent intensifies as labor markets tighten. The most talented workers are the most sophisticated consumers, looking for the best-tailored employee deals. Costs spiral as the workforce ages, health-care costs march upward, government mandates increase, and employers face the added effort and cost of handling complicated benefits options and customizing employee deals. In this whirlwind, employers and employees both face an unpleasant trade-off: each dollar spent on employee and retiree health care doesn't go to staff, equipment, or profits, and the more received in health benefits, the less received in wages, pensions, and vacation.[4]

The enormous retiree health-care liabilities of major corporations like the automobile makers have been in the news lately, and examples like Bethlehem Steel are fresh in CEOs' minds. At the time of Bethlehem's initial bankruptcy, its production costs were competitive, but the costs associated with a retiree-to-employee ratio of 5:1 proved unsustainable. The company has now liquidated, with retiree benefits much curtailed.[5] Companies in mature industries must choose between "changing the rules" for employee and retiree benefits and collapsing under untenable cost structures.

Facing this storm, employers must act now, when most labor markets still favor them, to reduce both long-term and short-term cost structures, especially around health-care costs. Many companies are, for example, abandoning defined-benefit pensions and raising employees' health-care contributions and out-of-pocket expenses. Of course, eliminating too much can compromise the role of compensation and benefits in recruiting and retention.

Overwhelming as the imperative to cut health-care and other benefits costs may seem, we recommend caution. Don't rush headlong into cutting benefits. Instead, adjust the deal to fit your business and workforce strategy. Organizations like SAS enjoy extraordinary employee loyalty and performance and attendant business results, because they buck the trend in benefits reduction and focus on enabling work/life balance for all employees.

What should an organization caught between cost pressure and employee demands do? Before you make tactical improvements in employer efficiency or employee accountability, we recommend looking at the big picture.

Start with business objectives. One objective is *enabling* employees to work productively, live their lives, and achieve work/life balance. This support comes mainly through base compensation, benefits, and work arrangements. Another objective is *motivating* employees to perform at the highest possible levels; to strive constantly to improve themselves, their organizations and processes, and their contributions; and to commit themselves to the success of the enterprise. This motivation comes mainly through variable compensation, learning and development opportunities, an organization's culture and leadership, and the stimulation of the work itself.

If you want to maximize the impact of compensation and benefits, you must recognize their limitations. Designing a new compensation option or adding a benefit of growing popularity (e.g., elder care) will have marginal effect when most employees view the deal in broader terms. Compensation and benefits enable employees to work and live, and are essential to employee satisfaction. But they usually don't necessarily motivate employees or secure their commitment. Thus, we recommend managing compensation and benefits in two larger contexts: the complete employment deal and the organization's performance management system—the set of methods for identifying, assessing, motivating, and rewarding employee performance. Employees are looking at the big picture, so employers must as well.

What Do Employees Want
in Compensation and Benefits?

Our nationwide survey showed, first of all, how essential compensation and benefits are to employees.[6] Two-thirds report dealing with financial issues, from trying to reduce debt to saving for purchase of a home or for children's education expenses. Over half are married, and over half have one or more children living at home. Twenty-seven percent report dealing with health issues for themselves or close family members. Ten percent have caregiving responsibility for an elder relative or adult dependent. So it's no surprise that direct compensation and the security of a benefits package rank extremely high among employee priorities. Employees still place high value on a traditional benefits package and—no surprise, given trends in health-care costs—especially the health coverage component.

When we polled employees on their relative preferences among ten basic elements of the employment deal, comprehensive benefits and retirement packages consistently topped the list, as table 11-2 shows.[7]

We described a *comprehensive benefits package* as "health care, dental, prescription drugs, disability, maternity, child care, elder care, wellness coverage funded primarily by employer." *Comprehensive retirement package* was "employer-funded pension and health-care benefits." These two basic elements of the deal rank a consistent one-two across many categories, including gender, race, and income level. There are, however, some exceptions. Among younger workers (ages eighteen to thirty-four), for whom retirement

TABLE 11-2

Overall preferences

Element	Relative weight
Comprehensive benefits package	18.5
Comprehensive retirement package	14.4
Work that enables me to learn and grow	11.7
Workplace that is enjoyable	11.5
Work that is personally stimulating	10.0
Flexible work schedule	9.0
10 percent more in total compensation	7.2
Two weeks' additional paid vacation	6.3
Work that is worthwhile to society	5.9
Flexible workplace	5.5

Relative weights add to 100

Source: *The New Employee/Employer Equation* survey

seems a distant prospect, today's benefits package ranks first, but a retirement package is down the list, below an enjoyable workplace, stimulating work, and work that enables learning and growth. Among mature workers (ages fifty-five and up), with retirement on the closer horizon, the retirement package ranks first, the immediate benefits package second. Among workers over age sixty-five, many of whom have pensions and benefits established, both elements move down the list. Finally, as we saw in the chapter on flexible learning, there is a cadre of employees—many of them high performers—for whom work that enables learning and growth is simply paramount, outranking even the security elements.

We surveyed preferences for more specific deal elements within the categories of financial compensation, health and wellness, and time off. In financial compensation (see Table 11-3), the theme seems to be "show me the money." Overall, employees showed the strongest preference for bonus compensation, above an annual pay raise, even though only 30 percent say their employers currently offer bonuses. The shorter-term payouts of bonus, raise, and stock outrank the longer-term payouts of pensions and life insurance. We suspect, however, that if we'd included just one pension option in the survey, it would have scored significantly higher.

TABLE 11-3

Financial compensation preferences

Element	Relative weight
Bonus compensation	26
Annual pay raise	19
Stock options or grants	18
Employer-funded defined-benefit pension	17
Employer-sponsored retirement savings plan	16
Life insurance policy	4

Relative weights add to 100

Source: *The New Employee/Employer Equation* survey

The breakdown of the health and wellness category (see Table 11-4) underscores how highly employees value—and worry about inadequacies in—health-care coverage, which carries three times the preference weight of the second-place element, retiree health-care coverage. The results for other elements may be deceptive—basic health care carries so much weight that there isn't much score left to go around. Still, wellness programs, elder care, and child care, while important or even essential for some employees, rank low. The message from employees seems to be, "Provide the basics first—and health coverage is most basic of all."

In the category of time off from the job, paid vacation understandably ranked first. People most crave more time off. It carried double the preference weight of the second element, paid maternity/paternity leave. Employees expressed quite low preference for the other two elements, unpaid leaves of absence and paid sabbaticals, even though both have proved invaluable at crucial points in individual careers.

We were also able to compare all of these specific deal elements as a group, apart from their categories. The results of that analysis reinforce what we've said. Health-care coverage ranks first, with half again the weight of the second element, paid vacation. The financial compensation elements, including pensions, come next, followed by the remaining health and wellness and time-off elements.

Our survey included having employees report on whether each of these compensation and benefits elements is available to them through their

TABLE 11-4

Health and wellness preferences

Element	Relative weight
Health-care coverage	47
Retiree health-care coverage	16
Prescription drug coverage	15
Short- and long-term disability coverage	10
Wellness program or fitness club membership	5
Elder care	4
Child care	3

Relative weights add to 100

Source: *The New Employee/Employer Equation* survey

employers. Note that we're tracking perceived availability, not whether employers claim the elements are offered, and not whether employees actually partake of them. Table 11-5 lists the elements by category in order of overall employee preference, and highlights the greater availability in large organizations (over five thousand employees), especially in comparison with small employers (under fifty employees).

This list reveals some apparent mismatches: items of high preference, such as bonus compensation, not generally available; and items of low preference (shortsightedly, some might argue), such as life insurance, regularly available. We note the low availability of some of the benefits—for example, child care and wellness programs—that get a lot of attention in the "best places to work" listings. We can see the transition under way from defined-benefit pensions to employer-sponsored savings plans like 401(k)s. Most striking of all is the contrast between large organizations and small. Large companies, with greater numbers and variety of employees to address, are more likely to offer every element on the list, often by wide margins. But that doesn't necessarily pay off in terms of employee engagement, of employee willingness to put forth extra effort to help the organization succeed. On our 100-point engagement scale, employees of small companies score 7 points above average and 11 points above their counterparts in large companies. Small organizations manage to connect with employees by means other than compensation and benefits.

TABLE 11-5

Perceived availability of compensation and benefits elements

	% overall	% large organizations	% small organizations
FINANCIAL COMPENSATION ELEMENTS			
Bonus compensation	30	44	24
Annual pay raise	55	74	34
Stock options or grants	19	50	7
Employer-funded defined-benefit pension	33	50	17
Employer-sponsored retirement savings plan	56	83	29
Life insurance policy	58	80	31
HEALTH AND WELLNESS ELEMENTS			
Health-care coverage	73	90	48
Retiree health-care coverage	25	36	11
Prescription drug coverage	63	82	38
Short- and long-term disability coverage	50	78	21
Wellness program or fitness club membership	18	31	7
Elder care	5	10	2
Child care	7	14	2
TIME-OFF ELEMENTS			
Paid vacation	76	92	53
Paid maternity/paternity leave	29	45	13
Unpaid leaves of absence	50	64	33
Paid sabbaticals	5	6	4

Source: *The New Employee/Employer Equation* survey

We conclude that adequate pay and benefits are necessary to employee satisfaction, but not sufficient for genuine employee engagement. Especially as job markets tighten, an attractive benefits package is a prerequisite for attracting and retaining employees. The perception that pay or benefits are inadequate or unfair can cause an exodus. So compensation and benefits may top the list, but they are increasingly table stakes. To engage employees' discretionary energy and deep commitment, however, you also must look elsewhere in the employment deal—in particular at work that is stimulating, work that enables learning and growth, and an enjoyable workplace.

Keep in mind that averages are deceiving. Workforce diversity is growing, and few people have "average" sets of needs and preferences. On the contrary, the employer's challenge is to recognize differences and individualize offerings to the extent practical within a set of (preferably modular) compensation and benefits options. A majority of employees may still be driven to seek the security elements. But significant minorities are driven by money, focused on flexibility in work arrangements, or connected with the work itself far more than with the employer.

Six Challenges in Managing Compensation and Benefits

In the course of our research into the management issues of a changing workforce, we have identified six major and interrelated challenges associated with compensation and benefits management: customization, segmentation, combination, integration, fairness, and accessibility. We discuss them in turn and offer recommendations on how to view and face each challenge.

Customization

Our study of the three workforce cohorts shows how their preferences for benefits and other facets of the employee deal vary based on a combination of age, generational attributes, and where they tend to be in their careers:

- *Young workers* often want and highly value time off for other pursuits. They prefer rewards that are instantaneous—if not literally, at least perceptually—and show little interest in the "old deal" (seniority-based pay, ritualized performance review, standard pension and benefits plan). As young workers marry and start families, child-care and family health-care benefits take on instant importance.

- *Midcareer workers* often focus on health-care, financial management, and wealth accumulation benefits. Some still (or again) need child care, some need elder care, and some need both. According to a Society for Human Resource Management survey, 25 percent of employees have some responsibility for caring for parents or other elderly family members, and another 25 percent anticipate having such responsibility in the future.[8] Midcareer workers also want time off for family and other pursuits, and relish sabbaticals, often for "the things they never got to do."

- *Mature workers* want affordable, age-relevant health-care and insurance benefits, as well as ample free time for personal pursuits. Many want to downshift their responsibilities, phase into retirement, or work in a flexible arrangement that satisfies their desire to contribute to an enterprise, to the community, and to family.

No fixed set of benefits options will affordably satisfy all three groups, and these worker cohorts represent just one possible workforce segmentation. With so much variety among employees and their needs, the employee deal in general—and benefits in particular—must be highly customizable. Perhaps the number-one challenge in benefits today is providing the set of options most meaningful and valuable to each employee while managing the overall program in a way that is cost-effective for the employer. In a sense, we're taking "cafeteria benefits" to the extreme and making that the norm. But customization has practical limits. The workforce may show infinite variety, but benefits can't. Crafting from scratch an individual deal for each employee in a large organization would be unmanageable and unaffordable. The compromise position is "mass customization," long familiar in manufacturing (where companies can produce seemingly endless variations of an item) and banking (where each customer's combination of services and terms seems uniquely tailored). Mass customization happens not because each item or service is built from scratch, but because it is rapidly assembled from a set of well-defined, modular, connectable components.

For benefits management, mass customization means that individual options must be well defined, with the legitimate connections and combinations known, and the underlying information systems must have the flexibility to represent options in modules. In assessing your organization's ability to customize benefits and other facets of the employee deal, be specific. How easily can people—both employees and HR staff—craft combinations? How do the information systems facilitate or impede this process? The goal is to *simplify* offerings, processes, procedures, and systems—and thus control costs—even while handling more variety in compensation and benefits packages.

Offering a valuable individual benefit to a significant number of employees is good. Anticipating employees' needs with new benefits is better. Providing flexibility to add, change, and phase out benefits options quickly and seamlessly is better still. Providing customization of benefits to maximize value for each employee is best of all.

Segmentation

One way to overcome the limits of customization is through better employee segmentation. The challenge is to identify meaningful and useful employee segments around which benefits options and combinations can be crafted. The traditional ways of looking at employees—by rank, function, skills, or tenure—are of declining usefulness for purposes of understanding needs and providing benefits.

Given the growing diversity in the workforce, and the growing challenge of work/life balance for so many workers, organizations need new forms of segmentation more in tune with people's needs both on the job and at home. We call this the "next frontier" in employee surveys and segmentation. The goal is to understand and appreciate employees' needs, expectations, and aspirations both on the job and off. The new variables in segmentation include age, generational cohort, life stage, lifestyle, and work stage.

Combination

In pursuit of work/life balance, employees look not just at individual benefits offered, and not just at the value and fit of the benefits package, but at specific *combinations* of benefits. A young worker might want extra time off for educational pursuits plus tuition assistance. A midcareer worker might want flexible hours that dovetail with child-care services. A mature worker might want part-time work plus help with financial management. These combinations usually draw from different "columns"—financial, health care, family support, time off.

The employer can increase the value of the benefits package to employees by making such combinations apparent and accessible. Using better segmentation, the employer might point out or package sets of benefits options as the "starter set" to satisfy a given life stage or lifestyle. The employer can also simplify the process for employees to find the right combinations on their own, as discussed later.

Integration

Compensation and benefits are just two components of the complete employee deal. As employees become more sophisticated and demanding consumers, they look at employee deals in their entirety. Employers must be able to view and manage deals the same way. That means the people and processes associated with compensation, benefits, work arrangements, learning opportunities, and overall performance management must work together as never before. It takes a cross-functional effort—and the active everyday in-volvement of line managers—to craft, adjust, and manage deals for key indi-vidual employees. It also takes cross-functional effort to outline and articu-late the overall deal offered by the employer.

To understand the need for and process of integration, ask a simple series of questions: Who works with employees in crafting their deals? Who works behind the scenes? What does the employee do on his or her own? How do information systems support the process? What can we do to simplify, streamline, and coordinate the cross-functional process called *deal making*? If you have an employer branding initiative under way, its work likely provides a head start in understanding your level of and need for integration across the elements of the employee deal. But the branding team is likely to focus on the external market and articulate what you offer as an employer. Perhaps a counterpart group should focus on the inside—bringing together the organi-zational pieces needed to craft employee deals and live up to the brand.

Fairness

This issue applies most visibly to compensation but also affects benefits and other facets of the employee deal. Many countries' laws mandate equitable treatment of workers, especially regarding benefits. Besides abiding by legal definitions of fairness, an employer must maintain the *perception* of fairness among employees—which is tough if executive compensation and perquisites appear excessive—because commitment, morale, performance, and retention can suffer, sometimes dramatically. People are generally happy with a pay sys-tem that seems fair across roles, ranks, responsibilities, and organizational units; that approximates "market rates" for the work performed and responsi-bility held; that depends on performance, including individual, group, and enterprise; and that values skills, experience, and productive behaviors.

With today's workforce, managers face potentially tricky issues of fairness at both ends of the age and experience spectrum. Young workers rightly want payment for performance and results. Since they don't expect a "job for life," they object when colleagues earn significantly more because of tenure, not performance. They have a valid point. When an employer shies away from rewarding an outstanding contributor—sometimes an outstanding innova-tor—because the person is new to the organization, then it is likely to lose that talent. If the employee has yet to demonstrate all the needed skills and traits but has produced outstandingly valuable results in an assignment or a project, then a flexible compensation scheme can finesse the situation by paying for that performance with a one-time bonus rather than the recurring benefit of a large raise in base pay.

At the other end, mature workers want payment for their experience, if not tenure. Whenever the enterprise can actively apply and share that experience—functional, organizational, marketplace—then the experienced employee should be rewarded. Mature workers also want to adopt various forms of flex retirement, but not suffer financially or in status. That entails compatible adjustments to pay, benefits, and pension calculations as they downshift to less intensive roles. Thus, the criteria for performance measurement and compensation calculation must cover results achieved, responsibility handled, skills and experience applied, and traits and behaviors demonstrated. The employer should pay youth for innovation, age for experience, and many employees for both—clearly and fairly to everyone.

Accessibility

We highly recommend providing employees with the "benefit of accessible benefits." Indeed, many employees will value assistance in understanding and maximizing the potential of their benefits package. Streamline and simplify the process for understanding what's available, choosing the best combination of benefits, and managing the consumption of those benefits. At the same time, educate (and maybe provide incentives for) employees to consume their benefits wisely and frugally, thereby curbing their own costs as well as the employer's. Making benefits more clear, accessible, and manageable also makes them more valuable to employees and increases their commitment to the organization.

Making the benefits offerings more valuable to employees while still closely managing the costs—sounds like a win-win and an obvious thing to do. It should not entail a lot of additional investment, since the employer is packaging and communicating what's already available. Unfortunately, we've found few organizations that really do this with purpose and excellence.

The challenge of accessible benefits is greatest, in the United States at least, with respect to the seemingly endless options and complications of health-care coverage. Highly capable and intelligent people get caught up in the funding options (premiums, MSAs, FSAs, etc.), provider variations (in-network versus out), coverages (various percentages usually less than 100), and co-payments (different for physician, pharmacy, etc.). Coping with health emergencies can drain an employee on the job and off. During such crises, employees need an advocate or agent to cut through the clutter and make the system work for them. Absent such employer assistance, a cottage industry has grown of consultant-facilitators who help people deal with their medical "benefits."

This need for accessibility extends beyond benefits to all facets of the employee deal. But benefits may be your company's place to start, especially if utilization and value to employees, and corresponding yield and value to the employer, seem low. Two pioneers are Saint Thomas Health Services and Humana, Inc.

Accessible Benefits at Saint Thomas Health Services

Saint Thomas Health Services (STHS) is part of Ascension Health, Inc., a national Catholic health ministry with a large network of hospitals and health-care facilities. Ascension Health is the largest not-for-profit health-care system in the United States. The STHS organization focuses on packaging and articulating employee benefits in ways that its ten thousand associates in the Nashville area can understand, appreciate, and fully use.[9] STHS found that its traditional benefits program, though thoughtfully designed, was not really being utilized, either by the employees for their own advantage or by the organization as a way to encourage loyalty, commitment, and performance. When Saint Thomas Hospital integrated an acquisition in 2001, it took the opportunity to update its HR practices and redefine its benefits to enhance associate value, while reducing areas of waste and abuse.

The result is a broad and rich program called LifeWorks! In STHS's view, too often benefits and other HR programs have centered on the offerings themselves, not on why they exist or how employees view them. The result is that people cannot understand them, don't use them, and don't value them. The fifty-five-page LifeWorks! Guide starts with the following mission statement: "LifeWorks! is a framework for developing and communicating a comprehensive partnership between Saint Thomas Health Services (STHS) and our associates. Our goal is simple: to empower you with the resources needed to help you achieve a healthy work/life balance through a wide variety of employee benefits and support programs."[10]

Perhaps as important as the details of the program is that it has been constructed to be understood and used by STHS staff. The LifeWorks! components and philosophy are communicated visually as a pyramid (see figure 11-1) containing "seven levels of support," beginning with basic life needs (fair and competitive pay) and evolving to higher-level wants and desires,

FIGURE 11-1

LifeWorks! pyramid

VII. Work/Life Harmony

VI. Whole Life Success

V. Recreation and Convenience

IV. Building Health and Wholeness

III. Programs to Build and Maximize Wealth

II. Programs to Protect Health and Income

I. Provide Competitive and Socially Just Wages

Source: Saint Thomas Health Services

such as health and recreation nearer the peak of the pyramid. The pyramid makes it easy for associates to grasp the entire program while also seeing all the parts and how they relate to one another to form a comprehensive package of "wholeness and healing" for the entire STHS community.

STHS has attempted to integrate—from the associate perspective—what had been discrete programs. LifeWorks! offers benefits and options for its staff at virtually any life stage, and the guide provides detailed descriptions of the rationale for each support level. For each level, the guide describes benefits, eligibility information, costs, and contact information. While offering the disclaimer that the guide is "not intended to serve as a Summary Plan Description" as defined by ERISA, it nevertheless delivers, in one publication, detailed information about every benefit available to associates in a clear, easy-to-read format, and that achievement alone probably makes it a most valuable communication from STHS.

The benefits redesign for STHS was done by a small team that used worker preferences as its data source. The goal was to expand the health and well-being aspects of LifeWorks! and make the financial components more relevant and useful to all participants. Work is ongoing to enhance financial well-being offerings and further associates' abilities to access and utilize the many parts of LifeWorks!

STHS's goal is to demonstrate its profound and tangible commitment to its workforce to create the environment needed to attract talent despite changing demographics. This means making benefits meaningful and accessible to associates at different life stages and with different needs. This includes appealing to younger workers, who tend to be focused on the here and now, and yet respond to opportunities for wealth accumulation and other benefits. A strong and easily understood benefits program should build loyalty and commitment among all workforce generations—and the expectation is that LifeWorks! will.

Accessible Benefits at Humana

Humana, Inc., headquartered in Louisville, Kentucky, is one of the nation's largest publicly traded health benefits companies, with approximately 6.6 million medical members located primarily in eighteen states and Puerto Rico. Humana offers coordinated health insurance coverage and related services—through traditional and Internet-based plans—to employer groups, government-sponsored plans, and individuals.

Humana test-drives new plans, new options, and new tools with its employees before it rolls them out to customers. Because Humana employees are engaged in both the business of the company and their own benefits plans and decisions, they are an ideal test base: they are knowledgeable and sophisticated about the company's business, products, and mission, and consumers of the company's products. In 2001, Humana launched a pilot "consumer-driven" health benefits program called SmartSuite for its five thousand employees in the Louisville area. The intent was to give employees more control over their health benefits choices and spending. In the pilot year, SmartSuite grouped six different health benefits plans into a single bundle for employees; options included traditional PPO and HMO, as well as CoverageFirst, Humana's first consumer-choice health plan offering. Following the pilot and extensive feedback from employees, Humana rolled out SmartSuite to its customers six months later.

In June 2002, the end of the pilot year with its own employees, Humana reported a savings of $2 million and an increase in medical claims costs of just 4.9 percent—versus a projected 19.2 percent increase and actual average claims increase experience of about 19 percent for other companies in the region. The savings are the result of three factors:

- *Communication and education efforts.* For example, Humana put a lot of effort into a campaign to demonstrate that double coverage (both wage earners in a family signing on for health-care benefits from their employers) did not produce double value. Almost all employees who had double coverage dropped the secondary coverage, which produced savings when the second plan was Humana's.

- *Plan design changes.* Humana modified personal physician and specialist visit co-pays, added a hospital co-pay for some plans, and added deductibles as an option to help employees lower payroll deduction costs.

- *Behavior modification.* The vast majority of the savings are the result of employees simply changing the way they use their health benefits plans. The company has found, for example, that while visits to personal physicians were up in the pilot year, hospital visits (which are usually more expensive) were down. Employees were choosing to have procedures done on an outpatient basis at their doctors' offices rather than in the hospital. They also made different pharmacy choices, opting for less expensive drugs. In short, "Employees are accessing care differently."[11]

At the same time that it introduced SmartSuite to help employees make choices of health benefits that best fit their life stage, family needs, and budgets, Humana also automated the process with the Wizard, an online benefits information and selection service available to employees through the corporate intranet or over the Internet. Many employees are becoming increasingly comfortable using online tools, so introducing the Wizard was a natural evolution in the company's use of online resources for employee communication. Using the Wizard, employees can narrow their plan choices by selecting variables such as hospital co-pay, deductible, plan coinsurance, pharmacy plan, and type of benefits—to customize a plan that closely meets their health-care needs and finances. The parameters for the Wizard are not infinite (employees cannot specify, for example, a specific dollar amount for a premium), but there are plenty of choices. They can balance out-of-pocket expenses against a monthly premium, for example. They can also view their actual usage information to help them decide how to adjust their benefits packages. Once employees have made their choices, they can compare various choice options, enroll, or start over to see new options compared.

Over the last three years, Humana has expanded the options in its employee benefits packages and the associated decision-making tools based in large part on employee feedback. Within two weeks of the enrollment period in June, Humana surveys employees about their experience in signing up for benefits and conducts focus groups among employees to drill down about their overall enrollment experience. In the first two years of SmartSuite, ending in June 2003, Humana received some seventy-five hundred lines of comments from employees (some just one word, others detailed critiques of the experience).

Following successful implementation of the Wizard for its own employees, Humana has rolled out the service to its corporate customers, along with training programs to teach customers and their employees how to get the maximum benefit from it. Humana also offers an online help desk for both its own associates and customers' employees who have health benefits questions, and delivers an online newsletter to all associates.

Performance Management Should Guide Changes in the Deal

Compensation and benefits work best—for both an organization and its employees—as part of a complete and coherent performance management system that enables and motivates people to perform well. The deal has got to be clear, and that's part of what performance management does. If the rewards and benefits of working are clearly tied to measurable performance, then employees perceive the system as fair, and the business can adjust the system for optimal results.

Performance management is a system of identifying, assessing, motivating, and rewarding employee performance, with a natural emphasis on serving and motivating top performers. It includes the process of individual and group performance appraisal, as well as orchestration—usually by the immediate manager—of compensation, benefits, other forms of recognition and reward, and other elements of the deal, such as work arrangements and learning opportunities that support and motivate employees. Performance management must be structured and consistently applied, but also flexible and responsive to the needs and styles of employees and employee segments. Every organization has a de facto performance management system, even if it is not explicitly designed and its motivational effects are inconsistent and ineffective.

Designing performance systems is never easy; changing them may be harder, if for no other reason than employees are used to the ones they have, like them or not. But it is the employees, especially high performers, whom you should listen to. They have the answers to your questions about what to include in a performance and reward system to attract, retain, and consistently motivate them. You will find that a foundation principle in any new organizational performance system is choice—informed choice—for employees, both in their deals and in how they relate to the performance system.

Put these trends together, and now may be a good (or overdue) time to revisit the design and operation of your performance management system. The following are hallmarks of the most effective recognition and reward systems. They describe how a successful performance management system operates:

- *Individuals receive continuous, personalized reinforcement and feedback throughout the year.* Managers and other feedback providers take the time to monitor, assess, and discuss an individual's performance regularly. Employees make the process work by turning feedback into improvement. Complaints such as "My supervisor is too busy to review my performance" and "The only feedback I get is when I've done something wrong" are sure signs of a performance management system that is neither functional nor respected.

- *Financial and nonfinancial factors determine incentives and rewards.* Even in the presence of clear financial indicators (e.g., revenue or profit), each employee is measured on a mix of factors, including behaviors that enable others to succeed (e.g., sharing experience).

- *Learning and innovation are rewarded, with both recognition and financial incentives.* Prominent in the measurement and reward mix must be an individual's learning on behalf of the organization (which implies sharing and acting upon what is learned) and innovating to improve the organization's performance.

- *Judicious risk taking is rewarded.* Failure upon taking a considered risk is tolerated (few organizations can bring themselves to reward such failure). The performance management system should note not just day-to-day production or results, but also the often bold, thoughtful, and creative attempts that fail.

- *Recognition is public.* The organization creates visible forms of acknowledgment, praise, and award that are held in high regard by employees, and that foster performance. Some forms of recognition are regular, others very ad hoc. For example, one international company had senior HR executives present their best practices at a corporatewide HR meeting, and the top three were recognized. The executive whose best practice was voted number one was then asked to go to any market in the world to implement that winning practice.

- *The reward system reinforces the corporate values, and vice versa.* If the organization claims to place value on learning and innovation, but there are no rewards or recognition for learning or innovation in the performance system, employees quickly see the disconnect. The performance system must "live" the organization's values—and motivate associated behaviors.

- *The bonus or incentive is at risk.* Incentives are linked to performance and are not automatic. They may be based on combinations of results (e.g., individual, team, businesswide) not entirely under the individual's control. But they must not be automatic, and money must be at risk, or the incentives lose their motivational power.

- *Executives' incentives are tied to the long-term success of the business and are consistent with the interests of shareholders.* Executive compensation can set the tone for a performance management system. Employees are well aware of the differences between their compensation packages and those of top executives. If executive compensation is out of alignment with the performance or interests of the organization, then people have reason for discontent, and the performance management system is automatically suspect.

Employee Recognition at CalPERS

California Public Employees' Retirement System (CalPERS) is putting many of our performance management principles into operation in a six-year-old employee recognition program, one of the most pervasive in any large U.S. organization. Only a handful of companies (Southwest Airlines, The Container Store) and governments (City of Seattle, State of Arizona) have institutionalized informal, day-to-day employee recognition the way CalPERS does. They recently received a national award as the Best Overall Recognition Program from the National Association for Employee Recognition.[12]

According to various studies, as many as 85 percent of employees leave their jobs because of the relationship with the immediate supervisor. This is one reason CalPERS has identified everyday employee communication and recognition as core competencies for its management team. It holds them accountable for making and maintaining connections with employees, and trains them to do so. The expectation is that supervisors will be attentive to employees and that all employees will support one another by giving recognition that is sincere, specific, timely, and personalized.

Recognition happens at three levels:

- Day-to-day recognition, the base or foundation of the program, consists of verbal or written feedback. "Rocks" (as in "your work is solid as a rock") in the form of a note card or an electronic "e-rock" serve as a means for employees and management to recognize one another.

- Informal recognition involves management-delivered, performance-based recognition for individuals and teams. Specific accomplishments or behaviors critical to business success are celebrated in a wide variety of ways, such as a management-catered barbecue or a personalized memento.

- APEX (Achieving Performance Excellence) is the organization's formal peer-driven recognition award. APEX awards, given annually to 1–3 percent of the organization, include a crystal trophy, a professionally taken photo of each recipient that is hung in the lobby until the next award cycle, lunch with top management, a public presentation, and $500. Receiving the APEX award is considered a major milestone in one's career, in large part because the program is peer driven—employees developed it and nominate and select each year's recipients.

CalPERS has turned its position as a governmental "low-cost" organization to its advantage through the recognition program. With little money for cash awards, the organization must excel at day-to-day and informal recognition, which is creative and delivered with sincerity. CalPERS tries to say regularly, "Here's what you did that made a difference, we value you, our customers value you, and here's how your work contributes to our success."

Employee satisfaction surveys are anonymous but broken down by unit, so the organization can see where there are supervisory strengths and weaknesses. Some supervisors are uncomfortable with giving and receiving recognition (e.g., if they haven't received much, if any, recognition throughout their personal careers), but CalPERS encourages them to work through their discomfort by finding ways to give recognition that best fit their personal communication styles (e.g., if note writing doesn't come easy, then drop by an employee's desk for a face-to-face thank-you). Through a 360-degree feedback process as part of their professional development, managers and supervisors receive the coaching and guidance needed to improve.

CalPERS worked for more than two years with cross-functional teams of staff, including union representatives and an outside consultant, on developing and rolling out the employee recognition program. The bottom-line results include improved employee and customer satisfaction, increased productivity, and a low turnover rate, compared with other California state agencies. Recognition has become a highly valued aspect of working at CalPERS, and helped make it an employer of choice in the state of California.

Is Your Performance Management System Working Well?

There are several litmus tests to gauge how well your performance management system is working. For starters, the performance system must motivate the best performers. Of course, performance management is for all employees, and general excellence in performance management means greater overall productivity. But it's especially important that the system work well for the employees who contribute the most.

The system must also accurately reflect business objectives. Employees should understand that their rewards derive from doing what the business values most. For example, a business cannot insist upon superior customer service but reward call center employees for call volume instead of customer satisfaction and retention. Employees must feel that their work matters toward business performance.

The performance system must also be transparent and understandable, especially to those at lower levels in the organization. If employees say, "I don't really understand how things work; I just get my automatic once-a-year raise," then they're not being influenced or motivated by the system. They must understand the performance management process to participate in it.

In particular, the system must be explicit about the baseline of performance that everyone must meet, and the consequences for failing to meet it. Finally, employees understand and fully appreciate the value of their total reward packages. They must know what benefits and choices are available, be able to make and manage their selections, and value their compensation and benefits packages.

We recommend periodically "taking the pulse" of the performance management system. Talk with a selection of managers, top performers, and representative employees about how and how well the performance management system meets its objectives. Then discuss ways to improve the performance, perception, and results of your system. Keep in mind that assessing and meeting people's needs and influencing their performance are not exact sciences. When designing or revising a performance management system, keep in mind these four underlying realities.

First, people have a wide range of needs and values when it comes to work and benefits. As we have seen throughout this book, these preferences and responses differ by career cohort, as well as by life stage, lifestyle, and work stage. Second, employees may not be able or willing to tell you what they value. This can be a major obstacle in developing the data needed to craft a performance system. Unaware of the possibilities, they may not know how to express what work arrangements, benefits, or learning opportunities might mean the most to them. Alternatively, if they do not sufficiently trust the organization, or sense that the organization does not trust its employees, they will withhold information about their preferences, suspicious of what the organization intends to do with it.

Third, employees' expectations condition their motivation. If people's expectations regarding the job and workplace are not being met, specific attempts at motivation—including monetary—have little effect. This factor can be especially important with young workers who do not yet know the ropes. That's one reason why rapid incorporation into both organization and job are so important. Finally, job satisfaction leads to "membership" in the organization. Membership is a choice. Some people work but never become real members of the employer organization. Others become not just members but leaders in the organization's operational and social structure. Commitment comes when employees are satisfied in all facets of their jobs—the work they do, the deal they have, the respect they enjoy. A performance management system encourages membership by helping an employee appreciate how all these pieces fit together.

ACTIONS TO TAKE

In Adjusting Compensation and Benefits

To maximize the effectiveness of compensation and benefits programs in the twin contexts of the employment deal and performance management, we recommend these four basic actions:

☐ *Probe with purpose.* First, gain real insight into the compensation and benefits most valued by employees now and in the future. Ask them, perhaps through surveys and focus groups, and research what other companies have discovered, particularly companies in your industry or competing for the same kinds of employees and skills. Second, evaluate the effectiveness of your overall compensation and benefits programs in meeting business needs. Find and eliminate the instances where compensation, benefits, and reward systems send mixed signals about performance expectations and organizational values.

☐ *Customize deals.* Now is the time to develop and deploy a sustainable and cost-effective plan for individualizing compensation and benefits. Within a few years, you will need the information systems, technology infrastructure, and business processes to implement individual deals broadly in your workforce. In the meantime, all progress in this direction adds to your employer-of-choice credentials.

☐ *Educate employees and retirees.* When surveyed, many employees will underestimate both the value and range of their benefits. Prepare them to manage the components of their benefits packages and make the trade-offs that are important to them and their futures. They must understand why and how they can help control costs, both out-of-pocket and the employer's costs.

☐ *Engage in the debate.* U.S. businesses must muster the political will and form the coalitions to enter and change the political debate around pension and health-care issues. They have a duty to shareholders and employees to address these issues for the long term. For a legislative agenda specifically around enabling flexible retirement, see chapter 4.

PART IV

Management Practices for the New Workforce

In order that people may be happy in their work, these three things are needed: They must be fit for it. They must not do too much of it. And they must have a sense of success in it.

—John Ruskin[1]

12

Meaningful Work and Engaged Workers

*How to Analyze Your Workforce
and Anticipate Your Needs*

Y OU CAN completely overhaul the employment deal to provide flexible
work arrangements, learning opportunities, and compensation and
benefits, but your best employees will still leave if their work neither
stimulates them nor brings out their best effort. Most of us have experienced
enervating work ourselves or through family and friends. It's monotonous,
homogeneous, meaningless, mindless, inconsequential, unremarkable, and
underwhelming—just check your brain at the door. Many people actually
prefer a routine, but where *routine* doesn't mean boring or unchallenging.

Common Characteristics of Interesting Work

- *Stimulation.* The work calls upon people to use their unique intellectual, creative, physical, and social skills and gifts, the very use of
  which stimulates and energizes them.

- *Variety.* It offers variety and at least occasional challenges when the worker can improvise, invent, or improve products, services, business processes, and policies.

- *Edification.* It involves learning new skills, honing existing ones, building new knowledge, and sharing it with others.

- *Connection.* It fosters interaction with others in and outside the workplace, thereby cultivating a collaborative, supportive work environment.

- *Control.* It provides a degree of control over the goals, methods, and timing of the activities performed or customers served.

- *Value.* Inherently important and meaningful, the work clearly benefits an internal or external customer and sometimes even the community itself—as when the worker can see the physical product or witness a customer enjoying a particular service.

When their work lacks these elements, employees tend to reshape it or recast their roles, regardless of the job itself. A local supermarket features two extraordinary grocery baggers. One is the authority on prices of sale items. He arrives a few minutes early, walks the aisles, and notes the markdowns so that he can help his colleagues to resolve discrepancies quickly. The other bagger uplifts colleagues through regular circulation, connection, and conversation—not banter.

Beware of the Satisfied Workforce

Satisfaction does not equal engagement. They're related and trend together, but they're different phenomena from different sources. Satisfaction is about sufficiency—enough pay, benefits, flexibility to work and live, and no major problems or unfair treatment to sour one's attitude toward the employer. Satisfied employees say, "Hey, it's an okay job; I could be doing worse." Engagement is about passion and commitment—the willingness to expend one's discretionary effort on the employer's success. For engaged employees, time flies. They identify with the task at hand, their enthusiasm infects others, the activity generates as well as consumes their energy, and they care deeply about the outcome. No compensation, benefit, or flexible arrangement can inspire such passion. It comes from the nature and challenge of the work itself—in the context of workplace, colleagues, and organizational culture—and from the individual's psychology.

The majority of employees tell us that they're somewhat satisfied with their jobs, describe themselves as reliable, hard-working, and confident, and prefer the state of engagement over the opposite. But only 20 percent of employees are genuinely engaged in their work and committed to their employers.[1] Well under 50 percent say that their work includes collaboration with bright and experienced people, provides opportunities to learn and grow, or is worthwhile to society. Fewer than 50 percent say their workplace is congenial and fun, that employees cooperate and teamwork is the rule, or that people are respected for their abilities and can exercise them. Two in five are looking to change careers or jobs. Forty-two percent feel burnout, and 33 percent find themselves at dead ends in their jobs, compared with 28 percent who are working on exciting new projects or assignments.[2] Clearly, many more employees are engageable than are currently engaged.

Why should employers care? Over the last several years, studies around the world have correlated employee commitment and business and financial performance. A Stanford University study of one hundred small companies found that those with high employee commitment are twelve times more likely to go IPO, and of those that went IPO, none failed.[3] The costs of low engagement are harder to gauge, but they are enormous. How does productivity change when employees don't expend themselves fully? What is the cost of lost recruits, employees, and customers when employees' disengagement permeates the organization and the customer and job marketplaces?

How Not to Redesign Work

Fifteen or so years ago, a well-known machinery manufacturer struggled to staff its customer service call center. The service center work was quite demanding because of the variety of callers and the information sought. Prospective customers called for descriptions and specifications of the machines and for comparisons with competitors' machines. Dealers called for similar information and the status of their scheduled shipments. Existing customers called to troubleshoot problems and schedule installations or repairs. Since some customers used independent service technicians or their own, the technicians called for spare parts, maintenance and repair manuals, and even advice on repairs. Thus, the representatives in the center had to know a lot about the company's products, processes, and customers and had to switch gears from call to call, and think on their feet whenever a caller posed an unprecedented variation on a request for information or service. Many had college credits or degrees.

Faced with a growing staffing shortage—the company was paying lots of overtime, and center employees were burning out—it devised a plan for re-automating the center. The company had recently succeeded with a major reengineering of its supply chain, including a new set of sophisticated information systems, and managers thought they could apply what they'd learned to the call center operations. With guidance from the most experienced customer reps, they built a much better organized "information engine" and a cleaner interface for the reps' workstations, enabling them to see the options and jump easily from function to function. They developed scripts for handling the various kinds of calls that commonly came in. Frontline reps would diagnose the very complicated calls and pass them to a "second tier," a small cadre of very experienced reps. With this higher level of automation, the company could hire less educated and skilled people as reps—and even *lower* the pay scales. It installed the improved information system, hired and trained a new group of reps, and piloted the "new service center" on a small scale within the old one.

It was a disaster. The reps often couldn't find information or combine or interpret information as needed. The average call took three times as long in the "new" center as in the "old," an unacceptable productivity level. Over one-third of the calls eventually went to—and overwhelmed—the second tier. Customers of all kinds complained, often vociferously, having once dealt with knowledgeable and versatile representatives. Additional training of the new reps, and even placing some experienced reps alongside the new ones (duty the experienced reps hardly relished) barely ameliorated the productivity and service problems.

The company quickly backtracked, closing the new center and rethinking its goals and strategy. Curtailing service to customers—in a competitive industry where substitute products were readily available—was not an option. They severely underestimated what it took to do the job and overestimated how much of it could be automated. They overlooked the extent to which the reps made connections, assembled information (in ways computers couldn't) into personalized solutions for customers, and shared knowledge and tricks of the trade in the service center's informal network. In short, the company tried to dumb down the work when it should have been enriching it.

So the company pursued an alternative—and better—set of results. The combination of the improved information systems and the skilled reps in the old center proved extraordinarily productive. Reps spent less time on finding information and moving between information systems for different functions, and more time communicating with customers and customizing solutions. Average call time declined considerably, and customers' satisfaction with service, already high, went higher. Since the average rep could now do more, the company didn't need to staff up as much or as fast. The new arrangement worked well because the reps helped design it; they could focus their time and creativity on the customers. In the end, the company upgraded the rep jobs (and pay scales) and focused recruiting on college graduates, both recent ones and workforce reentrants.

What should we learn from this cautionary tale? First, work design makes or breaks productivity, and good work design mixes human skill and automation to get the best of both. Second, companies should enrich jobs and enable people to use their skills rather than routinize work and treat people as automatons. Enriched work engages people's intellect, energy, effort, and commitment. Reengineering business processes should always yield more interesting and challenging work for employees. So, unlike the process reengineers of the late 1980s and early 1990s who largely ignored the human element, you can combine flexible technology with engaged employees and create the work of the future.

Improving Your Workforce Assessment

We've looked at the nature of work itself. Now let's look at the nature of the workforce. What should you know about yours? How diverse is it, in terms of gender, ethnicity, age, and background, as well as employment needs and expectations? How must you adjust workforce management practices to handle this variety? How will you customize employment deals, including work arrangements and compensation and benefits? How will training, development, and on-the-job learning fit the individual's as well as the organization's needs and styles?

How do you find out? Most large organizations survey their employees to determine attitudes, needs, and satisfaction levels. They also model their workforces to some extent, often to anticipate capabilities needed. They often study their local, and sometimes national and international, labor markets to understand sources of labor supply and anticipate how to succeed at recruiting. Here, we focus on what new or additional information organizations should obtain to anticipate workforce demographic shifts and mitigate the effects of labor and skills shortages.

We recommend enriching your workforce information and assessment in four basic areas.

Employees and their aspirations and preferences. This area includes more information about what people want and need from the employment deal and what motivates them to stay or leave. In addition to understanding what employees generally and employee segments want, it's also essential to track how well they make use of what's available to them. How well do employees understand, appreciate, and utilize available components of the deal, including work arrangements, benefits, and learning opportunities? The goals of this analysis are to be able to craft more attractive deals, discover emerging needs, and identify significant workforce segments.

Employee segments. To visualize patterns of workforce change, most organizations should categorize employees and "slice and dice" employee information more meaningfully, segmenting by age and other facets of diversity, by employee needs and preferences, by current skills and training needs, by turnover/retirement patterns, and so on. Organize the information by business unit, function, role (e.g., associate, manager), and profession (e.g., engineering, accounting). Then determine which segments matter most to business success, or seem in short supply, and develop labor/skills demand-and-supply profiles for them.

Employee performance and potential. Review performance measurement and management methods and all the other places where individual evaluation (including subjective assessment) shapes decisions around employees. How precise and how consistently applied are the evaluation criteria? How do you gauge the value and replaceability/irreplaceability of an employee to the enterprise? How do you determine who should be on the "high potential" and "high retention" lists? This review should reveal opportunities for both better measures and more systematic evaluation methods. See the discussion of performance management in the chapter on compensation and benefits.

Labor markets. Expand your tracking and analysis of current and potential recruiting pools, especially if you anticipate the need to recruit from nontraditional groups such as workforce reentrants, career switchers, and retirees. As with market research generally, it's important to understand the potential prospects—those you're not yet in relationship with and those you haven't considered marketing to in the past—as well as current "customers."

How can organizations go about gathering some of this new information and deepening their understanding of their workforces? An obvious first step is to expand what they ask and learn in employee surveys. We recommend surveying key employee groups—including those on the high-potential and high-retention lists—more often and in more detail to understand more fully what matters most to the employees who matter most. We also recommend seizing more occasions for *opportunistic inquiry*:

- *New hires.* Don't just say, "Welcome aboard." Find out why they accepted the positions. What in the work itself, the employer brand, and the employment deal attracted them?

- *Failed hires.* When people choose not to accept a job offer, find out why. What is it about the job, the organization, or the offer that led the candidate to decline?

- *Departing employees.* Be serious about exit interviews and find out what, if anything, went wrong in the employment deal, and what needs or expectations were not being met.

- *Mature workers.* For those approaching retirement age, get a sense of their intentions, their interests in partial retirement, and what changes to the employment deal would encourage them to stay.

- *Employees seeking changes.* When people ask for transfers, seek training, or express interest in new roles, find out what triggers those needs or desires.

- *High-potential employees.* Most organizations pay extra attention to people who may make the greatest contributions to the business. But not many survey their high potentials on a regular basis.

As the saying goes, you can learn a lot just by asking. A health services organization surveyed its top performers, asking not about satisfaction with pay and benefits, but rather about what they want in the work environment—leadership, culture, development opportunities—and how effectively the company delivers these. Work/life balance, work arrangements (like having more say in scheduling), and more involvement in decision making were high on the list, and so was more fun, excitement, and enthusiasm on the job. The results are informing both workplace improvement and employer branding initiatives.

Another company we worked with, this one in the medical technology field, was surprised by what its employees were *not* focused on. As part of a study of the young employee cohort, those under thirty-five, the company convened a focus group of twenty-five high-potential people. It learned, rather predictably, how highly these individuals valued flexible work arrangements, ongoing learning opportunities, and the chance to work with mentors. But contrary to what the company expected to hear (and counter to generational stereotype), the state of the organization's technology was not a significant factor for them.

Workforce Planning at General Motors

General Motors is leveraging workforce analysis in fundamental ways. The Human Resource Planning group, created in 2000 and staffed with twelve people, is responsible for planning across all of GM's North American functional areas. The group includes planning representatives from engineering, manufacturing, information systems, and other functions, who work with the company's central planning group to forecast employee supply and demand up to two years into the future. They are strategically linked to the various functional leadership teams to understand the needs of the organization (both current and long term), their specific business strategies, and the focus of their internal human capital strengths and weaknesses. The group covers all salaried workers; a separate planning group deals with hourly workers, who are covered by union contracts.[4]

HR Planning has helped "lower the water line" on resource requirements throughout GM North America (GMNA), avoiding oversupply and undersupply, and optimizing the flow of people into and out of critical skill areas, including a variety of engineering disciplines. Careful planning enables GMNA to perform *cadenced hiring*—adding just-in-time resources in response to specific business needs and to avoid the wasteful practice of "precautionary staffing."

The planning group helps control people costs by carefully linking human resource flows to the budgets of the individual functional units while attempting to optimize the enterprise as a whole. Since GM operates under a functional matrix structure, HR Planning has the difficult task of performing simultaneous resource planning both functionally and organizationally. In the past, GM's decentralized operating units developed their own plans and did their own hiring and flow analyses location by location and organization by organization. The result was that HR simply could not effectively align available people with the work to be performed.

Today the detailed plans reflect many variables, including production and workload forecasts, expected retirements, projected hiring needs, and future skill set requirements. To develop function-by-function labor supply information, up-to-date data and sophisticated attrition models are utilized, incorporating, among other variables, age, type of work, and economic conditions. Demand is much harder to predict, since it involves more speculative variables, such as production volumes and workload units. The HR Planning group looks, for example, at engineering staffing needs based on a complex modeling of workload. These forecasts are performed by functional planners using their own models, but HR Planning then relies on their output to determine how many people and what types of skills will be needed to perform the anticipated work.

Every annual human resources plan begins a year in advance and goes through several iterations to adjust for changes in production forecasts, the product portfolio, the economy, and many other factors. In addition, the planning group does a large number of what-if scenarios and must be able to completely revise a plan at a moment's notice. Nearly instantaneous scenario planning allows group and functional leaders to make timely, data-driven people decisions whenever required.

One difficult element in the process is timing: HR prepares its plans six months to a year in advance, to provide direction to functional units for worker flow, including hiring plans. Preapproved recruiting plans provide ample time for the organization to gear up for the college-recruiting efforts and to be on campus with offers in hand to attract the best candidates early in the season. Another complexity is that GM has about thirty vehicle development programs under way at any time, and more than twenty-five basic skill set groupings are required at each development stage. The number of design engineers and chassis engineers, for example, must be determined on a quarterly basis, so HR Planning looks at the flow of skills by type and seeks to consistently match demand and supply.

At the outset, the planning group had to make substantial changes to existing databases and upgrade the quality and accuracy of human resources data throughout GMNA. This was a critical step, since data was often untimely or unreliable for the kind of HR forecasting and planning expected of the group. Information provided to the functional unit leaders from HR is now much more accurate and more easily retrievable than in the past. The ability to provide meaningful data to the functional areas has enabled top leadership to make better decisions with regard to people. It has allowed them to foresee changes in the workforce and to address future skill requirements—in other words, to constantly optimize their human capital.

The proof of HR Planning's success is GM leadership's request to expand its work globally. The potential for productivity improvement in engineering alone is huge if the global product portfolio plan can be linked to a workforce optimization model. It may be possible, for example, to move work, not people, from engineering center to engineering center across distant regions as supply (skills) and demand (workload) ebb and flow at each center. For a company of GM's size, lots of people and money are at stake in developing this linkage.

Toward New Segmentations

Better segmentation represents the next frontier in workforce assessment and modeling. With so much variety among employees and their needs, the employee deal must be more customizable. But crafting an individual deal for each employee in a large organization is unmanageable. So the challenge is to identify meaningful employee segments defined not by rank, function, skills, or tenure, but by needs, expectations, and aspirations both on the job and off. By understanding the patterns of what different types of employees seek in the workplace and the employee deal, organizations can craft work arrangements, compensation and benefits, and career development opportunities to be most effective and attractive from the employees' perspectives. In short, understand employees as you would customers, and apply techniques of consumer market research and marketing to current and prospective employees.

The key variables in this expanded analysis and fresh segmentation of the workforce include:

- *Age.* This variable matters more as the workforce and general populations age, and as the age mix and range of organizations shift. Age is a significant factor because people's physical abilities and health-care needs may change as they grow older. Age is also the basis for a series of (rather arbitrary) checkpoints that shape the terms of employment, such as reaching retirement age. According to a recent Conference

Board study, two-thirds of employers don't even have detailed age profiles of their workforces.

- *Generational cohort.* On the one hand, we must recognize that generational boundaries are arbitrary, must avoid stereotypes, and must
  not assume that generational characteristics apply to any individual.
  On the other hand, generations such as the boomers do, in the aggregate, share specific experiences and exhibit certain attributes. How
  people learn, work, interrelate, even think is conditioned in no small
  part by the culture, dominant events, technology, and educational
  methods of their youth. Thus, it's very useful for employers, without
  being deterministic, to understand the generational mix of their workforces, including "*when* people are from" and how different cohorts
  are likely to behave and interact.

- *Life stage.* What employees seek in an employment deal, especially
  the compensation and benefits they need, is often driven by where
  they are among life's major phases. Are they unattached and highly
  mobile, raising young children, putting kids through college, empty
  nesting, or sandwiched between commitments to parents and children? Are they readying themselves for retirement? In the past, life
  stage tracked somewhat predictably with age. But as more people
  delay marrying or having children, and more people divorce and start
  second families, the pattern is broken. An employee at almost any
  age can be in any life stage.

- *Lifestyle.* This includes personal preferences, patterns, pursuits, and
  style. Are people extravagant or Spartan, stay-at-home or highly trav-
  eled, rural or urban, fast paced or leisurely? Lifestyle is an especially
  important variable at the intersection of work and the rest of life. For
  example, some employees want different patterns of time off for specific recreational or educational pursuits, and dual-career couples
  must manage their work/life balance in tandem.

- *Work stage.* Where are employees in terms of their careers and
  relationships with the current employer? Are they fresh and eager
  or getting stale or burned out? Are they established and comfortable
  or emerging as leaders? As with life stage, the correlation between
  age and work stage is breaking down. More people change employers
  and change careers. They may be well established from a career

perspective but uncertain in a new role with a new employer. This variable shapes what employees need in the workplace, including feedback and learning opportunities. Perhaps the most useful yet elusive variable upon which to base a segmentation model, it best represents how employees relate to their work and their employers.

With so many influential variables shaping employee needs and preferences, managers must understand their interconnections, find meaningful employee segments, and customize employee deals efficiently.

Workforce Segmentation at Tesco

U.K.-based retailer Tesco wanted to learn as much about its employees—two hundred sixty thousand people in the United Kingdom, Continental and Eastern Europe, and Asia—as it knew about its customers.[5] Employee survey data revealed that while 82 percent of employees agreed that Tesco put customers first, only 64 percent felt valued by Tesco. This gap troubled management, given the strong correlation between how positively employees feel about the company and how satisfied customers are. Management also knew of significant trends in its workforce, including more people wanting to work part-time, a decline in the number of twenty-six- to forty-four-year-olds available for hire, the workforce becoming more ethnically diverse and better educated, more women working in management, and more employees working remotely from stores and offices. All these trends pointed toward a growing demand for more "nonstandard employment contracts," with better work/life balance becoming a high priority for many.

Drawing on the experience and expertise of its Consumer Insight Unit (CIU), Tesco developed an Employee Insight Unit (EIU) to deepen its understanding of attitudes toward Tesco as an employer. EIU interviewed more than one thousand people outside Tesco, held focus groups with representative employees, and surveyed some sixteen hundred employees on "Your Life . . . Your Future." The unit wanted to know what employees valued in work, what they perceived Tesco as offering, and the trade-offs they currently made between the two. EIU also incorporated results of the company's other ongoing employee surveys. As a result, it identified five distinct types of workers among Tesco employees:

- *Work/life balancers* want to work flexible hours or part-time. They are not necessarily interested in promotions but want challenging and stimulating work and a fulfilling job with responsibility and the opportunity to learn new skills.

- *Want-it-alls* want their work to be challenging and varied, and want the company to be successful. They are ambitious and want promotions. Money is an important part of the deal for them. They are one of the most demanding and mobile groups; they tend to leave Tesco if the job fails to challenge them or if they can increase their salary elsewhere.

- *Pleasure seekers*, more likely to be single men, had the least commitment and loyalty to Tesco. This group is ambitious and keen to travel overseas and to enjoy their leisure time. But they do not take enormous pride in their work and do not want work to affect their personal and social lives. They are the most mobile segment, likely to leave Tesco if they can join a higher-paying competitor. EIU also concluded that more and more workers in the coming decade are going to be pleasure seekers.

- *Live-to-work* employees, not surprisingly, are the most ambitious employee segment with the highest loyalty and commitment. They want to work long hours, desire promotions, seek challenging jobs that offer variety and responsibility, and are willing to put work before their home life. They do not see work as a place for fun or for developing deep friendships.

- *Work-to-live* employees are not interested in working long hours or promotions and don't mind working on repetitive tasks; for them the opportunity to work close to home is important. EIU concluded that work-to-live employees will represent a declining proportion of the working population over the coming decade.

These surveys and additional focus groups also suggested that there were four major motivators for commitment at Tesco. Employees are motivated by the *social context*, more committed when they have colleagues and a manager with whom they enjoy working. They value the *opportunity* associated with a pay and benefits package and career advancement. They are motivated by the *help* they receive in the form of training and development that increase their skills, the opportunity to control their workload, and the communications between them and their manager. Finally, they are motivated by job *content*, a most important theme for many workers. Uninteresting job content was found to be one of the major reasons people leave Tesco.

With the EIU's conclusions and data, the Tesco board could determine how to tailor the employment proposition in a cost-effective and targeted manner to maximize retention over the coming decade. It decided upon a portfolio of offerings and initiatives to present people with more choices that reflected the values and motivations of different employee types. For example, young parents can use child-care vouchers, and the highly ambitious person can choose share options. Earlier initiatives had offered choice mainly in compensation and benefits structure. Now Tesco is building on existing training and development initiatives to expand choice in other aspects of work and the employment deal. So Tesco met its goal of differentiating its employee deal from those of its competitors. The board has since authorized the development of additional technologies, methodologies, and resources to support the Employee Insight Unit, including, for example, datamining analytics developed for customer insight that Tesco is now applying to its groundbreaking employee profiling work.

Analyzing Your Workforce Demographics

Workforce analysis should be an ongoing business process (not an occasional extraordinary effort) to ascertain best actions (both short- and long-term), to ensure adequate talent supply, and to communicate with an organization's leadership in concrete terms what they should know and do about the workforce situation. The process has five basic steps:

- *Diagnose* your business symptoms related to the workforce. Key questions include these: Can your workforce respond in a timely manner to shifting market and business conditions? Are you experiencing high turnover rates—especially in specific professions, functions, roles, or age, gender, or ethnic groups? Are you having trouble filling specific openings? Do you have difficulty identifying and effectively deploying talent? Do you know what the right mix of talent would be?

- *Assess* your current workforce characteristics. Determine employee characteristics and preferences, and make this information as "local" as possible—by business unit, geography, function, role, and profession. Determine your local age distributions, turnover, and employee cost patterns. Try to understand not only employees' preferences, attitudes toward the organization, and overall satisfaction, but also how they define success on the job.

- *Review* your workforce practices. Inventory and evaluate the effectiveness of current employee management processes. How do they facilitate (or sometimes hinder) the flow of talent? Examine practices throughout the "employee life cycle"—identifying and attracting, hiring and incorporating, training and developing, rewarding performance, engaging and retaining, and sustaining relationships (even after employees have departed). Look to best-practice organizations for useful practices that you have not yet deployed.

- *Envision* your future workforce. On the basis of business strategies, objectives, and projections, as well as understanding of local labor markets, describe the workforce you'll need in three to five years. Break it down by capability, function, profession, and location. What would be the ideal demographic mix? How do you want the labor markets to view you as an employer? Insofar as possible, translate this vision into tangible and measurable goals.

- *Move forward* by identifying gaps, prioritizing needs, and implementing solutions. As with any serious initiative, establish accountability, commit resources, and measure progress.

In addition to this ongoing workforce analysis, you may well perform a version of the process centered on a specific known business problem or need. For example, more organizations must determine how to deal with a retirement wave. They should begin by analyzing employee age, turnover, and retirement data and anticipating retirements and the associated organizational risks. As one HR executive told us, "Knowing these statistics helped us to prioritize our programs and also to up-sell them to top management." Next, survey employees to better understand their retirement intentions and refine your projections. Identify which factors will be most important in retaining and motivating mature workers. Then zero in: assess how potential retirement losses among key personnel may impact team performance and corporate knowledge. Identify departments, roles, and skills most susceptible to retirement losses. Assess the experience and capabilities needed for these roles, the amount of training required, and mature workers' fit with these needs.

Now look outside. Analyze the demographics of your traditional talent pools and recruiting communities. Will there be enough candidates to meet projected needs from attrition and business growth? Then put the pieces together, set specific goals, and take action. Describe the age distribution and retirement pattern that you'd like to maximize business performance and continuity. Prioritize retention, succession-planning, and recruiting efforts to target mature employees who will make the most difference to business performance. Take actions such as retaining the part-time services of retirees through a retiree-return program; sharing knowledge and expertise before it walks out the door via coaching, mentoring, and other forms of structured collaboration; and adjusting recruiting, development, and succession-planning processes to offset labor and skills shortages.

From Analysis to Action at the U.K. National Health Service

Health care is in crisis in many Western nations—because of a combination of an aging population (meaning more people with need for care and fewer people to provide it) and increasingly sophisticated treatment (which increases demand and pushes up costs). In the United Kingdom, the National Health Service (NHS) workforce of 1.3 million is subject to the same demographic changes as the population it serves.[6] The average age of health service workers is increasing, and there is a chronic shortage of skills and personnel, particularly nurses and doctors. Financial resources are currently available, but where and how will the Department of Health (DH) and NHS find the skilled people to meet the fast-growing demand for health services? Read on.

Diagnosis: Workforce Modeling

In 2001, DH and NHS established twenty-eight local Workforce Development Confederations to develop workers in their health communities, then integrated them into the twenty-eight Strategic Health Authorities set up in 2003. There has been a major program of change within the NHS involving process redesign, the development of new roles, and a major shift in emphasis in workforce planning from projecting growth trends (i.e., "more of the same") toward focusing on what workforce skills are really needed to meet patients' needs. One of the outcomes of this approach has been to show that the unavailability of the specialist skills of the smaller allied health professions often causes critical blockages in the system. For example, analysis of patient pathways in cancer showed major delays in diagnosis and treatment caused by shortages of radiographers.

Several factors further complicate the issues of physician supply and careers. Younger trainees and practitioners (more than half women) have changing attitudes toward the profession, and many are not interested in a traditional apprenticeship followed by a "buy into a practice" career path. European working-time directives call for reduction in doctors' average working hours to forty-eight hours per week, thus increasing pressure on recruiting and training. Finally, reliance on foreign recruits is increasing, but some of them complain of encountering a glass ceiling limiting their advancement.

Modeling of the nursing workforce has shown that there are significant demographic problems ahead, with the numbers of nurses retiring each year from the workforce set to double between 2005 and 2015. Although the numbers entering nurse training in England each year have been increasing from sixteen thousand in 1995 to around twenty-five thousand now, this figure will not be sufficient to match the predicted annual loss from the workforce by 2015. While further increases in training levels are planned, the NHS would have to hire close to 20 percent of the United Kingdom's college graduates for the home-trained supply to match demand.

Although the majority of health care in the United Kingdom is provided by the NHS, private health-care providers grew rapidly in the 1990s, particularly in the private nursing-home sector, to the point where 25 percent of nurses were employed in the private sector. The NHS has been poor historically in understanding the impact of private sector employers, but with the likelihood of an increasingly mixed economy in health-care provision, it must increasingly understand the whole labor market.

Treatment: Recruiting and Retention

A major aim of the policies to improve recruitment and retention has been to make the NHS the employer of choice. A range of initiatives have been brought together under the Improving Working Lives program:

- *International recruitment.* International recruitment has long been a feature of the medical workforce in the United Kingdom, but in recent years it has become more necessary to recruit overseas for nurses and other allied health professions. There is free movement of labor within the European Union, and the number of recruits from this source has increased in recent years. The largest proportion, however, comes from developing countries, particularly where English is widely spoken, such as the British Commonwealth and the Philippines. Conscious of its need to operate ethically, the British government has negotiated intergovernment agreements with source countries such as South Africa to prevent brain drain of skills in short supply. Consequently, the NHS cannot recruit there. The government has acted to reduce dependence on overseas recruitment for doctors by increasing the number of medical school openings in England by around 40 percent. However, the extent of the nursing workforce makes it extremely difficult to reduce dependence on international recruitment.

- *Broadening the recruiting base.* The NHS has focused on marketing health care as a career to young workers. It offers good job security, a system of lifelong learning, and competitive wages for many entry-level positions. Such programs as the nursing cadets let young people experience the profession before entering professional health-care education. The NHS has targeted the groups significantly underrepresented in the workforce, particularly men and certain ethnic minorities. It has launched a Positively Diverse program to address different equality and diversity issues, including age diversity, and formed Black and Ethnic Minority Staff Networks. Other initiatives will develop more attractive roles for men by, for example, expanding the responsibilities of ambulance paramedics.

- *Recruiting midcareer workers.* Over the last few years, a number of initiatives aimed at midcareer workers have been developed within the NHS. For example, in Greater Manchester an initiative called Delivering the Workforce—The Introduction of Assistant Practitioners targets thirty- to fifty-year-olds, many of them unemployed for some time. To date, the program has attracted mainly women, some of whom have been raising families and undertaking other caring responsibilities. Many of the individuals lack the usual qualifications of the NHS or its education providers. So the trainee assistant practitioners undertake a service-based program of learning to earn a two-year foundation degree, after which they can work as assistant practitioners in the NHS. Greater Manchester already enjoys four hundred fifty trainee assistant practitioners, with another fifteen hundred in the pipeline over the next two years.

- *Flexible work arrangements.* One of the effects of current labor shortages has been a dramatic rise in the use of staff supplied by agencies. Staff are often attracted by the flexibility of working through an agency, combined often with higher rates of pay, particularly for working less desirable shifts (or "unsocial hours," as they're called), weekends, or public holidays. Agency staff is not, however, eligible for the NHS pension scheme and other benefits. NHS Professionals is an initiative aimed at offering individuals the flexibility of agency work combined with access to the pension and other benefits of NHS staff. This not only gives NHS employers greater control over the supply of temporary staff, but also is seen as a way of encouraging agency workers to rejoin the regular workforce in time.

- *Flexible retirement.* NHS pensions are already getting more flexible. For example, while it is a final-salary scheme, the final salary is calculated at the full-time level so as not to penalize part-time workers. There are also tax incentives for continuing contributions between sixty and sixty-five. Managers and employees are being encouraged to understand and make maximum use of those flexibilities already available, and a major review of pension arrangements is currently being undertaken, which should remove most of the remaining barriers to flexible retirement. There are also financial incentive packages for a number of key groups, such as general practitioners, to delay retirement. Older hospital consultants are encouraged to agree to new job plans that reduce the stress of their roles (e.g., spend more time teaching and less time operating).

With these initiatives and a range of others around flexible work, the Improving Working Lives program is having a significant impact on retention.

Treatment: Skills Escalation

The DH and NHS increase the utilization of existing personnel in two innovative ways. The first is *delegating tasks.* Health-care organizations have long strived to make selected tasks doable by less skilled personnel. For instance, X-ray and ultrasound machinery is gradually getting less expensive and complicated and thus more usable by less skilled staff, while the diagnoses themselves must still be done by highly trained personnel. A number of research studies have shown that up to 40 percent of the tasks carried out by doctors and other health professionals do not require their level of training. The creation of new roles can tap underutilized recruitment sources—a good example being the expansion of paramedic roles, which are more attractive to men than some traditional health-care roles.

The second key tactic is *upgrading skills*. The aptly named Skills Escalator program enables interested and capable employees to undergo continued studies and on-the-job training to prepare for performing higher-level, scarce-supply jobs. For example, orderlies escalate their skills to become nurses' aids, and aides escalate to become nurses. The Skills Escalator provides both the mechanisms and the atmosphere that enable and encourage the movement from one career trajectory to another. The Skills Escalator has been underpinned by a radical restructuring of the pay-and-reward scheme for all NHS employees except doctors and top-level managers. This provides direct financial rewards for staff who increase their skills or expand their roles. Pay bands are based on job evaluation, but progression within them is based on an individual assessment against a national knowledge and skills framework. This is underpinned by a commitment to appraisal and personal development plans for all staff, and these policies support a strong drive to produce an upwardly mobile workforce.

Treatment: Physician Career Paths

While physicians are not within the same pay scheme, radical changes are also taking place in medical careers. The traditional training arrangements for doctors in the United Kingdom meant that doctors spent up to fifteen years or more in junior training-grade roles before eventually achieving the status and earning power of a consultant physician. Supply was regulated by time—the more popular the specialty, the longer it took to achieve consultant status. Many who failed to go the distance, disproportionately women and ethnic minorities, were often left stuck in career-grade posts that lacked the status or pay of consultants. This contrasts with the situation in the European Union and the United States, where doctors are required to undergo only three to five years' training after medical school. The U.K. system both discriminates against overseas-trained doctors and potentially restricts the supply of home-trained specialists. The solution is a radical restructuring of medical training into a shorter time-limited sequence. Combined with a move to competence-based assessment, this will free up supply by moving doctors through training faster and making it easier for individuals to reenter training following a break, including many of those currently stuck in career-grade posts.

In summary, the DH and NHS are in a challenging position. They face—on an extraordinarily large scale—the upheavals of population demographics, workforce demographics, and the health-care industry. As public agencies, they can see their priorities and funding shift with the political landscape. They are, however, in the advantageous position of being charged with both delivery of health-care services and training of health-care professionals. Thus, guided by workforce models and plans, they can pursue creative ways, such as the Skills Escalator and the careful distribution of talent, to shape both sides of the workforce supply-demand equation.

Applying What You've Learned

This book has described many actions to improve the performance and retention of different age cohorts and to respond to demographic changes in the workforce. Here are the most important ways to improve your workforce analysis, and then to act upon that information:

- *Enrich your workforce assessment* with both better information and new segmentation—each aimed at understanding how employees really relate to their work and the employer.

- *Get your workforce assessment in motion*, anticipating changes in workforce composition and labor market conditions. Don't just study today's employees.

- *Consult with people in customer research* on how to conduct better employee research.

- *Identify and share best practices.* In the process of analyzing in depth a workforce, or any facet of an enterprise, you inevitably uncover many examples of what works and what doesn't. Don't lose this opportunity to capture best practices and adopt or refine them for use elsewhere in the organization.

- *Measure and track employee engagement*, both overall and by major and important employee segment. Depending on your organization's profile, you might fine-tune work and workplace, or you might address the thoroughly disengaged through outreach and attrition.

- *Measure work enrichment.* Insist that every business improvement initiative—automation, systems implementation, process redesign—set and meet goals for the new work to be more stimulating and responsible than the old.

- *Involve employees in work design.* They are an essential source for understanding the nature and potential shape of work. Involving them in work design, of course, doubles as a means of enriching their work.

- *Automate what you can* and let people do what they're good at—empathizing with customers, applying their cognitive, emotional, and creative intelligence and social skills to communicate, collaborate, and solve complex problems.

- *Insist upon action.* Workforce planning and analysis should shape the goals and operation of all the basic HR processes—recruiting, retention, and so on. Don't make workforce analysis an academic exercise.

13

The Manager's Agenda
for Change

*Setting Strategies in Motion
to Avert a Workforce Crisis*

U NPRECEDENTED CHANGES in workforce demographics pose the threat
of skills and labor shortages. The symptoms—unwanted turnover,
localized labor and skills shortages, retirement waves, a brain drain,
and poor bench strength—are already appearing. To address and forestall these
problems, employers must engage and maintain, in different ways, the commitment of workers at all career stages: young, midcareer, and mature. Along
the way, they must revamp the employment deal to make it more flexible in
meeting employee needs and expectations. That includes not only traditional
compensation and benefits, but also work arrangements and learning opportunities. Changing workforce composition presents both threats and opportunities to large organizations. Early action—which hinges upon overcoming inertia and tackling a seemingly postponable management problem—can turn

the threats into business opportunities in productivity, retention, and customer service. Organizations that put the right management practices in place ahead of the point of necessity or crisis will enjoy both the short- and long-term benefits of superior talent supply.

Three Core Questions for Corporate Leadership

What, then, must organizations and their leaders know and do? There are three basic sets of questions to address:

- *What's our situation?* What shortages will we face? Will they be shortages of skills, labor, or both? When will we face them? How severe will they be? And what are our corresponding opportunities?

- *What are our potential sources of labor and skills supply?* How much relief will each source provide? With what implications and side effects? For example, tapping an underskilled labor pool entails a commitment to training.

- *What actions should we take and when?* How can we mitigate or prevent shortages? How can we cope with or recover from them if they occur? What should we do now to gain business advantage?

Six Core Perspectives

As you determine what actions to take—to cope with changing workforce demographics, to better engage employees of all ages, and to make the most of the employment deals you offer—don't let the actions be isolated efforts. Instead, amplify their impact by shaping them via a coherent and ongoing workforce strategy. And let your strategy be guided by these six perspectives on workers and organizations. They form the basis for our approaches to employment engagement.

- *Consumerism has found the workforce.* People are more informed than ever about labor markets, pay scales, and facets of the employee deal. They are more willing than ever to "shop around" for the right deal, and quite often the most valuable people have learned to "ask for it all." As workforce growth slows, it becomes a buyer's market. Employers must meet people more on their own terms.

- *People want and benefit from organizational affiliation.* We've all heard the prediction of almost all workers becoming "free-agent contractors" without permanent affiliation with any one employer. While worker mobility and part-time work are both on the rise, the need for affiliation remains, even (and sometimes especially) among work-at-home employees. Corporations are far less paternalistic than in the past, and employees far more independent. But people still have a very fundamental and important desire for affiliation, it's good for business performance, and organizations must find ways to satisfy it—for full-time and part-time employees alike.

- *The best source of skilled labor is often people you already know.* Retirees, ex-employees, mature workers who prefer not to retire and employees who can expand their skills—all can be great candidates for increasing your labor pool. Many of the techniques we discuss center on reengaging the people already in affiliation with an organization.

- *The employment deal must be relevant and comprehensive.* There are many ways for employers to fail in the eyes of employees. Employees want engaging work, the opportunity to learn and grow, fair and comprehensive compensation and benefits, work/life balance, supportive management style, a congenial workplace, and an organization with a worthwhile mission and positive image. Serious shortcomings along any of these dimensions can lead employees, especially younger ones, to find more satisfying deals elsewhere.

- *The employment deal must be customized.* Handling an increasing variety—of employees and therefore employee deals—is key to talent management and business success. One-size-fits-all doesn't work anymore in employee management practices, but infinite variety is impractical. Employers must be more flexible and provide more options—in work arrangements, learning, and benefits—for more granular employee segments. This in turn demands that the information systems supporting HR processes be both robust and modular. In the ways they represent information about employees, work processes, performance, and benefits, these systems create—or inhibit—workforce and therefore business flexibility.

- *Human capital is the ultimate business asset.* The organization with the better workforce wins—performing better and changing more readily. But don't equate *better* with only skills and expertise, because that's only one dimension. Human capital has three dimensions, all of which factor in the performance equation. *Intellectual capital* is what people know and learn. *Social capital* is how people form connections and share. *Emotional capital* is how much people are committed to the organization and how much of themselves they're willing to invest in its success.[1]

Five Courses of Action

We recommend that employers do the following to position their organizations for tomorrow's labor market and to improve performance along the way:

- *Get in touch with your workforce demographics.* Develop a better understanding of your workforce and how its characteristics, and those of your potential labor sources, are changing. Put this knowledge in the business context of the workers, skills, and performance levels needed to thrive. Chapter 1 described the demographic forces at work and the challenges they present, and chapter 12 focused on understanding your own organization's workforce demographics.

- *Refine your workforce strategy.* Determine how you will ensure that your supply of labor and skills is going to meet future business demand. Borrow techniques from marketing and determine what brand or brands the organization must promote among employees and in the labor marketplace. Determine how you will leverage changing workforce demographics to forward business strategies in areas like growth, innovation, and customer relationships. Chapter 2 discussed the challenges for management and outlined the components of a workforce strategy.

- *Adjust management practices to enhance both engagement and productivity.* Improve your ability to refine and customize all facets of the employment deal—including work arrangements, learning opportunities, and compensation and benefits—to meet the changing needs and motivate the performance of workers of all ages and backgrounds. This is the heart of the analysis, recommendations, cases, and techniques that we have shared, first with a perspective on career cohorts in chapters 3 to 8, then with a perspective on the employment deal in chapters 9 to 11.

- *Make the work itself engaging.* The most influential driver of employee engagement, day in and day out, is the work itself. Is it

personally fulfilling and worthwhile? Does it enable people to exercise
their capabilities and develop new ones? In order to retain the best
employees in tightening labor markets, and to motivate some to continue working past the point of possible retirement, organizations
must build upon a foundation of relevant, flexible, and enjoyable
work. Chapter 12 explored this issue.

- *Lobby for pension and benefits reform.* All of the actions we've
  recommend in this book are within a corporation's control. However,
  a central recommendation—to offer flexible retirement as a means
  of maintaining your talent supply—would be much easier for corporations to implement if pension laws and benefits coverage were re-
  formed and simplified. We urge employers in the United States to
  lobby, individually and collectively, for changes (discussed in chapter 4) that would make it easier and more attractive for mature people
  to continue working. But don't wait for Washington to act—you can
  and should establish retiree-return programs and other variations on
  flexible retirement today.

The Executive Agenda

Fundamental shifts in workforce demographics will affect every part of your
organization, demanding changes not just to human resources practices, but
also to management methods generally. The temperature of change is increasing gradually, and many organizations are lulled into ignoring the heat.
But the time to sense the heat and get moving has arrived. CEOs, general managers, and HR leaders must help their organizations address the challenges of
changing workforce composition and turn the threats into opportunities.

To do so, you must think both long term and short term about these
issues. On one hand, plan on leaving your organization the legacy of a secure
talent supply; on the other, insist on results from *every* workforce management initiative. You must treat workforce composition as both a human
resources challenge and a marketplace opportunity—can you present a better face to the customer than the competition can? You must develop other
leaders who appreciate changing workforce demographics and know what to
do about them. Talent supply should hold a permanent and prominent place
in the executive agenda. And you must charter your HR organization to make
the enterprise more flexible. HR isn't about personnel administration—it's

about attracting talented people and developing the capabilities for business performance, growth, and change.

Even if your organization is not yet facing serious skills or labor shortages, you still must be ready for a different, older, and more varied workforce. Demographics move at the speed of life. Organizations that adapt to the evolving workforce mix early and effectively will attract and retain better talent and thus hold competitive advantage. They will turn potential threats into realized opportunities.

Best of all, you can apply these management techniques *now* to improve business performance, cost structures, and employee retention today.

Readers' Discussion Guide

T HIS BOOK covers demographic and related trends that will significantly affect corporations and their workforces, our lives outside the workplace, and the economic and social well-being and political policies of societies around the world. The book also gives managers practical advice for thriving during the coming shortage of skills and talent.

This section of the book guides readers through the process of reflecting upon and discussing the trends and their implications for organizations, and then setting organizational priorities and action plans.

The guide is organized thematically, with sets of questions corresponding to individual or pairs of chapters. The first section offers a series of personal questions that will help you to ground later discussions in your own experience and that of your colleagues. The second section looks at the big picture—assessing your organization's workforce situation and developing its workforce strategy. We invite you to discuss these questions as a management team, then work through the remainder of the guide, then revisit these big-picture questions at the end in light of all intervening discussion.

Reflecting on Your Work and Career

Whatever your age and career stage, think back on your work experiences, your employers, and the roles of work in your life. Answer and discuss these questions.

1. What has been your most exciting and personally fulfilling work experience? The least? What were the major factors behind each situation?

2. What has motivated you to change jobs, employers, or careers? Has your career ever stalled and then been rekindled? Under what circumstances and by what means?

3. Which job or organization has enjoyed your fullest engagement—that is, your going the extra mile for the enterprise's success? What motivated such engagement?

4. At which stages of your life have you had a satisfying balance of work and the rest of your life? At which stages have you struggled with work/life balance or mix?

5. Think about your generational traits, including the most formative experiences of your youth. How have these early experiences and attitudes shaped you as an employee? How do you see these generational traits affecting today's multigenerational workplace?

6. Have you tried flexible work arrangements? When and why? What did the arrangements do for or mean to you?

7. At which points did learning dramatically affect your career? How did you learn—through formal training, a stretch assignment, a management development program, a mentor?

8. At which points has your compensation and benefits package best suited your needs and lifestyle? When did it seem inadequate or disjointed, and how did you compensate?

9. What does *retirement* mean to you, and how do you envision spending your time? Do you even plan to retire? When? How would your spouse (or significant other or best friend) answer these questions?

10. When *can* you retire? Have you evaluated your financial situation and current employment deal to determine when and where you can afford to retire?

11. Reflecting on earlier stages of your career, how have your needs, attitudes, and motivations as an employee evolved? How has your relationship to work itself changed?

12. If you had the next thirty years to begin a whole new career, what would you do?

Assessing Your Situation and Developing Your Strategy
(see chapters 2 and 12)

To avoid the otherwise inevitable workforce crunches, organizations must have forward-thinking strategies. That requires understanding your organization's demographic trends—not just the statistics but also the drivers of performance and retention. Answer these questions for the organization at large and, where appropriate, for specific important employee segments, such as high performers and key managers.

1. What's your workforce situation? What shortages will you face? Involving which skills? When?

2. Where and when will retirement waves hit you the hardest? Which key skills and experience must you retain?

3. What motivates the people in your organization? What are their passions? Why do employees join, stay, and leave your organization?

4. Which skill sets will drive the success of your business strategy? Which types of talent will help you to meet your long-term business objectives? Which values and attributes will best support and align with your organization and leadership?

5. What are your potential sources of labor and skills? How much supply will each source provide? With what implications and side effects?

6. What feeder programs (schools, degrees, work experience) are most critical to the development of your key talent pools? How "well stocked" are these feeders?

7. What do your organization's older employees want to do when they retire, and under what circumstances might they still want to work? Which jobs in your organization are most suitable to older, project-based, or part-time workers?

8. What are some of the actions you might take to mitigate or prevent shortages? To cope with and recover from existing shortages, if you have them already? To attract and retain employees with the values and attributes you need most?

9. Review the "Checklist of Trends to Count On." Do you have a handle on each—on how it will affect your organization and what you must do to prepare for or cope with it?

Retiring Retirement for Mature Workers
(see chapters 3 and 4)

To prepare for the coming shortage of skills and talent, organizations must learn how to use the skills and energy of mature workers—retaining them, revitalizing them, and even attracting new ones to the organization. As individuals, we must plan for a long period (often twenty-plus years) of active, healthy life post traditional "retirement." How individuals choose to spend those years, and how corporations create conditions for productive employment, will seriously affect corporate success and overall economic health.

1. What is the age profile of your organization's new hires? What is your track record in hiring other companies' retirees? Workforce returnees age fifty-five and over? How well are you tapping these varied talent sources?

2. What are your working assumptions about the pros and cons of hiring mature workers? For which roles do you seek mature candidates? For which roles do you avoid them? Why? On average, are you more or less likely to offer a job to a mature candidate instead of a younger one? How do you account for any difference?

3. What's your pitch to mature workers? What do you offer that meets their needs at their career stage? I'm a sixty-year-old job candidate. Recruit me.

4. Do you have retirees working as contractors? If so, are there patterns in the disciplines contracted and the arrangements made with them?

5. Are there signs of age bias in your organization? Do older workers have equal access to promotion and training opportunities, for example?

6. What do mature employees want in work opportunities and benefits, both before and after the point of retirement? Who wants to postpone retirement or return as working retirees, and why?

7. Do your pension or benefit plans—and any proposed changes to them—facilitate or impede the hiring of mature workers and the implementation of flexible retirement? Do these plans motivate or discourage those who want to phase into or postpone retirement? What are the implications for employee and talent retention?

8. How do government regulations restrict the structuring of your pension and benefit plans or inhibit them from meeting your business goals and your employees' needs? What would you like the government to change? Are you making your voice heard among policy makers and legislators?

Rekindling the Careers of Midcareer Workers
(see chapters 5 and 6)

As the large bulge of baby boomers encounters midcareer frustrations, organizations must creatively rekindle the work experiences of this workforce cohort. To understand and encourage career rejuvenation among midcareer workers in your organization, ask the following questions.

1. Do you know who your keepers are? Beside those in the leadership or management track, who has the skills, experiences, attitude, and adaptability that you need most?

2. How many of your midcareer employees need some rejuvenation of their skills or careers? Which renewal methods hold greatest potential in your business?

3. How freely does the lifeblood of experience and talent flow in your organization? Can employees move around? What is clogging the arteries? Would a more systematic approach to mentoring improve the flow?

4. How well do you make each job assignment a win-win for business performance and employee growth? Can you tap people for fresh assignments when their personal circumstances change?

5. Can you and do you encourage employees to change careers within your organization? If not, why not?

6. Do you offer sabbaticals? Under what circumstances, and with what results? If not, why not?

7. What is your track record in hiring midcareer workers? Do your hiring practices seem in or out of proportion within your overall hiring mix?

8. For which jobs do you avoid interviewing midcareer people? Why? For which jobs are midcareer people the best candidates? What implicit biases are influencing you and fellow managers?

9. Do you actively recruit people who are reentering the workforce, changing careers, or downsized (despite their skills and talent) by other companies? If not, why not? What special provisions would help you to incorporate them and rekindle their careers?

10. What's your pitch to midcareer workers? What do you offer that meets their needs at their career stage? I'm a forty-year-old job candidate. Recruit me.

Retaining the Talent of Young Workers
(see chapters 7 and 8)

If your business needs a sizable influx of young talent, then you must excel at attracting, incorporating, and satisfying this demanding workforce cohort. To gauge your ability to connect with young workers, ask these questions.

1. Which changes, if any, have younger job candidates and new hires requested? Which recruiting channels do they prefer?

2. How long do new employees take to learn their jobs, assimilate into the organization, contribute to results, and feel part of the enterprise?

3. How have you accelerated and improved the incorporation process? What works and what—such as current assumptions about learning curves—gets in the way? Which incorporation strategy—trial by fire, boot camp, mentored entry—best fits your business and each major employee segment?

4. How do young employees experience your organization? What do they like least about the company and its operations? What does the corporate brand mean to them?

5. What are your tenure levels and turnover rates for employees under thirty-five? What are reasonable targets? Specifically, what percent of new hires under thirty-five stay with your organization for more than three years? For those who get over the three-year hump, which aspects of their experience influenced them most?

6. How are you doing on the three Ss (say, stake, stimulus) and three Rs (responsibility, recognition, respect)? What are your strengths and weaknesses?

7. How well do you communicate (two-way, not broadcast) with young workers? Do you engage in the types and frequencies of communication that they prefer?

8. What do your physical work spaces say about who you are and how you operate? What messages do they send to young workers?

9. How often are managers in your organization surprised when young employees quit?

10. When you have an unwanted departure, do you understand why the employee is leaving? Do you track and act upon this information? Do you keep the door open and encourage the person to return?

11. Do you know which ex-employees you'd really like to rehire? Where they are now?

Implementing Flexible Work Arrangements
(see chapter 9)

Flexibility emerges as a common theme across all three workforce cohorts—each for somewhat different reasons, but all important to meeting employees' needs. You are likely to find that the flexible work arrangements described in this book are already in evidence, here and there, in your organization. But they probably aren't being offered systematically or managed to maximum benefit of the business. To gain an understanding of how flex retirement and many other forms of flexible work arrangements can work more effectively in your organization, ask the following questions.

1. Where do your operations lend themselves to flexible work arrangements? Which types and patterns of flex work make sense for you?

2. What are the potential business benefits of flexible work arrangements—in terms of cost, performance, and employee engagement and retention?

3. Which work arrangements do your employees want and need?

4. How far are you from implementing flex work at a scale that makes a difference to the business? What barriers, both physical (work design, technology) and attitudinal ("I need to see my employees working"), are in the way?

5. How strong and consistent is management's commitment to make flex work succeed for both employees and the business? How do you demonstrate and document that commitment?

6. Where might you target initial flex retirement efforts for maximum business benefit?

7. How can you smooth people's transition from traditional full-time work to flex retirement?

8. What's already going on with respect to providing people with more flexible work arrangements or career deceleration opportunities? Do you have a systematic program, or is each such arrangement ad hoc?

Enhancing Learning and Development
(see chapters 10 and 6)

The role of corporations in adult education will rise, as more employees look to their work experiences for new learning and continued development. To understand the current and potential role of learning in your organization— as an approach for rapid incorporation, a mechanism for reengagement, or an essential means of retooling the workforce with new skills for new challenges—ask these questions.

1. What must the business learn to meet performance expectations and execute strategy? Which areas of knowledge and expertise must be absolutely cutting edge?

2. What and how do different segments of your workforce want and need to learn? Where does the lack of skills and knowledge hamper business performance?

3. How well—and consistently—do you meet employees' needs and expectations for learning and development?

4. Is learning an everyday thing in your organization? Embedded in the daily work and interactions of employees? Or do you equate learning with an infrequent classroom session?

5. How must your learning content and methods change as workforce composition changes?

6. How full is your leadership pipeline? Where is it leaking? Is it delivering leadership talent and experience as you need it? Is development of the next two generations of leaders on track? Must you act now to accelerate their development or tailor it to today's business conditions?

7. What is the age mix of employees participating in your leadership development program? Is this mix right?

8. Are you leveraging your leadership development program to rekindle careers and reengage key employees?

9. How steadily have you committed to and invested in leadership development? What must you do to stay the course?

10. Do all employees genuinely believe that they have development and career advancement opportunities?

Customizing Compensation and Benefits
(see chapter 11)

As the variety of needs and preferences of employees increase, and as competition for talent heats up, the ability to customize employment deals will differentiate the winning organizations from the also-rans. This evolution from "equal" to "fair, but not necessarily equal" will break new ground in human resources management. To assess how compensation and benefits serve employees and employer alike, ask the following questions.

1. Do you pay employees for a clearly articulated mix of performance, skill, experience, attitude, and behavior? Do employees sense that their compensation is genuinely earned?

2. How well do compensation and benefits fit into your overall performance management system? How healthy is that system to begin with? Is it driving top performance from your top employees?

3. How do compensation and benefits support your goals, not just in recruiting and retention, but also in business performance?

4. How much variety can your system support?

5. What's your strategy for controlling health-care, pension, and other benefits costs without compromising your business goals, including employee satisfaction and retention?

6. How do compensation and benefits programs enable—or impede—flexible work arrangements and flexible retirement in your organization?

7. How will you adjust compensation and benefits as the workforce ages and its composition changes? Can you handle increasing variety?

8. How much do employees understand, utilize, and value your compensation and benefits offerings?

Excelling at Employee Engagement
(see chapter 12)

Low engagement is a significant—and growing—issue, especially among the baby boom generation, who, as they enter their forties and fifties, are increasingly questioning the role of work in their lives. To understand how work drives engagement in your organization, ask the following questions.

1. How engaged are your employees? Do you know? Especially for those you rely on most? Are you measuring the most important indicators of engagement?

2. Which factors drive engagement up and down in your organization? How does this vary by employee group?

3. Do employees find their work stimulating? Where in the organization is this most the case? Least? What can you learn from the comparison?

4. Which work can you structure more efficiently or automate altogether, to free workers for more "knowledge-able" and engaging tasks?

5. Have you overly structured and automated aspects of work so that workers cannot really exercise their capabilities?

6. Do your business improvement projects seek the optimal mix of people and automation? Where have you optimized? Where not? What does the comparison teach you?

7. Do you really understand the portfolio of work that your organization does and how this mix is changing? Where and how often do your organizational structures, information systems, and management methods interfere with employees' work?

8. Describe the workplace atmosphere. (Groups should write down some descriptive words individually, then compare responses.) Is it congenial? Do you yourself enjoy it? How does the work shape the workplace, and vice versa?

Further Reading

If you would like to continue exploring the major themes we have discussed, we recommend the following books:

Age Power: How the 21st Century Will Be Ruled by the New Old. Ken Dychtwald, New York: Putnam, 1999.

Age Works: What Corporate America Must Do to Survive the Graying of the Workforce. Beverly Goldberg, New York: Free Press, 2000.

The Democratic Enterprise: Liberating Your Business with Freedom, Flexibility and Commitment. Lynda Gratton, London: FT Prentice Hall, 2004.

Geeks & Geezers: How Era, Values, and Defining Moments Shape Leaders. Warren G. Bennis and Robert J. Thomas, Boston: Harvard Business School Press, 2002.

Generations at Work: Managing the Clash of Veterans, Boomers, Xers, and Nexters in Your Workplace. Ron Zemke, Claire Raines, and Bob Filipczak, New York: American Management Association, 2000.

A Nation at Work: The Heldrich Guide to the American Workforce. Herbert A. Schaffner and Carl E. Van Hord, eds., New Brunswick, NJ: Rutgers University Press, 2003.

The Power Years: A User's Guide to the Rest of Your Life. Ken Dychtwald and Daniel J. Kadlec, Hoboken, NJ: Wiley, 2005.

Notes

Part I

1. Peter F. Drucker, "The Next Society," *Economist*, November 3, 2001.

Chapter One

1. In its 2003 "Older Workers Survey," the Society for Human Resource Management (SHRM) reports that one-third of HR professionals say their companies are doing nothing to prepare for demographic change in the workforce. Those who say they are preparing are focused on training and succession planning. Only 7 percent have plans to deal with an anticipated retirement wave.

2. Unless otherwise cited, all of the data in this chapter on size, growth, participation, and composition of the U.S. workforce is drawn from the Bureau of Labor Statistics.

3. Committee for Economic Development, "America's Work Force After the Baby Boomers: The Surprising Role that Immigration Will Play," *CED in Brief*, http://www.ced.org/newsroom/brief.shtml; and the Segal Company, "The Aging of Aquarius: The Baby Boom Generation Matures," *Segal Special Report*, February 2001.

4. The study, *Demography Is De$tiny*, was led by the Concours Group and Age Wave and was sponsored by thirty major organizations. It led to a companion project, *The New Employee/Employer Equation*, in which Harris Interactive conducted a poll of over seventy-seven hundred employees nationwide.

5. The estimate was based on Bureau of Labor Statistics labor force projections but was not made by the BLS. See Howard N. Fullerton Jr. and Mitra Toossi, "Employment Outlook: 2000–2010," *Monthly Labor Review*, November 2001, 21, for the labor force projections. This original estimate of 10 million was often cited. See, for example, Carroll Lachnit, "Brave New World," *Workforce*, March 2003, 8; and Peter Francese, "The American Workforce—Number of Service Workers Still Growing," *American Demographics*, February 1, 2002.

6. Testimony of Edward E. Potter, president, Employment Policy Foundation, before the Special Committee on Aging of the U.S. Senate, September 20, 2004, 5.

7. Employment Policy Foundation, "Challenges Facing the American Workplace, Summary of Findings," *The Seventh-Annual Workplace Report*, 2002, http://www.epf.org/pubs/labordayreports/2002/ldrsummary2002.asp.

8. Jon E. Hilsenrath, "Forrester Revises Loss Estimates to Overseas Jobs," *Wall Street Journal*, May 17, 2004; and Brent Schlender, "Peter Drucker Sets Us Straight," *Fortune*, December 29, 2003.

9. Stephen Baker, "The Coming Battle for Immigrants," *BusinessWeek*, August 26, 2002; and "The New Demographics," *Economist*, November 3, 2001.

10. Employment Policy Foundation, "Challenges Facing the American Workplace."

11. Ibid.

12. Peter Cappelli, "Will There *Really* Be a Labor Shortage?" *Organizational Dynamics*, August 2003, 221–233.

13. *NACE Journal* (National Association of Colleges and Employers), Summer 2004.

14. "Strategies to Retain Older Workers: Balancing Retirement Promises with a Changing Workforce," Watson Wyatt presentation at Wharton School conference "Reinventing the Retirement Paradigm," April 26–27, 2004.

15. Testimony of Edward E. Potter, 7.

16. Employment Policy Foundation, "Challenges Facing the American Workplace."

17. Amie Jamieson, Hyon B. Shin, and Jennifer Day, "Voting and Registration in the Election of November 2000," *Current Population Reports*, U.S. Census Bureau, February 2002.

18. Ken Dychtwald, *Age Power* (New York: Putnam, 1999), 20.

19. Note that the 15 percent increase in working-age population from 2000 to 2020 is half the rate experienced in 1980 to 2000. In absolute terms, the 2000–2020 increase in working-age population is roughly 10 million people fewer than the increases of 1960–1980 and 1980–2000. The working-age population in the United States is growing far more slowly than the accustomed pace.

20. *Demography Is De$tiny* and *The New Employee/Employer Equation*.

Chapter Two

1. Unless otherwise cited, all of the data in this chapter on size, growth, participation, and composition of the U.S. workforce is drawn from the Bureau of Labor Statistics.

2. "Feds Undercount Illegal Aliens," United Press International, March 16, 2001, http://www.newsmax.com.

3. *The New Employee/Employer Equation* survey, conducted in 2004 by Harris Interactive for the Concours Group and Age Wave, found that 66 percent of employees plan to work at least part-time after retiring. AARP reports similar findings in "Staying Ahead of the Curve 2003: The AARP Working in Retirement Study," September 2003.

Part II

1. Confucius, *Analects* 2:4.

Chapter Three

1. Material in this chapter is based on Ken Dychtwald, Tamara Erickson, and Bob Morison, "It's Time to Retire Retirement," *Harvard Business Review*, March 2004.

2. Danny Hakim, "With Pedal to the Metal and Stogie in His Pocket, Bob Lutz Is Back," *New York Times*, October 23, 2002.

3. David Welch, "GM's Design Push Picks Up Speed," *BusinessWeek*, July 18, 2005.

4. Bernard Weinraub, "Rock's Bad Boys Grow Up but Not Old," *New York Times*, September 26, 2002.

5. William Safire, "Never Retire," *New York Times*, January 24, 2005.

6. AARP, "Staying Ahead of the Curve: The AARP Work and Career Study," September 2002.

7. On the topic of strengths and limitations of older workers, see, for example, Deborah Parkinson, "Voices of Experience: Mature Workers in the Future Workforce," The Conference Board, 2002, 64–69; Sandra E. Rix, "Health and Safety Issues in an Aging Workforce," AARP Public Policy Institute, May 2001; Michael Weinper, "Catering to the Silver-Collar Crowd Can Create a Golden Workplace Opportunity," *Managed Healthcare Executive*, December 2001, 38–41; Tara Parker-Pope, "Health Matters: Work May Hold One Key to a Longer Life," *Wall Street Journal*, June 28, 2004; Alice Dembner, "New Research Affirms Seniors' Mental Abilities," *Boston Globe*, December 22, 2003; and testimony of Dr. Sharon A. Brangman, professor and division chief, geriatric medicine, SUNY Upstate Medical University, before the Special Committee on Aging of the U.S. Senate, September 20, 2004, 7.

8. "American Business and Older Employees: A Summary of Findings," AARP, 2000.

9. Testimony of Joseph Eichelkraut, president, Southwest Airlines Pilots' Association, before the Special Committee on Aging of the U.S. Senate, September 14, 2004, 3; and Sally B. Donnelly, "Is 60 Too Old?" *Time*, September 30, 2002.

10. David Wallis, "Act 2.0," *Wired*, May 2000.

11. Unless otherwise cited, all statistics in this section are drawn from *The New Employee/Employer Equation*. This research project included a nationwide survey of over seventy-seven hundred employees conducted in June 2004 by Harris Interactive for the Concours Group and Age Wave. Note that all these statistics describe the fifty-five-and-over working population, not the population at large.

12. AARP, "Staying Ahead of the Curve 2003: The AARP Working in Retirement Study," September 2003.

13. Bureau of Labor Statistics. See also the University of Michigan's ongoing "Health and Retirement Survey," http://hrsonline.isr.umich.edu/, for data on early retirees and retirement patterns.

14. Interviews with Stephen Wing, December 2002 and November 2003.

Chapter Four

1. Dayton Fandray, "Gray Matters," *Workforce*, July 2000.

2. AARP, "Staying Ahead of the Curve: The AARP Work and Career Study," September 2002.

3. Material in this chapter is based on Ken Dychtwald, Tamara Erickson, and Bob Morison, "It's Time to Retire Retirement," *Harvard Business Review*, March 2004.

4. Stephen M. Wing, "HR Voice: CVS Hiring/Training Program Helps Disadvantaged," *Human Resource Executive*, September 10, 2002; and Joe Mullich, "They Don't Retire Them, They Hire Them," *Workforce*, December 2003, 49–54.

5. Alison Maitland, "Inside Track: A Fresh Start for Older Employees," *Financial Times*, January 22, 2002.

6. Wing, "HR Voice"; Mullich, "They Don't Retire Them, They Hire Them"; and interviews with Stephen Wing, December 2002 and November 2003; Jim Wing, November 2003; and Jean Penn, November 2003.

7. Interviews with Stephen Wing.

8. Catherine Johansson, "A Store of Experience," Orange County Register, May 8, 2004; http://www.homedepot.com; and Bruce Shutan, "Feeling Right at Home: Home Depot Dangles a Broad Benefits Package to Woo Older Workers," http://www.agewave.com/media_maddy/press11_04.html.

9. http://www.walmartstores.com and Senior Employment Program, http://www.sremploy.org/older_workers.html; and Robert S. Menchin, *New Work Opportunities for Older Americans* (New York: toExcel, 2000), 123.

10. "Employment Trends: As the Workforce Ages . . ." BusinessWeek.com, June 28, 2001.

11. Committee for Economic Development, "New Opportunities for Older Workers," 1999, 43; and interview with Jack McCarthy, November 2003.

12. "Capitalizing on an Aging Workforce: Phased Retirement and Other Options," William M. Mercer, April 2001.

13. http://www.mitre.org and interviews with Bill Albright, December 2002 and November 2003.

14. Interview with Ronald Coleman, December 2003.

15. Interview with Bob Bennie, December 2003.

16. Interview with Theresa Powers, December 2003.

17. Interviews with Liz Thien-Reich, December 2002 and November 2003. Interview with Jim Fornango, November 2003.

18. Kevin Johnson, "FBI Taps Retiree Experience for Temporary Jobs," USA Today, October 3, 2002; and Richard B. Schmitt, "Exodus of Staff Hobbles the FBI," Los Angeles Times, December 13, 2004.

19. Interviews with Nancy Tootle, December 2002 and November 2003.

20. Maitland, "Inside Track."

21. Employment Policy Foundation, "Phased Retirement: Its Time Has Come," *the balancingact*, April 15, 2003.

22. For a detailed discussion of the impediments, see the Urban Institute, "Legal and Institutional Impediments to Partial Retirement and Part-Time Work by Older Workers," November 2002.

23. Employment Policy Foundation, "The Facts Behind Retiree Health Benefits," *factsheet*, October 7, 2004.

24. Testimony of Vincent E. Kerr, MD, director, health-care management, Ford Motor Company, before the Subcommittee on Employer-Employee Relations of the Committee on Education and the Workforce, U.S. House of Representatives, May 16, 2002.

25. "The Age Wave," CBSNews.com, August 10, 2003, and *60 Minutes* segment, http://www.cbsnews.com/stories/2003/08/08/60minutes/main567331.shtml.

26. Employment Policy Foundation, "Phased Retirement."

Chapter Five

1. Carol Hymowitz, "Baby Boomers Seek New Ways to Escape Career Claustrophobia," *Wall Street Journal*, June 24, 2003.

2. Unless otherwise cited, all statistics in this section are drawn from *The New Employee/Employer Equation*. This research project included a nationwide survey of over seventy-seven hundred employees conducted in June 2004 by Harris Interactive for the Concours Group and Age Wave.

Chapter Six

1. Interviews with Nancy Tootle, December 2002 and November 2003.

2. Joe Mullich, "Let Your People Go," *Workforce*, February 2005, http://www.workforce.com.

3. Carol Hymowitz, "Baby Boomers Seek New Ways to Escape Career Claustrophobia," *Wall Street Journal*, June 24, 2003.

4. Rick N. Garnitz, "Semiretirement: A Practical Alternative for Boomers," *Employee Benefits Journal*, June 2002; and interviews with Sandy Aird, December 2002 and Daniel Gruber, December 2003.

5. Interview with Sandy Aird.

6. "Forever Young: Don't Go Yet," *Economist*, March 27, 2004.

7. Interviews with Michael Wren and Tim Sands of the Department of Health, and Rachael Charlton of the Greater Manchester Workforce Development Confederation, April 2003.

8. Thea Singer, "Radical Sabbaticals," *Inc.*, August 2002.

9. Fara Warner, "Inside Intel's Mentoring Movement," *Fast Company*, April 2002, 116.

10. CSX is described in Marilynne Miles Gray and Dr. William A. Gray, "Mentoring the Many Faces of Diversity," CMSI Corporate Mentoring Solutions, Inc., http://www.mentoring-solutions.com/pdfs/many_faces_diversity.pdf. Case studies on Intel, Agilent,

Southwest Airlines, and others are available from MediaPro, Inc., http://www.mediapro
.com/services/mentoring/mentoring-CaseStudies.html.

11. Matt M. Starcevich, "What Is Unique About Reverse Mentoring, Survey Results," Center for Coaching and Mentoring, 2001, http://www.coachingandmentoring.com/reversementoringresults.htm.

12. E-mail exchanges with Marguerite Foxon, March and August 2005.

13. Interview with Anne Knapp, March 2005.

14. Hewitt Associates, "Managing Time Off 2000/2001," 2001.

15. "Time Out for Workers," *Innovation*, July 10, 2002.

16. Gene Koretz, "Hazardous to Your Career," *BusinessWeek*, January 17, 2000.

17. http://www.intel.com; and "Best Companies to Work For," *Fortune*, January 20, 2003.

18. http://www.arrow.com; Gail Repsher Emery, "A Rest for the Best," *Washington Technology*, July 30, 2001; http://www.linchris.com/sabbatical.htm; and Jeff Mauzy and Richard Harriman, "Creating a Climate in Which Corporate Designers Can Flourish," DMI eBulletin, May 2003.

19. Singer, "Radical Sabbaticals."

20. Interview with Joan McDade, August 2003.

21. Toni Kistner, "ARO's Sweet Success," *Network World*, February 10, 2003.

22. Interview with Michael Amigoni, November 2003.

23. Interview with Joe Frick and Rob Croner, June 2003.

24. Douglas A. Ready, "How Storytelling Builds Next Generation Leaders," *MIT Sloan Management Review*, Summer 2002, 63–69; and interview with Zabeen Hirji, June 2003.

Chapter Seven

1. Unless otherwise cited, all statistics in this chapter are drawn from *The New Employee/Employer Equation*. This research project included a nationwide survey of over seventy-seven hundred employees conducted in June 2004 by Harris Interactive for the Concours Group and Age Wave.

2. "Survey: The Young," *Economist*, December 23, 2000.

Chapter Eight

1. Vladimir Pucik and Alum Kahn, "People Practices at Cisco Systems," International Institute for Management Development, 2000; and K. Subhadra, "Recruiting—The Cisco Way," Icfaian Centre for Management Research, 2002.

2. Charles Fishman, "Whole Foods Is All Teams," *Fast Company*, April–May 1996, 103; and Charles Fishman, "The Anarchist's Cookbook," *Fast Company*, July 2004, 70.

3. Matthew Boyle, "Joe Galli's Army," *Fortune*, December 17, 2002; e-mail exchange with Cari Davidson, July 2005; and http://www.newellrubbermaid.com/newellco/careers/phoenixInitiative.jhtml?id=id4.

4. Chuck Salter, "Insanity Inc.," *Fast Company*, January 1999; Noel Tichy, "No Ordinary Boot Camp," *Harvard Business Review*, April 2001; Thomas J. DeLong and Michael Paley, "Trilogy University," Case 9-403-012 (Boston: Harvard Business School, 2002); "Trilogy Software: High Performance Company of the Future?" http://www.wiley.com/college/man/schermerhorn332879/site/tour/ic/page00.htm; and e-mail exchange with Eric Levine, July 2005.

5. Laird Harrison, "We're All the Boss," *Time*, April 8, 2002; Glenn Hasek, "The Right Chemistry," *Industry Week*, March 6, 2000; Dawn Anfuso, "Core Values Shape W. L. Gore's Innovative Culture," *Workforce*, March 1999; Paul C. Judge, "How Will Your Company Adapt?" *Fast Company*, December 2001; and e-mail exchange with Heidi Cofran, March 2005.

6. Hasek, "The Right Chemistry."

7. Interview with Steve Nesbitt, March 2003.

8. On GE Capital, see Alan M. Webber, "How Business Is a Lot Like Life," *Fast Company*, April 2001; on Intel, see Sumantra Ghoshal and Christopher Bartlett, *The Individualized Corporation* (New York: HarperCollins, 1997), 118; and on Continental Airlines, see Robert F. Harley, *Management Mistakes and Successes* (New York: John Wiley & Sons, 2001), 116.

9. Ron Zemke, Claire Raines, and Bob Filipczak, *Generations at Work* (New York: Amacom, 2000), 171–174.

10. Anthony DiRomualdo, "The Next Generation Company: Creating a High Performance, High Fulfillment Workplace," Next Generation Consulting, 2003; Scott Kirsner, "Total Teamwork: SEI Investments," *Fast Company*, April 1998; and e-mail exchange with Dana Grosser, March 2005.

11. Janet Wiscombe, "Rewards Get Results," *Workforce*, April 2002.

12. Andy Law, *Open Minds: 21st Century Business Lessons and Innovations from St. Luke's* (London: Orion Business, 1998); and e-mail exchange with Liz Vater, May 2005.

13. Zemke, Raines, and Filipczak, *Generations at Work*, 166–170.

14. Vladimir Pucik, "People Practices at SAS," case study, International Institute for Management Development, December 1, 2001.

15. Interview with Stacy Goetzmann, April 2003.

16. Jennifer Koch Laabs, "Thinking Outside the Box at The Container Store," *Workforce*, March 2001; http://www.thecontainerstore.com; interview with Carolyn McMannama, June 2005; and Benchmark Communications Ltd., "Best Practices in Managing HR," 2002.

17. Interview with Steve Nesbitt, March 2003.

18. Christopher A. Bartlett and Meg Wozny, "Microsoft: Competing on Talent (A)," Case 9-300-001 (Boston: Harvard Business School, 2001).

19. Scott Kirsner, "Hire Today, Gone Tomorrow?" *Fast Company*, August 1998.

20. Ibid.

21. Ibid.

22. Ibid; and e-mail exchange with Laura Masset, March 2005.

Part III

1. Mary Barnett Gilson, *What's Past Is Prologue* (New York: Harper, 1940).

Chapter Nine

1. "22nd Annual Patterson Lecture," Northwestern University Transportation Center, April 9, 2003.

2. "Blue Pumpkin and JetBlue Airways Reinvent Customer Service," *CRM Today*, October 16, 2002. For details on JetBlue, see Chuck Salter, "Calling JetBlue," "On the Runway," and "And Now the Hard Part," *Fast Company*, May 2004.

3. Based on Thomas G. Moehrle, "The Evolution of Compensation in a Changing Economy," *Compensation and Working Conditions*, Bureau of Labor Statistics, Fall 2001, which was expanded to become chapter 2 of *Report on the American Workforce 2001*, Bureau of Labor Statistics, 2002.

4. SHRM/SHRM Foundation, "2003 Benefits Survey." A 2002 survey by Hewitt Associates returned similar results; Sally Roberts, "Companies Slow to Adopt Alternative Work Options," *Business Insurance*, April 8, 2002.

5. *The New Employee/Employer Equation* survey, conducted in 2004 by Harris Interactive for the Concours Group and Age Wave.

6. Interview with Michael Amigoni, November 2003.

7. Sarah Fister Gale, "Formalized Flextime: The Perk That Brings Productivity," *Workforce Week*, October 10, 1999.

8. Bruce Shutan, "Feeling Right at Home: Home Depot Dangles a Broad Benefits Package to Woo Older Workers," http://www.agewave.com/media_maddy/press11_04.html.

9. Watson Wyatt, "Report Summary: Human Capital Index: Human Capital as a Lead Indicator of Shareholder Value," 2002.

10. Jeff Hill, "Work and Family Harmony: Toward a New Paradigm," World Family Policy Forum 2001, 53.

11. CCH, Inc., "2002 CCH Unscheduled Absence Survey," http://www.cch.com/press/news/2002/2002101601h.asp

12. Unless otherwise cited, all statistics in this section and the accompanying box are drawn from *The New Employee/Employer Equation*. This research project included a nationwide survey of over seventy-seven hundred employees conducted in June 2004 by Harris Interactive for the Concours Group and Age Wave.

13. IBM's Global Work/Life, Flexibility and Mobility Project Office. Interview with Andrea Jackson and Mike Shum, April 2003.

14. Interview with Brad Allenby, April 2003; see also Brad Allenby and Joseph Roitz, "Implementing the Knowledge Economy: The Theory and Practice of Telework," Batten Institute Working Paper, 2003.

15. Ibid.

16. Fay Hanson, "Truth and Myths of Work/Life Balance," *Workforce*, December 2002, 34–39.

17. Based on frameworks developed by Karen S. Grove, PhD.

Chapter Ten

1. http://www.bp.com; and Chris Collison and Geoff Parcell, *Learning to Fly: Practical Knowledge Management from Leading and Learning Organizations* (Chichester, U.K.: Capstone, 2005).

2. GE Annual Report 2000.

3. Employment Policy Foundation, "Challenges Facing the American Workplace, Summary of Findings," *The Seventh-Annual Workplace Report*, 2002, http://www.epf.org/pubs/labordayreports/2002/ldrsummary2002.asp.

4. Interview with Marvin Bressler, December 2003.

5. Unless otherwise cited, all statistics in his section and the next are drawn from *The New Employee/Employer Equation*. This research project included a nationwide survey of over seventy-seven hundred employees conducted in June 2004 by Harris Interactive for the Concours Group and Age Wave.

6. David A. Garvin, *Learning in Action: A Guide to Putting the Learning Organization to Work* (Boston: Harvard Business School Press, 2003).

7. Interview with Martha Soehren, August 2005.

8. Interviews with Stephen Wing, December 2002 and November 2003.

9. Howard Muson, "Valuing Experience," The Conference Board, 2002, 18.

10. Interview with Steve Nesbitt, March 2003.

11. Interview with Sally Hartmann, May 2003.

12. Interviews with Michael Wren and Tim Sands of the Department of Health, and Rachael Charlton of the Greater Manchester Workforce Development Confederation, April 2003.

13. Interviews with Nancy Tootle, December 2002 and November 2003.

Chapter Eleven

1. Gary H. Anthes, "Pillar of the community," *Computerworld*, November 24, 1997.

2. Charles Fishman, "Moving Toward a Balanced Worklife" *Workforce*, March 2000, 38–42.

3. Charles Fishman, "Sanity, Inc.," *Fast Company*, January 1999, 84

4. Howard Gleckman, "Welcome to the Health-Care Economy," *BusinessWeek*, August 26, 2002.

5. Robert Guy Matthews, "A Retired Steelworker Struggles with a Health-Insurance Crisis," *Wall Street Journal*, May 12, 2003.

6. Unless otherwise cited, all statistics in this section are drawn from *The New Employee/Employer Equation* survey. This research project included a nationwide survey of over seventy-seven hundred employees conducted in June 2004 by Harris Interactive for the Concours Group and Age Wave.

7. For purposes of this ranking, we assume base salary and vacation time as given, and offer for comparison increments of each. Preferences within the categories of compensation and time off are discussed in the following paragraphs.

8. SHRM/SHRM Foundation, "2002 Benefits Survey."

9. Interview with Glenn Carnathan, April 2003.
10. Saint Thomas Health Services LifeWorks! Guide.
11. Interview with Deborah Triplett and LaQuesha Dillingham-Spivey, June 2003.
12. Interview with Heidi Evans, May 2003.

Part IV

1. John Ruskin, *Pre-Raphaelitism*, 1851.

Chapter Twelve

1. *The New Employee/Employer Equation* survey, conducted in 2004 by Harris Interactive for the Concours Group and Age Wave. Surveys of the U.S. workforce by Towers Perrin and Gallup show similar results. See "Working Today: Understanding What Drives Employee Engagement," Towers Perrin 2003 Talent Report; and Jim Harter, "Strengths, Engagement, and Outcomes in the Workplace," at the 2004 International Positive Psychology Summit, http://www.gallup.hu/pps/2003/Harter.pdf.

2. *The New Employee/Employer Equation* survey.

3. Jeffrey Pfeffer, Graduate School of Business, Stanford University, from the Stanford Project on Emerging Companies (SPEC), http://www.gsb.stanford.edu/spec/findings/index.html.

4. Interview with John Bridge, July 2003; and Howard Muson, "Valuing Experience," The Conference Board, 2002, 12–13.

5. Adapted with permission from Lynda Gratton, *The Democratic Enterprise* (Upper Saddle River, NJ: Financial Times Prentice Hall, 2004), 119–124.

6. Interviews with Michael Wren and Tim Sands of the Department of Health, and Rachael Charlton of the Greater Manchester Workforce Development Confederation, April 2003; for additional information, see http://www.nhsemployers.org.

Chapter Thirteen

1. For a complete discussion of the three types of human capital, see Lynda Gratton, *The Democratic Enterprise* (Upper Saddle River, NJ: Financial Times Prentice Hall, 2004), 83–94.

Acknowledgments

Our deepest gratitude to Ron Christman, Chairman and CEO of the Concours Group, for bringing the authors together, helping to shape our ambition, and enthusiastically supporting our work

The authors would like to extend our appreciation to the following people for their support and their contributions to this book:

David Baxter for his foundation research on the mature worker cohort and his major contributions throughout this effort. The other members of the Age Wave team for their unrelenting intelligence, compassion, vision and hard work: Maddy Dychtwald, Elyse Pellman, Robyn Hamilton, Daniel Veto, Erin Pritchett, Luke Van Meter, Aaron Vance, Neil Steinberg, Joel Westbrook, Catherine Fredman, Sal Mesa, Matt Mucklo, and Diane Barde.

The entire Concours Group and particularly Lynn Keehan for her superb management of relationships with all of our research clients, and Maira Galins and Sharon Randall for their incomparable skill and composure in keeping the research projects and authors on track. Many current and former Concours Group consultants, researchers, and staff members assisted in our research and the development of this book. They include: Espen Andersen, Eileen Antonucci, Allison Bacon, Tim Bevins, Maryann Billington, Eileen

Birge, Cheryl Fields-Tyler, Amy Griffin, Karen Grove, Maggie Hentschel, Mark Martin, Kristen Palson, Jennifer Piel, Mollie Reding, and Shauna Satrang.

From Harris Interactive, Humphrey Taylor, Chairman of the Harris Poll, for lending his incomparable expertise to our nationwide employee survey; David Krane for skillfully managing the survey project; and Kristina Hanson, Michele Salomon, and Steve Struhl for lending their great talent to the effort.

Tony DiRomualdo, for his research and insight on the young workers cohort, and Glenn Mangurian for his research and insight on the employment deal. Ed Potter and Mike Chittenden of the Employment Policy Foundation and Mitra Toossi from the Bureau of Labor Statistics for helping us interpret the numbers.

The management educators and practitioners who advised our research or shaped our thinking in a big way: Marvin Bressler, John Seely Brown, James Cash, Peter Drucker, Lynda Gratton, Lester Thurow, and Dave Ulrich.

Our wonderful and gifted editor, Kirsten Sandberg, for her insightful handling of our manuscript; Jen Waring for seeing the book smoothly through production; and all of the professionals at Harvard Business School Publishing who helped this book see light of day. Danny Stern for putting us together with the HBS Press and playing the catalyst for this book. And our thoughtful and talented literary agent, Owen Laster.

At *Harvard Business Review*, editor Tom Stewart and our senior editor, Ellen Peebles, for publishing "It's Time to Retire Retirement," and for their ongoing support of our work.

In addition, this book and the research behind it would not have been possible without the active participation of the following organizations and their representatives:

Aerospace Corporation	Blue Cross & Blue Shield
Agere Systems	CalPERS
Allianz Life Insurance Company of North America	Cardinal Health
	Clayton, Dubilier & Rice
ARO	CVS/pharmacy
Ascension Health	Deloitte Touche Tohmatsu
AT&T	

Department of Health (U.K.)

Diageo

Dow Chemical

Fidelity Investments

FPL Group

General Electric

General Motors

Georgia-Pacific

GMAC Residential Funding

Hewlett-Packard

HSBC Finance

Humana

International Business Machines

Johnson & Johnson

Lincoln National

Lucent Technologies

MDS

Merrill Lynch

MITRE

Monsanto

Pfizer

Pharmacia

Pitney Bowes

Prudential Insurance

RBC Financial Group

Rockwell Automation

Sears, Roebuck and Co.

Sprint

Starwood Hotels and Resorts

Textron

Thomson

Tyco International

Wells Fargo Bank

Xerox

Finally, and most importantly, our families for your ever-present support, encouragement, love, and emotional nourishment: the Dychtwalds, Kents, and Fuscos—Maddy, Casey, Zak, Pearl, Seymour, Alan, Sally, Ray, Richard, Linda, David and Joel; the Ericksons—Tom, David, and Kate; Muriel and Bob Morison, Lynne Barrett, and James Barrett-Morison.

Index

About the Authors

Ken Dychtwald, PhD, has emerged over the past thirty years as North America's foremost visionary and original thinker regarding the lifestyle, marketing, and workforce implications of the "age wave." A psychologist and gerontologist, he is the author of twelve books on aging-related issues, including *Age Wave* and *The Power Years: A User's Guide to the Rest of Your Life*. He is the President and CEO of Age Wave, a company whose services include groundbreaking research, business development guidance, and a wide range of communications programs. Over the course of his speaking career, Dychtwald has addressed more than two million people worldwide.

Tamara J. Erickson is an innovative expert on strengthening the relationship between employees and corporations. Her work blends a deep understanding of organizational dynamics, business strategy, and technology-driven change to help corporate leaders understand the changing workforce, enhance engagement, and increase productivity. She is also a respected authority on technology and is a coauthor of *Third Generation R&D: Managing the Link to Corporate Strategy*, a widely accepted guide to making technology investments and managing innovative organizations. She is President of The Concours Institute, the research and executive education arm of The Concours Group, an innovative advisory services firm. She is also a member of the Board of Directors of The Concours Group and of PerkinElmer.

Robert Morison is an executive vice president of The Concours Group, a founding employee of the firm, and its director of research. For the past twenty years, he has been leading breakthrough research at the intersection of business, technology, and human asset management. He has worked with over 300 major organizations in North America and Europe and written or overseen more than 130 research and management reports on topics ranging from business reenginnering to electronic business to workforce demographics.

The authors together directed the two major research projects behind this book, *Demography Is De$tiny* and *The New Employee/Employer Equation*. And they wrote the influential *Harvard Business Review* article "It's Time to Retire Retirement" (March 2004), which received the McKinsey Award as the best HBR article in 2004.